Film and Attraction

From Kinematography to Cinema

André Gaudreault

Translated by Timothy Barnard

Foreword by Rick Altman

Followed by
Kinematographic Views (1907)
by Georges Méliès
Edited, with an Introduction and
annotations, by Jacques Malthête

University of Illinois Press
Urbana, Chicago, and Springfield

André Gaudreault. *Cinéma et attraction: Pour une nouvelle histoire du cinématographe.* © CRNS Editions, 2008.
English translation © 2011 by the Board of Trustees
of the University of Illinois
Manufactured in the United States of America
1 2 3 4 5 C P 5 4 3 2 1
♾ This book is printed on acid-free paper.

Library of Congress Cataloging-in-Publication Data
Gaudreault, André.
[Cinima et attraction. English]
Film and attraction : from kinematography to cinema / André Gaudreault ;
translated by Timothy Barnard; foreword by Rick Altman.
p.   cm.
Includes bibliographical references and index.
ISBN 978-0-252-03583-8 — ISBN 978-0-252-07805-7
1. Motion pictures—France—History.
I. Barnard, Tim. II. Malthête, Jacques. III. Méliès, Georges, 1861–1938.
Vues cinématographiques. English. IV. Title.
PN1993.5.F7G37513   2011
791.430944—dc22   2010051031

For Sylvie and Grégoire

Contents

Foreword

Rick Altman

What is cinema? As everybody knows, cinema is a form of entertainment based on the projection of moving images. Think again, says André Gaudreault. Traditional notions of cinema are severely lacking, he claims. No serious history of moving images can be built on this kind of definition.

When did cinema begin? As everyone certainly knows, cinema started in the 1890s, both in the United States and in Europe. Think again, says André Gaudreault, who insists that we need nothing short of a total reconsideration of received notions on the early history of moving images.

Just how do we know when cinema started? Easy. When the moving picture camera and the moving picture projector were invented, that's when cinema started. Think again, says André Gaudreault. Cinema is not an affair of cameras and projectors, but of something entirely different.

Who invented cinema? Well, there may be some doubt about whether the credit for inventing cinema belongs to the Edison team or to the Lumière brothers, but as we all know it's certainly one or the other. Think again, says André Gaudreault. Cameras and projectors may have been invented, he maintains, but nobody invented cinema.

In *Film and Attraction: From Kinematography to Cinema*, André Gaudreault asks us to put aside virtually all our supposed "knowledge" about the beginnings of cinema. Instead of thinking about early moving images as predecessors to—or a beginning version of—the phenomenon that we know as cinema, Gaudreault suggests that we read early moving images in the context of the many "cultural series" with which contemporary viewers identified them. The Lumières didn't think of themselves as making what we call "films," Gaudreault points out; they thought of themselves as making photographs. A new kind of photographs, perhaps, but photographs nonetheless. Retrospectively, we all too easily identify moving images with what we now call cinema, but at the time moving images were just one of several sorts of "views" that regularly shared a stage, a tent, or a lecture hall with attractions of the widest possible nature. With our own notions of cinema in mind, developed in a more recent context, we confidently identify one of these attractions as cinema and the others as lantern slides, vaudeville turns, or illustrated lectures. André Gaudreault challenges us to strip ourselves of any apparent knowledge we might have about cinema, and to examine instead the connections and the vocabulary that moving images inspired in the late nineteenth and early twentieth centuries.

As Gaudreault sees it, cinema was not a late-nineteenth-century invention, but dates instead from around 1910. One of the essential foundations of this claim is the notion that cinema is not a technical, but a cultural category. The existence of cinema depends not on the invention of new physical devices, but on the development of broad-based cultural practices. Instead of telling us tales of invention or showing us pictures of cameras or projectors, Gaudreault gives us analyses of contemporary vocabulary, the establishment of disciplinary norms, and the institution of cultural codes. Strikingly, he concludes that the moving images of the late nineteenth and early twentieth centuries are not a form of cinema at all, but the result of an entirely different practice, which he dubs "kinematography," borrowing (as he often does) from contemporary terminology. In passing, he performs a delightful deconstruction of the words now used in both French and English to designate the moving images of this era. Demonstrating that neither the French expression "le cinéma des premiers temps" nor the English label "early cinema" appropriately covers the phenomena in question, Gaudreault challenges us to think in new ways about films and practices that we thought we understood. Creatively deploying the concept of "attraction," a notion that he introduced (along with Tom Gunning) some two decades ago, Gaudreault suggests that we consider early moving images not as an incipient form of cinema, but as something radically other. Unless we do, he insists, we will never succeed in comprehending practices and products around the beginning of the twentieth century in all their cultural detail and historical specificity.

But how can we tell when kinematography stops and cinema starts? Gaudreault offers a fascinatingly simple yet powerful standard for making this determination. For many years, moving images were treated not as a separate cultural practice or independent category but as a form of representation inspiring comparison to several different already existing practices. As long as moving pictures were regularly consumed and considered in the context of these already existing "cultural series," as Gaudreault calls them, nothing meriting the new name of "cinema" could be said to exist. But when moving images began to be perceived as their own separate cultural series—a process that took place around 1910—the term and category of "cinema" may appropriately be invoked. Gaudreault's use of the notion of "cultural series" thus provides a new and intriguing way of thinking about the process of institutionalization that moving images underwent in the years surrounding 1910, resulting in the development of what may appropriately be termed "cinema."

Just what is involved in Gaudreault's notion of kinematography, based as it is on recognition of an altogether other category of moving images, preceding cinema without representing in any sense an immature or early form of cinema? And what benefits does Gaudreault draw from his determination to use period terminology in describing this phenomenon? A useful case in point is Gaudreault's treatment of the process of exhibition during the kinematography period. In his original French, Gaudreault distinguishes between two types of exhibitor. An "exploitant" is someone who simply exploits the ready-made products distributed by film producers. But, as he correctly points out, this is not how kinematography worked. During the eighteen-nineties and nineteen-aughts, exhibitors regularly treated purchased or rented films as so much footage to be reconfigured according to the needs of the exhibition situation. These "exhibiteurs," as they were called in contemporary French technical terminology, thus took an active part in deciding what images should be seen by their audiences, and in what order. Serving as producers as well as exhibitors, these "exhibitioners" (as Tim Barnard calls them in his excellent translation) were a familiar feature of the kinematographic approach to moving images—fundamentally different from the cinematic approach championed after about 1910. *Film and Attraction: From Kinematography to Cinema* is chock full of analyses like this one, sensitive not only to the current cultural context but also to the very vocabulary used by contemporary producers, exhibitioners, and audiences.

Because contemporary terminology looms so large in Gaudreault's arguments, the book's Appendix is an especially welcome addition. First published in 1907, "Kinematographic Views" constitutes Georges Méliès's longest and most complete reflection on the production and status of moving images. The Méliès text is presented in Appendix B as edited by Jacques Malthête, along with an introduction and annotations by Malthête. As Gaudreault repeatedly notes, Méliès deploys a vocabulary differing substantially from the technical terminology that would be adopted by those involved with cinema after 1910. Whereas later commentators would write about *cinéastes* (film directors), by which they meant the people who made films, Méliès writes about *cinématographistes* (kinematographers), by which he means those who produce "views," a term applied around the turn of the century to images of all sorts, and not just those that move. From beginning to end, "Kinematographic Views" strongly supports Gaudreault's insistence that in order to understand moving images before 1910, we need a new vocabulary and a new set of standards.

Thanks to Tim Barnard's fine translation, ever-sensitive to the importance of precise vocabulary for Gaudreault's careful arguments, a far larger audience will now have access to this important book.

Acknowledgments

The following pages were written, at least in their present form, from June 2002 to April 2007 in Vieux-Bourg (Fréhel), Brittany, and Montreal, Quebec. They reflect my thinking and some of my research into the emergence of cinema over the past twenty years, since the initial publication of my book *Du littéraire au filmique: Système du récit*[1] in 1988 (which was in turn the product of my work immediately following the Brighton congress of 1978).

The present book has been made possible by the direct and indirect contribution of many people. I would like to express my thanks first of all to those colleagues with whom I have collaborated on conference papers, articles, and books over the past few years, whether in the preparation of texts I have been able to incorporate in part here (Tom Gunning, Frank Kessler, Philippe Marion, Roger Odin, and Denis Simard) or others (François Albera, Jean Châteauvert, Pierre Chemartin, Stéphanie Côté, Elena Dagrada, Nicolas Dulac, Anne Gautier, François Jost, Germain Lacasse, Jean-Marc Lamotte, Jean-Marc Larrue, Églantine Monsaingeon, and Jean-Pierre Sirois-Trahan). I am greatly indebted to them, because our discussions, carried out to the point that our ideas began to intermingle, have enabled me in various ways to formulate the ideas I present here. I am also greatly indebted to the students who have attended my seminars since 1988.[2] The explanations one is called upon to provide and the clarity one is obliged to maintain when communicating with university students play a large role in the final form of any scholar's work, as does the exchange of ideas between students and professor. The forms of interaction to which teaching gives rise are fundamental to the kind of research that academics carry out.

I would also like to thank all the other people who have supported my work in one way or another: my research assistants[3] and all those with whom I have worked over the past few years in GRAFICS (Groupe de recherche sur l'avènement des institutions cinématographique et scénique) and CRI (Centre for Research into Intermediality), two bodies at the Université de Montréal I have (or have had) the honor and pleasure of directing. Their collaboration at all times and the assistance they have provided me have been a help in more ways than one, especially with respect to finding new resources to make academic research possible and easier to carry out, but also for contributing to advancing our understanding of the phenomena we study.

Thanks are due also to Leonardo Quaresima, who was behind the publication of the Italian version of the present volume and who, by inviting me year after year to the Udine International Conference on Film Studies, which he organizes, has enabled me to refine my thinking on the emergence of cinema. In fact, parts of this book began as papers I have delivered at various editions of the Udine conference.

I must also thank those experts on early cinema who, since Brighton, have been putting their shoulders to the wheel of this immense movement of scholarly and inspired rediscovery of early cinema—in particular the members of DOMI-TOR, an International Association Dedicated to the Study of Early Cinema. Their work, because it affords us an overall understanding of the phenomenon of the emergence of cinema in a new light, makes the work of others like me possible.

My thanks also to Nicolas Dulac and Santiago Hidalgo, who, under my supervision, compiled the bibliography of the present volume, and to Viva Paci, a member of GRAFICS, who discussed with me various sticky points among the ideas advanced here (particularly with respect to attraction, the topic of her remarkable doctoral dissertation).[4]

I am also grateful to the people most immediately responsible for the French edition of the present publication, from which this English translation was prepared: Laurent Creton (editor of the series in which it appeared) and Maurice Poulet (my editor at CNRS Éditions), who were patient enough to read and comment on the various versions of the manuscript and who offered judicious advice. Similarly, Jacques Malthête not only agreed to prepare the critical edition of the article by Georges Méliès appended here, but also went over my manuscript with a fine-tooth comb. My thanks also to Roger Odin, who offered valuable advice.

My thanks to the Cinémathèque Méliès for their gracious authorization to reproduce photographs and illustrations of Star-Film productions. Special thanks are due in this regard to Madeleine Malthête-Méliès, Jacques Malthête, and Anne-

Marie Quévrain. Thanks also to the late Pierre Courtet-Cohl and to Laurent Mannoni and Charles Musser for providing me with illustrations to the present volume.

I would like to extend my most heartfelt thanks to all those guardians of cinematic treasures who, while I was working in their institutions or from a distance, have facilitated my access to period documents these past few years. Among these I must single out here Michelle Aubert and Éric LeRoy of the Archives du film at the Centre national de la cinématographie in France; Eileen Bowser, formerly of the Museum of Modern Art in New York; David Francis, formerly of the Library of Congress in Washington, D.C., and the National Film and Television Archive in London; Madeleine Malthête-Méliès of the Cinémathèque Méliès; and Laurent Mannoni of the Cinémathèque française.

Finally, I would like to express my indebtedness to the Département d'histoire de l'art et d'études cinématographiques at the Université de Montréal, where I "officiate" daily, for its support at all times.

A large part of the present volume is the product of research I carried out in 1997–98 while I was the recipient of a Killam Research Fellowship from the Canada Council for the Arts. More precisely, this volume was written as part of my work with GRAFICS at the Université de Montréal (http://cri.histart.umontreal.ca/grafics), which is funded by the Social Sciences and Humanities Research Council of Canada (SSHRC) and the Fonds québécois de recherche sur la société et la culture (FQRSC); GRAFICS is a part of the Centre for Research into Intermediality (CRI). These groups, institutions, and infrastructures have made my work possible, for which I am deeply grateful.

This English version of my book has been made possible by the passionate devotion to the translator's craft by Timothy Barnard, who, in addition to being a fabulous translator, is a genuine scholar of early cinema. My thanks to Rick Altman, who kindly agreed to put my work in context for the English-speaking community, to Joan Catapano of the University of Illinois Press for her persistence on the winding path to this book's appearance, and to Lisa Pietrocatelli and Carolina Lucchesi Lavoie for their assistance. Last but not least, I am most grateful to the initiating spark behind the project of an English edition of this book, Jane Gaines of Columbia University, who believed in the importance of translating it into English and who made it possible. If it had not been for her faith in the necessity of the project, the book you are holding in your hands would not exist.

Introduction

The ideas expressed in this book owe a great deal, as the reader will discover, to the tremendous growth over the past thirty years in research into early cinema, a field that has come to occupy center stage in the small world of film studies. This movement got underway at the Cinema 1900–1906 congress held in Brighton in 1978.[1] At that conference, film scholars were invited to examine film history in the years 1900–1906 by way of a highly documented approach using a great many films of the period. Indeed, nearly 600 films were screened to a small group of specialists.[2] Seeing these films, which had not been screened for decades, was a true revelation. It quite turned people's ideas about the early years of kinematography on their head.[3]

In the present volume, I will propose a series of theses and hypotheses inspired by the many years of research I have devoted to this topic since the Brighton congress. I will propose a new way of looking at this now well-established field of study into early cinema. My new approach also carries with it new propositions that will at times call into question or reject established viewpoints or take the form of seemingly simple questions of semantics and our choice of words. My reappraisal will go so far as to question the very term we use to describe this field of study, "early cinema." Like many other scholars, I am convinced that our choice of words to designate a phenomenon is indicative of our attitude toward that phenomenon. I would not be saying anything new if I were to state that the words in a given discourse reveal the speaker's relationship to his or her object of study. Whenever we place words in syntagmatic sequences to express ourselves, we are making paradigmatic choices. Hence the great care with which I chose the title of the present volume.

Indeed, the title and subtitle of this book caused quite a few problems for its author. What to call a historical book on periods of history is often a problem, especially when one ventures to name the periods in question, as I implicitly do in my subtitle. In most cases, the name of the period under study pertains more to the discourse of the person studying it than it does to the objects that make it up. The present case will be no exception, because one of the expressions I have chosen to designate my object of study, "kine-attractography," is derived from one used in the 1920s (on this topic, see chapter 3), whereas the events and phenomena I will discuss extend just to the 1910s. (The more user-friendly word found in the book's subtitle, kinematography, dates from the period under study.) At the very most, we can say that this expression has the merit of having been proposed, albeit after the fact, by a major figure in the period under study. This, as it turns out, is not its only merit, as I hope to demonstrate in the pages that follow.

The names historians give to their object of study often reveal their position on it. These names can also reveal some of their assumptions. Most often, the name of the period being analyzed by the historian is not taken from the period under study but from what we might call the historian's "historicizing" present. Thus to write a study of Picasso's so-called "blue period" is to acknowledge from the outset that one believes that such a thing as Picasso's blue period exists. It is also to acknowledge that one accepts that the work of the painter in question can be divided into periods. Finally, it accepts the idea that the pieces produced during this period conform to the principle of "blueness" postulated by the name used. When we subscribe to these principles of periodization, we must remember, as Jonathan Crary remarks, that "there are no such things as continuities and discontinuities in history, only in historical explanation."[4]

At first glance, one might think that the title of this book could have been *Early Cinema*. Such a title might have seemed contradictory, since I have subjected this expression to a fairly radical critique[5] (although this does not prevent me from using it from time to time for the sake of convenience). It could also have been entitled *Primitive Cinema*, *The Beginnings of Cinema*, *Cinema at the Beginning*, or, as it was in the Italian edition, "Cinema at its Source" (*Cinema delle origini*).[6] This is why, in addition to the fact that I was unaware of all the connotations each of these possibilities could carry with them in Italian, I preferred to leave the choice to the editor of the series in which the book appeared, Leonardo Quaresima. Thus, in Italian the book title used a term that was somewhat more widely used than other terms in that language, it appears, and one with fewer connotations.

The sense imparted by the Italian title of the book was thus more "genetic" in nature: The use of the term *origini* (source) suggests a search for the connection among various phenomena over a period of time. "Cinema at its source" indicates that there are at least two things, located at opposite ends of a temporal spectrum: on the one hand, in the present, *cinema*, and on the other, in the past, its *source*—in other words, a conclusion (cinema today) and its source, and between them a connecting thread.

The underlying principle of this approach is simple: Cinema today grew out of cinema yesterday. Despite the simplicity of this formulation, it carries with it various problems. How can we seriously propose, without raising thorny questions, that the first animated pictures were the source of the cultural formation that we know today as "cinema," cinema as it is regulated by the contemporary institution that goes by that name? How is it possible to assert, without exposing oneself to criticism, that there is an unbroken continuum of one hundred years and more of history separating us from the invention of a technical device? How is it possible to assume that film history is a single, uninterrupted block? How is it possible to believe that Georges Méliès's *Voyage dans la Lune* (*A Trip to the Moon*, 1902) can in some way account for and be at the source of George Lucas's *Star Wars*?

To do so would be to overlook, despite the resemblance between these two films on a thematic level, the way the production of a film, or rather a series of films like *Star Wars*, is carried out in keeping with the rules of the game established by an institution, in this case Hollywood cinema. This institution is an unavoidable frame of reference for the authors of the film or films in question, something that Méliès did not have to deal with when he made his animated picture back in the days when kinematography, because it was not yet subjected to an institutional framework of its own, was in a sense free to do as it pleased.

To speak of the beginnings of a sociocultural phenomenon as being the source of the phenomenon in question is necessarily and voluntarily to place oneself in the service of a fundamentally evolutionist and quite possibly mechanical conception of history. It is to risk overlooking, consciously or not, the ruptures and continuities that make up history, or to risk not noticing them. It is also to subscribe to a conception of history wherein what comes before necessarily explains what comes after. It is to expose oneself to the dreadful consequences of deceptive hindsight, determinism, and teleology.

Indeed, we may well ask ourselves what so-called early cinema really has in common with institutional cinema. Not only was the former not usually accompanied by recorded sounds; in addition, its viewers were not always seated closely in rows or subjected to strict injunctions to remain silent. Not only did this cinema use unknown actors, it was viewed in the gray shades of black and white (or, on the contrary, in brilliant colors applied directly to the film). Not only was this cinema viewed in screenings lasting less than an hour, but these screenings were made up of a dozen or more individual views.

Was this cinema really cinema? Are we not, rather, in the period I describe here as kine-attractography (roughly 1890–1910), on the threshold of cinema?

This is one of the fundamental hypotheses of the present volume: that in the case of kine-attractography, which dominated the world of animated pictures until about 1908–1910, we have not yet entered the history of cinema. For the simple reason that "cinema"—cinema as we generally understand it today—was not a late-nineteenth-century invention. The emergence of cinema, in the sense we understand the term today, dates instead from the 1910s. The principal task of the present volume is to validate this hypothesis.

Figure 1. The Edison Kinetograph in operation. Source: GRAFICS.

The So-Called Invention of Cinema

My hypothesis is that "cinema" was not invented in 1890 by Thomas Edison and W. K. L. Dickson with their Kinetograph, nor by Auguste and Louis Lumière in 1895 with their Cinématographe, nor by any other supposed inventor of cinema. The only things invented by those who are generally recognized as having invented cinema were the devices to make cinema. It is a subtle distinction, but the device used to make cinema is not the same as cinema itself.

Edison's Kinetograph was a device for taking sequential photographic views of moving subjects: views that, enlarged by a lens, could be reproduced in uninterrupted form for anyone who put their eye to a Kinetoscope peephole. In the end, what Edison invented at the turn of the 1890s was animated pictures. He did not invent cinema.

Neither did Louis and Auguste Lumière invent animated pictures as such, because those had existed for some time prior to their arrival on the scene. Nor did the Lumière brothers invent cinema. What they invented was a device,

Figure 2. An 1894 Kinetoscope transformed into a Kinetophone in 1895 by placing an Edison phonograph inside. Source: Cinémathèque française (Will Day collection).

completed in 1894 and patented in 1895, that made it possible to project the images it recorded onto a screen or wall. We are thus indebted to the Lumière brothers for enabling Edison's animated pictures to be set free from the box in which they were confined (the Kinetoscope) and take flight. The Lumière brothers have many accomplishments of which they can be proud, but I believe it is time to take back from Caesar what is not Caesar's. The generally accepted idea that the Lumière brothers invented cinema appears to me to be pure usurpation.[7] Their camera, the Cinématographe, was certainly a fine piece of work. It was equipped, for example, with a mechanism whose regularity and stability made it possible to project their views, something the Kinetograph did not allow. But cinema does not consist merely in projecting photographic images onto a screen to give an illusion of movement!

Edison and Dickson's invention of animated pictures and the Lumière brothers' invention of a device for projecting them are, on a diachronic level, two important milestones in the history of moving pictures. Nevertheless, we must realize which of these two milestones is the more important. While historians should make every effort to avoid overly historicizing the phenomena they examine, they must also make a minimal effort to realize the quite relative importance that projecting moving pictures onto a screen will have a few hundred years

Figure 3. The Lumière Cinématographe. Source: Cinémathèque française.

from now. Once our movie screens have been replaced by screens produced by a completely different kind of technology—a process that has already begun—we may no longer be quite so interested in who it was who found the means to project moving pictures onto a screen for a relatively brief historical period.

It may someday no longer matter who was able initially to give life to these images, to make them move in a seemingly autonomous manner, to give them life (to give them anima). We owe tribute to Edison and Dickson (Edison's assistant, who by all appearances had a larger role than his employer in developing the device) for achieving this as early as 1890. And yet this pair, whom we can credit with inventing animated pictures, cannot be seen as having "invented" cinema any more than the Lumières: for the simple reason that cinema is not the product of an invention. This is one of the cornerstones of the edifice I intend to construct here: Cinema did not come into the world in the nineteenth century, even if Edison's Kinetograph was developed in 1890 and the Lumière Cinématographe in 1895. Cinema came into the world in the 1910s.

Between these two dates (1890 and the 1910s), there was a time when what I call kine-attractography reigned. The principles and products of kine-attractography have little in common with those of cinema, apart from the fact that each paradigm is based on the use of moving pictures. One thing the intensive research of the past few years agrees upon is precisely the specificity of so-called early cinema's animated pictures. This specificity is so pronounced compared to the films produced under the institutional paradigm that it is impossible to correlate the production and exhibition circumstances of the short views produced at the beginning of the twentieth century with those of the feature-length films produced, say, during World War I.

From Kinematography to Cinema

The invention of the "basic apparatus" (1890 in the case of Edison, 1895 in the case of Lumière) was certainly a turning point in the evolution of photographic technology. We must ask ourselves, however, whether the invention in question brought about a new state of affairs: Was the appearance of the Kinetograph or Cinématographe a true break with the past? I don't believe it was, as I will explain later. Ruptures and changes of paradigm do not necessarily occur at the same time as the invention of new techniques or new devices, or even with the introduction of new procedures such as editing. The question we should be asking in such cases is whether the sudden availability of a new technology revolutionizes behavior and practices, whether it transforms the cultural landscape, whether it brings about significant changes and makes it possible to pass to a new cultural or artistic level within the medium in question. Nothing could be less certain. In fact, it is well known that a new medium starts out by adopting the logic of existing media and by reproducing in rather mechanical fashion the medium or media from which it is largely derived. The kinematograph does not appear to depart from this model.

I will thus argue in the course of this book that it is completely pointless to connect the terra incognita known as "early cinema" to the immense continent that is cinema itself. I will also advance the idea that the kinematograph was transformed into cinema by means of a radical metamorphosis, a true mutation. This mutation came about as a result of a change of paradigm of such wide-reaching effect that it would be justified to view both phenomena as standing back to back.

In the following pages I will explore some of the questions raised by these hypotheses. Throughout, I will be helped by one of the most important figures of the period: Georges Méliès himself. I will call the magician of Montreuil as a witness at various points in my argument by referring periodically to his article "Kinematographic Views," first published in the *Annuaire général et international de la photographie* in 1907,[8] the first important article on cinema in its pages. This article is reproduced in its entirety in a new translation in the present volume, a critical edition prepared by Jacques Malthête, a specialist with an encyclopedic knowledge of Méliès. Since the book you are reading was completed in 2007, this is a fine way to celebrate the hundredth anniversary of this essential contribution to thinking about the ways "kinematographic views are made," as Méliès put it in the language of the day.[9] An essential contribution, for me at least, because I see it as an implicit manifesto for kine-attractography, even if this expression was not a part of Méliès's vocabulary.

Chapter 1

Looking at Early Cinema
in a New Light

"Traditional" film history, which the new generation of film scholars began to dispute following the Brighton congress, was known for an idealist conception of cinema and a teleological vision of its history. In this vision, events are only stages at various degrees of distance away from the ideal to be attained: so-called "classical" cinema. Because of this ideal standard of a cinema yet to come, early cinema, for traditional film historians, could only be a "primitive" cinema whose sole goal was to strive toward its cinematic potential. In the eyes of traditional film history's critics, such a conception, because of its idealist nature, could only deform the reality of the phenomenon under study, because it consisted in measuring it against standards completely foreign to it. For these new scholars, what was needed was a radical new approach to film history and especially toward so-called early cinema. From that moment on, it was no longer a question of understanding film history on the basis of established cinematic norms but of understanding how these norms came into being and were institutionalized. To this end, these new film historians, or at least a good number of them, quickly realized that it would not do to impose norms on cinema itself; rather, new norms would have to be imposed on their own discipline.

This is why this new generation of scholars wanted to reexamine, in light of the recent upsurge in archival activity and advances in film theory, both the suppositions and quality of historical inquiries in the field on the one hand and newly available empirical data on the other. Renewed interest in research into early cinema in the 1980s contributed largely to this transformation, enabling historical issues to resume their place in film studies alongside theoretical speculation. This renewed interest also contributed to changing scholars' views of the approach they should take to their object of study.

After the efforts of the first great film historians—men such as Georges Sadoul,[1] Lewis Jacobs,[2] and Jean Mitry[3]—to make film history a recognized field of study, historical analysis had become relatively undervalued in film studies by the late 1970s. In the 1960s and '70s there had been a strong upsurge in theoretical work, whose principal model was semiotics. To simplify matters, we could say that these beneficent years for theoretical speculation were the product of the domination of a shared paradigm, that of the "film language" that could be found in the "filmic text." In other words, it was no longer a case of seeking film language in a supposed "ontology of reality" (André Bazin) or even in an "aesthetic and psychology of cinema" (Jean Mitry) but rather in the structure of the filmic text itself, apart from any contextual consideration and by eliminating as much as possible the normative aspect that had always accompanied the concept "film language."

In those years a number of scholars, myself included, seeking to call into question the seeming naturalness of film language, became interested in early kinematography. Their goal was quite plainly to join recent advances in film theory with rigorous study of film history. Because the norms of film language had not yet been defined at the beginning of the twentieth century, "early cinema" was a natural choice as a field of study with great heuristic value, one that made possible this new way of thinking about the supposed naturalness of institutional film language.

We might view the return in force of historical issues in film studies in the early 1980s as a result of a typically "1980s" tension between synchrony and diachrony and between structure and development, which is nothing other than a form of the tension between theory and history. This historical turn was not made at the expense of theory, however, because what was distinctive about the renewed interest in historical questions in the field was the way it coalesced to a large extent with theoretical inquiry.[4] This alliance of history and theory in the field of early cinema studies is even more interesting in that it did not merely employ a theory of history (although this in itself was a new approach to film studies); it also made possible a theory of the subject—cinema—whose history it wished to write.

Today, then, film history is no longer practiced the way it was before 1970, and while it was rare for a member of the previous generation of film historians to also be a theorist, today the opposite is true.[5] This is one of the reasons for the relative success of new historical studies in the field, which have been infused with new life by theory. Theory is the oxygen any form of history requires, while history has the same function for theory. As Jean-Louis Comolli wrote in a series of articles in the early 1970s,[6] in which he unleashed a forceful attack on traditional film history, "Whatever the difficulties of this work (and they are great), it is no longer possible to maintain the history and the theory of cinema in separate watertight compartments."[7]

An Alliance of Theory and History

When you think about it, it is quite natural that questions about early cinema would be of interest to both film historians and film theorists. All film historians, whether they like it or not, are also film theorists, although to varying degrees of course. This was made quite clear by Ron Mottram in his comments on Lewis Jacobs and the latter's claim for what he saw as the "first" close-up insert in cinema:

> The question needs to be raised, why does the historian make this claim? Or, rather, why is such a fact being affirmed? To point it out in the first place implies that a cut within a scene is significant. Considering it significant reveals an attitude toward the cinema that gives value to a scene made up of more than one shot and that places the multiple shot scene in relationship to other kinds of scenic constructions. Does not the historian who makes this point do so on the basis of a theoretical consideration?. . . . Inevitably the historiographer is a theorist, perhaps not a good one, but some kind of theorist.[8]

It is true that there has been at least one film historian who was also a film theorist, and an important one at that: Jean Mitry, whose work is fairly evenly divided between film history and film aesthetics.[9] Despite this exception to the rule, film theory and history have never been as symbiotically joined as they have been in the recent movement to rediscover early cinema.[10] What's more, this situation is perhaps attributable as much to the intrinsic qualities of the object of study, early kinematography, as it is to the research that has been carried out in film studies since the late 1970s.

Comolli's articles were one of the rare studies to give a thrashing to "official history" at such an early date and in such a systematic and forceful manner. Judge for yourself the list of this history's misdeeds, which Comolli delights in retailing: "[L]inear causality, claims for autonomy on the two-fold basis of cinema's 'specificity' and the model of 'idealist' art histories, a concern with teleology, the idea of 'progress' or 'improvement', not only of technology but also of 'form.'"[11]

This veritable dressing-down was preceded—at the other end of the ideological spectrum, it's true—by what was promised as a historical undertaking of "a new kind," although this latter project was interrupted along the way and got only as far as the year 1906. I am referring to Jacques Deslandes's study *Histoire comparée du cinéma*, published in two volumes in 1966 and 1968.[12]

Future work on the history of other periods will probably be marked by the approach recently adopted by the new generation of scholars of the early days of cinema. The method of this approach extends and combines the work of Comolli and Deslandes.[13] It is because of research into early cinema that there has arisen over the past twenty-five years the most systematic critique of the work of traditional historians, whom no one wanted to touch before (except in the case, precisely, of Comolli and Deslandes). This critique has been necessary for there to be any new approach to film history in general and all its periods.

"Post-Comolli" criticism, which continues in the same vein, is mostly concerned with the approach historians should take to their object of study. The new generation of historians has thus declined to judge early cinema in any other way than on the basis of the practices of the elements in play at the time (individuals, institutions, practices, customs), which back then had the force of law. The novelty of their approach consists in judging early cinema only by criteria recognized in its own day.

Indeed, it would be theoretically and historically indefensible to take the measure of early kinematography using as our yardstick the norms of classical narrative cinema. These norms, which are indisputably proper to cinema, at least to a certain extent, cannot alone be held as constituting the entire specificity of cinematic expression; hence the increasing hesitation to view what is commonly referred to as "film language" as the ne plus ultra of cinematic expression. In the final analysis, the norms that Noël Burch calls the "Institutional Mode of Representation"[14] are just a historical moment, despite their apparent durability (after all, cinema is barely a hundred years old). The traditional historians, although they may not have been aware of this on a theoretical level, acted as if there were only one, necessarily limited, "film language"—as if the early years were only an incubation period that made it possible for this "film language" to be revealed and as if this kind of cinema was destined to dominate film practice.

It is thus not surprising that the movement to rediscover early cinema has been accompanied by a veritable revolution in the ways we write film history— to the extent that Dana Polan, writing in 1984, remarked: "Attempt(s) to think about early cinema have surely become the dominant activity in present-day historical research into film. Above all, we see there not simply historical writing itself but also an examination of what it is to write history."[15]

This new context has not only made possible the development of a new "historical-theoretical" way of thinking about film; it has also opened the door, during this same period, to many important studies that have led to the preparation of detailed and rigorous filmographies (identifying films and determining the date and place of their production). In this way the inevitable approximations of the earliest film historians have been superseded.[16]

An Alliance of Archivists and Film Scholars

Allying history and theory appears to be the main factor in the recent recognition of early cinema as a specific field of study. Two other factors might be seen to be at play, however, and to have contributed significantly to this recognition: the way in which archivists, since Brighton, have worked more closely with scholars not directly connected with archives; and what we might call the "institutionalization of cinema studies."

The alliance between archivists and scholars rests on a strictly material aspect, the willingness of the former to make their archives more accessible to the latter. This spirit of openness began to be seen in the very late 1970s, and the Brighton congress was its most visible manifestation. Archives, where applied study is carried out, began a series of exchanges with universities, where fundamental study is carried out. Before then, it was a well-known fact that many film archives were impregnable fiefdoms where films were secluded and kept apart from the world. The renewed interest in early cinema came at exactly the same time as new attitudes were taking hold in both the archiving and research domains, giving rise to new forms of collaboration between the two. Film archives were no longer content to find copies of films and store them away in some dark vault; they became places where films are restored and shown, without hesitation. Better yet, several film archives began to grant special privileges to scholars.

Archivists and scholars can now be seen working together regularly in most of the fields in which film history is studied. This is the case of the indispensable festivals in Pordenone-Sacile and Bologna,[17] which don't stop at cultivating cinephilia, because critical, theoretical, and historical reflection always has a strong presence there in the form of publications, panel discussions, workshops, et cetera. The same is true of the mostly academic conferences held in various places on themes having to do with film history. Scholars are no longer content simply to engage in writing film history and are taking advantage of the opportunity that these international gatherings offer to show films, over and over again.[18]

Over the past thirty years, these conditions have had a major impact on our familiarity with and understanding of film. The results of such a revolution in attitudes and practices were not long in coming: never before have film historians been as "cultivated" and well documented as they are today! And to think of the huge efforts that traditional film historians had to make, even to see a single archival film.

The creation of film archives is a relatively recent phenomenon. These institutions are extremely valuable for film historians, who owe it to themselves to consider the riches that lie within them as a way of adding to their understanding of historical phenomena. In this sense, the work of film archivists is indispensable to historians, especially since they are responsive to historians' arguments in their work. The previous generation of historians had no choice but to lobby archive directors to restore the work they felt to be particularly important. The choice of which films to restore depends not only on physical criteria (the chemical composition of the film stock, for example) but also on aesthetic, cultural, and temporal criteria (the label "cinematic masterpiece" naturally varies from one era to another). Thus in the 1970s, American archives gave precedence to restoring the many films produced and directed by D.W. Griffith. Choices such as this are not without effect on how film history is written, and in this way archivists can play a leading role and influence the new historians, because it is the archivists who, in the end, "create" the physical traces upon which historians work.

The Institutionalization of Film Studies

One of the factors behind the emergence of the early days of cinema as a specific field of study is the institutionalization of film studies. Over the past thirty years, the study of film has seen a strong push toward institutionalization, visible not only in the increased interest in archival preservation but also in the emergence of university-level cinema studies. This institutionalization has made it possible, first of all, to consolidate and update our knowledge of film through its transmission to new generations of scholars. This process has also brought about a process of specialization in specific fields, making highly focused research possible. The new generation of historians, by virtue of their willingness to join history and theory, their increasingly close collaboration with archivists, and their high standards of precision and thoroughness in the way they handle research data is thus a product of this institutional growth.

In its scope and precision and in the resources it puts to use, the work of the new generation of historians is distinctly different from that of the previous generation. Sadoul, Jacobs, and Mitry, for example, did not have at their disposal the great number of films available to today's historian. They did not have videos or DVDs, catalogued archives, or research groups for gathering and interpreting data. In short, they worked under completely different material conditions than those found in institutions of higher learning about cinema today. Like true pioneers, they generally worked alone with very few resources and often had to make do, for their documentation, with only their memory of the films they had seen over the course of their lifetimes. The new generation of historians, working under the aegis of the university, is distinctly more demanding when it comes to the reliability of their sources. With the growth of film studies at the university level in the 1960s and '70s came an advance in research methods and improved critical faculties.[19] We might say that these developments also influenced in turn film archives and the way film history is written. Archivists were required to devote increasing efforts to restoring films in their care and to provide these new scholars with an environment wherein more precise and exacting research could be carried out.

The Filmography, Where Historians and Archivists Meet

The interdependence of the respective labors of scholars and archivists motivates and justifies the need for close collaboration between them, particularly in designing the tools used by both. Filmographies are precisely one of the places where the two distinct but neighboring spheres historical research and archival preservation meet. One of the effects of the rise of new approaches to film history is precisely, as I remarked above, the proliferation of filmographies. For the first time, these are now reliable. The research carried out to establish a filmography has become a form of collaboration between individuals in both spheres, thereby giving much more conclusive results than what was obtained previously. I believe we must promote an even greater interpenetration of the work of archivists and historians. Filmographies are the linchpin of this interpenetration. Isn't one of the purposes of a filmography to enable archivists, when they are not historians themselves, to identify, date, and catalogue the films in their collections? Might not the hypotheses arrived at by historians when compiling filmographies serve to guide the restoration of films?

If this is to be the case, it is clear that "filmographers" must respect two fundamental principles.[20] The first is that the ideal filmography must collect various kinds of knowledge about a film and thus establish what is known about it in the present day on an international scale. This collection of knowledge is an objective we cannot overlook. It is an essential condition if film history is to advance. It may, for example, become important in the case of films that exist in a complete version only in virtual form and whose restoration involves gathering together fragments scattered about the world. The second principle is that the ideal filmography must be a clear and precise means of communication among present-day scholars and, especially, between present-day and future scholars, as well as between scholars and archivists; hence the need to ensure that every filmography is accompanied by a selection of notes and annotations that give clear, precise, methodical, and unequivocal indications of the source of all information found within it.

An Epistemological Break

The three conditions that made possible the recent recognition of early cinema as a specific field of study (the joining of history and theory, the collaboration between archivists and scholars, and the institutionalization of the discipline) have influenced research in the field to the point of introducing a break it would not be exaggerated to describe as epistemological. As we have seen, the new historians were opposed to traditional film history and the very basis of its approach; their attempt to define their project was based on this opposition and borrowed, consciously or not, from Comolli's shaking up of official history. Comolli's acerbic critique of empirical historians who, in Dana Polan's words, "continue to write texts in which history is seen as the exact and transparent reflection of historical events,"[21] attracted considerable attention. In my view, it was a true historical turning point. It is as if Comolli's work, in rising up against worn-out conceptions of film history (linear causality, idealism, the notion of progress, etc.), was a user's manual for the scholars who were soon about to express an interest in the early days of cinema.

Is it not also the fate of every conception of history, moreover, to be cast aside one day as out-of-date? What historians of each new generation do is not "simply" right wrongs; they also, especially, interpret the historical subject, or rather reinterpret it, interpret it in a different way than it had been by the historians who came before them. Of course, for each new generation new facts are dying to have their say and demolish some of the hypotheses of the previous generation, but there is also at play, in particular, a new way of seeing things, new approaches to things. And these new methods, these new approaches adopted in our day were just as inaccessible to the historian of yore as, for example, past historical objects are to today's historians.

Traditional Film Histories

The new ways with which we now approach film history delineate new fields of research and raise new questions. This is the case, for example, with the great debate over periodization. It is hard to believe that this is one of those things that has to be hammered out anew twenty times over. And yet this has been its fate! Every new conception of history establishes, in one way or another, a new periodization of its own. We will see in chapter 3 my own approach to this age-old question, which has always been the Achilles heel of traditional film historians. In this respect, one need only read the table of contents of their books to see how this question, rather than attacking a true problem, becomes truly problematical.

We could begin with Lewis Jacobs's book, *The Rise of the American Film*,[22] published for the first time in 1939, whose schema is as follows:

1. Fade-In (1896–1903)
2. Foundations (1903–1908)
3. Development (1908–1914)
4. Transition (1914–1918)
5. Intensification (1919–1929)
6. Maturity (1929–1939)

We should note, first of all, that Jacobs's ambition is not to cover international cinema as a whole, unlike Sadoul and Mitry. This American author restricts himself to a critical history of the rise of American film alone (the full title of his book is *The Rise of the American Film: A Critical History*). If we take this table of contents as our guide, history for Jacobs is like a story one tells, a narrative. What these chapter headings tell the reader is that they should expect to follow the "development" of American cinema from its "foundation" to its "maturity." I will not dwell on this book, except to point out a recurring penchant among all traditional film historians: their annoying tendency to make us think that empirical reality should conform to the dates of a calendar! Indeed events in their systems often seem to leap by decade with breaks arriving exactly (or almost) at the turn of each new decade, or exactly in the middle of a decade. This is the case with Jacobs, who calls his last two periods "Intensification"

(1919–1929) and "Maturity" (1929–1939). The same is true of Georges Sadoul, whose six-volume *Histoire générale du cinéma*[23] sets out the following schema (note in particular the period that concerns us here, the way history is broken up between volumes two and three):

1. The Invention of Cinema (1832–1897)
2. The Pioneers (from Méliès to Pathé) (1897–1909)
3. Film Becomes an Art (1909–1920)
   Volume One: Before the War
   Volume Two: The First World War
4. Silent Film Art (1919–1929)
   Volume One: The Post-war Period in Europe
   Volume Two: Hollywood and the End of Silent Film

Jean Mitry's five-volume *Histoire du cinéma*[24] follows a similar pattern. Mitry cuts film history up in a fairly mechanical way into ten- or fifteen-year periods, with one exception:

1. Art and Industry I: 1895–1914
2. Art and Industry II: 1915–1925
3. Art and Industry III: 1923–1930
4. Art and Industry IV: The 1930s
5. Art and Industry V: The 1940s

We might ask ourselves whether a book by a historian who treats historical phenomena by leaps of ten or fifteen years is not more a chronicle than a history.[25] We might also ask ourselves how historians can arbitrarily arrogate to themselves the right to decree that a film from 1926 forms part of the same group as a film from 1920, while a film from 1918, closer in years to the film from 1920, is dealt with in another chapter or another volume. The faults we may find with such a method are too numerous to enumerate here. Suffice to say that historians who propose such schema have not, by all appearances, asked themselves the proper questions with respect to diachronic phenomena and that they didn't trouble themselves to base their division of film history into chapters or volumes on a true analysis of the issues at stake.

Kinematography and Cinema

One of Jean Mitry's ideas concerning periodization appears to me to be particularly interesting with respect to my discussion here: Mitry postulates the existence of a break around 1915, about when what is now widely seen as the institution "cinema" was established. Mitry's first volume distinguishes between what he calls, in the heading to chapter 4, the "pioneers" (a period lasting from 1900 to 1908) and what he describes in the heading to chapter 5 as the "discovery of cinema" (from 1908 to 1914):

1. Moving Pictures before Lumière
2. Moving Pictures after Lumière
3. The Kinematograph before 1900
4. The Work of the Pioneers (1900–1908)
5. The Discovery of Cinema (1908–1914)[26]

Mitry's explanation for this breakdown, if we are to go by what he says in the second volume in the series, is quite simply this: "It is no less obvious that cinema as an art, as a valid and coherent means of expression, when it finally arrived at its true nature, appeared only in 1915."[27]

Thirty years ago, a statement like this made many a young scholar, including myself, bristle.[28] Yet it remains current in many respects. For Mitry, cinema arrived at its "true nature" only in 1915. This suggestion, which is not that far removed from the position I adopted in my Introduction, deviates from it just the same by its resolutely essentialist aspect: "cinema arrived at its true nature only in 1915," Mitry writes. In my view, it is not cinema's "true nature" that appeared in 1915; what changed, in places where cinema was present, was what the dominant culture of the day made of it. There is a difference between these two things, and it is an important difference.

Mitry, as he is at pains to explain throughout his writings, believed that the efforts of film's "pioneers" only served in the end to reveal "film language," a natural code, an essence that already existed potentially from the moment of the invention of the kinematograph. It was enough to draw it out of the undifferentiated magma of early kinematography. Back in 1978 Noël Burch, in an article on Edwin S. Porter he presented at the Brighton congress, tackled this attitude head-on: "There is the prevailing thesis concerning these beginnings, according to which a language gradually emerged out of a sort of primordial chaos generally described as 'theatrical': the language, cinema's NATURAL LANGUAGE, innate in the camera from the outset, but only brought into the *light of day* as a result of determined efforts by certain 'pioneers of genius.'"[29]

Mitry asserts, more or less, that at a given moment in its history, around 1914–15, cinema attained the status of art. We might say that this new status coincided with its institutionalization; such a claim is pretty much in keeping with some of the ideas I will develop in the present volume.

Mitry was not the only historian to think this way. A few years earlier, in 1946, Georges Sadoul had described similar views, although Sadoul has the merit of contrasting the kinematograph with the cinema: "For the kinematograph to become the art we now call cinema, it had to employ and adapt the means of theater: scripts, sets, costumes, make-up, actors, and staging."[30]

Basically, what irritated the "moderns" (the new, post-Brighton scholars) about Sadoul and Mitry's position was their sovereign and perhaps mistaken disdain for what was for them "early cinema," in combination with their attempt, which at the time seemed absurd, to exclude such a phenomenon from the very realm of cinema or, worse yet, from the realm of cinematic art. While it is still worthwhile to criticize the main underlying assumptions upon which such arguments are based, and to criticize the exclusion that follows from them, Sadoul's idea of separating the period of "early cinema" from the rest of film history by referring to it as "kinematography" (cinématographe) remains interesting, especially since it respects the vocabulary of the day. Indeed in the first decade of the 1900s the word "kinematograph" was fairly widely used to describe various activities involved in making and exhibiting animated pictures, without necessarily implying any direct reference to the Lumière brothers or the device they invented, the Cinématographe.

Finally, the idea of making a diachronic division between kinematography and cinema is in keeping with the dichotomy created when we speak of cinema before and after its institutionalization (which occurred, as is now generally agreed, at the outset of the 1910s). This is all the more true when we consider that this distinction is found, in French at any rate, throughout the history of thinking about film history. This contrast is forcefully explored by Edgar Morin in his masterful book *Le Cinéma ou l'homme imaginaire* (*The Cinema, or the Imaginary Man*),[31] where it forms the basis of the book's argument. It would thus be possible to advance, following Morin, that the period known today as early cinema saw the kinematograph transformed into cinema by means of a fairly radical change in paradigm obliging us to distinguish clearly between the two and to see the movement from one to the other as a break, a rupture.[32] A distinction such as this would make life easier for anyone bound and determined to see the earlier paradigm as a period whose sole intrinsic quality was to have served as an antechamber to the later paradigm. This is a point of view of which the new generation has long been aware and has strived with difficulty to combat systematically. Effort has been expended to conceptualize this project, which the present volume seeks to express.

This division between kinematograph and cinema has always played an important role in film history (by this I mean in the history of writing film history), whether people have been aware of it or not. We find this division, symptomatically, in Mitry's distinctions between "primitive cinema," which for him is not really cinema, and the cinema of the 1910s, which became an art. He thus draws a line somewhere around 1914–15, just as the sounds of cannon fire in World War I were beginning to sound—a war, we know, that spelled the end of French hegemony in the film industry and during which the feature film was born, alongside that key element of institutional cinema, the star system.

Putting Things in Context

One of the most revealing ways in which film historians' attitudes changed after the Brighton congress, where many films that had lain unseen for nearly a century were discovered, is the role attributed to D.W. Griffith's films in establishing what we have come to call "film language." Many of the extravagant judgments rendered by film historians of previous generations were based on "facts" that were later found to be erroneous. Griffith did not "invent" the procedures or techniques that people too often attribute to him (the close-up, the shot-countershot, crosscutting, etc.). In essence, Griffith served as the mythical figure traditional film historians needed for their concept of history to function the way it did. The new historians came to see this conception as outdated. Even so, Griffith's role was absolutely fundamental to the development and establishment of the form of representation that would come to dominate film practice. But while Griffith systematized, standardized, and perfected certain procedures and techniques, he did not invent them.

The goal of putting things into context in this way is not, however, to create a "pantheon" that would acknowledge artistic merit in an ostensibly more precise manner than earlier film historians did. Rather, it is a matter of using these corrections to pin down as concretely as possible the conditions in which a filmmaker such as Griffith, along with other filmmakers of his day, was able to carry out a radical transformation of the dominant mode of representation during the period of so-called early cinema. Only when we have completed this task will we be in a position to understand every aspect of the manner in which cinema became institutionalized. This process will also make it possible to better understand how cinema's supposed specificity, which arose in the 1910s, is not necessarily the ne plus ultra of film discourse and, especially, that it is not "natural," contrary to what has too often been stated.

If there is one constant in every traditional film history, if there is a theoretical supposition that presides over demonstrations of the arguments these histories offer, if there is a kind of irreducible premise guiding the work of the previous generation of film historians, it is, as I mentioned earlier, that there is a single and intrinsic film language, a "natural" way to arrange its visual (and later audiovisual) signifiers. This language is said to have won out over every other kind of organization of the materials of the medium principally because it is best suited to the task of expressing cinema's supposed specificity. It is true that a certain way of telling stories through film developed over the years, which the institution ended up adopting. A number of relatively binding rules were thus instituted as norms. The origin of these "codes," which historically came to dominate film practice, was essentially cultural. In the end, there is nothing natural about them, contrary to what an earlier generation of film historians believed, consciously or not. This explains these historians' propensity to see the work of kinematographers (as camera operators and the earliest filmmakers described themselves in their own time[33]) as a taste, a "preview," of a supposedly embryonic film language that had to be discovered and revealed. The mission these historians accorded to kinematographers was thus to pave the way for their successors, film directors, and to place at their disposal a series of narrative codes, or subcodes, one of whose virtues was to make it possible to tell a story more efficiently.

It is thus not surprising to find a litany of "firsts" in a great number of film histories, rhymed off like incantations to bring out the awaited god, film language. Tom Gunning has summed the matter up in the following way:

> The essential gesture of the recent reexamination of the history of early film lies in a rejection of linear models. Rejecting biological schema of infancy and maturity that were abandoned long ago in the histories of other art forms, researchers avoided viewing cinema's first decades as embryonic forms of later practices or stuttering attempts at later achievements. Instead of a linear and organic model of development, a jagged rhythm of competing practices emerged, practices whose modes and models were not necessarily sketches or approximations of later cinema. Instead of continuity we discover difference, and rather than organic development, a series of contrasting conceptualizations of cinema's social role, mode of exhibition, and method of address.[34]

Once upon a Time Came the First Time

Jean Mitry, to take only his work as an example, built his historical system on a linear model of the sort the new historians tossed out of the discipline. His premises include statements such as "the principle underlying all of Méliès's work . . . turned out to be going in the wrong direction"[35] and the claim that, at the time of the *film d'art* (c. 1908–11), "film language was still in limbo."[36] Nevertheless, we must acknowledge that Mitry sometimes displays a great deal more theoretical and historical subtlety than his predecessors. In particular, he came up with the idea that, between 1903 and 1911, cinema was divided into two major tendencies, the theatrical and the narrative. Despite the reservations I have expressed elsewhere about this hypothesis,[37] it must be admitted that it is a real effort at historical theorization whose goal is to bring out the specific features of the successive systems at work between 1895 and 1915.

This does not prevent the same author, unfortunately, from sometimes showing signs of a remarkable degree of blindness. This is the case when he argues: "*L'Incendiaire* [Pathé, 1905] . . . is also a great step forward. In the first place because the sensational news story it illustrates is plausible and its narrative is generally credible, and because it was the first drama Pathé shot out of doors."[38] And again: "Porter's film [*The Great Train Robbery*, Edison, 1903] . . . although considerably out of date, contained the seed of cinematic expression and remains the first true example of cinema in film history."[39]

At a time when "animated pictures" were in full force, the plausibility of the news item, the credibility of the narration, and the recognition of the merits of shooting out of doors were criteria of an age yet to come, not as something transcendent the way they are described by Mitry. To say that a 1905 film was a "great step forward" or that one from 1903 was "out of date" means adopting the linear logic Mitry constantly employs, especially when he advances the idea that the *film d'art* was a backward step with respect to the films of G. A. Smith, James Williamson, and Edwin S. Porter,[40] or that Smith's film was "inferior" to those of Méliès or Pathé.[41] These quotations from Mitry also amply demonstrate how he succumbed to what Comolli described as the "fetish of the first time."

Mitry responded to Comolli's criticism and offered an exemplary mea culpa— albeit a somewhat paradoxical one, as we shall see—in an article published in 1973:

> The truth is that historians take note of present events the same way they take note of past events. They then research, discover, and analyze the series of causes

Figure 4. *L'Incendiaire* (Pathé, 1905). A film Mitry describes as a "great step forward." Film still. Source: GRAFICS/NFTV/Renn Pathé Catalogue.

and effects that make up the past. But these continuous series of events do not entail a linear development unfolding from the less perfect to the more perfect according to a logic both determinist and unequivocal. They do not suppose an objective that retrospection can suggest was immediately foreseeable, even if the present state of the phenomenon is the conclusion of a series of more or less confirmed, thwarted, or varied intentions throughout the ages. There is a progression, but not necessarily progress. Progress is a value judgment imposed on historical events; it is not these events themselves.[42]

Had Mitry learned something from Comolli? It would appear not, because, in the same article, he reaffirmed, despite the long "lapse" quoted above, the importance and even preeminence for him of a linear conception of history: "I have devoted myself to following the constant development of the means of cinematic expression through manifestations that, as different from each other as they may be, gradually perfected it."[43]

He could not have been more clear: Jean Mitry's vision of film history, as late as 1973, still involved the concepts continuity, progress, and perfection.

Thus the agenda of each new generation of film historians is laid out: to find one or, better yet, several new "firsts," making us revise backward by a few years the first appearance of the close-up, the tracking shot, or any other technical and narrative procedure of importance. I believe it is better to abandon such thoroughly teleological conceptions and to study early kinematography in the context in which it was created and to employ boundaries imposed by this context: in a word, on the basis of its own specificity, not the specificity of institutional cinema from a later period.

The Historian's Orientation

Of course the propositions in this book will not solve every problem that arises when we address a terra incognita belonging to the past. They are simply a theoretical and methodical framework that may make possible a reasoned approach to various aspects of film history—and, more precisely, in the present case, of the history of early kinematography. I have tried to ensure that my approach is a reasoned one, but it remains no less limited. Any historical approach will be. In this sense, the only distinction we can make between various historical approaches is one that explicitly recognizes their specific orientation. The advocates of some approaches, like the one proposed here, acknowledge this from the outset and take this essential condition of writing history into account, while others naively cling, most often implicitly, to a vain hope for complete objectivity.

The historian cannot, however, claim transitivity or transparency, for the simple reason that the discipline is, above all else, a discursive activity. History truly is a discourse (and not, contrary to what one would expect, a story, to employ Émile Benveniste's typology),[44] in the sense that the historian's discursive present, if we were to examine it closely, is always riddled with signs of utterances. History is a discourse, to employ Benveniste's sense of the term once more, because the present of the past, to which the historian's activity gives rise, is, precisely, a discursive present a thousand miles from Benveniste's historical utterance (i.e., a story). From a strictly linguistic viewpoint, a historian's discourse can of course take on the appearance of a historical utterance, but it remains riddled with traces of discourse hiding beneath the surface of the "(his)story" it tells.

If history is thus always a discourse, in Benveniste's sense of the term, it is quite simply because at the same time, as Hans-Georg Gadamer remarked in his hermeneutic project,[45] writing history is always an act of interpretation. The task historians set themselves may appear to be "merely" to restore and recreate, but it remains the case that this restoration or recreation is the fruit of a complex labor of interpretation. And historians necessarily work on the basis of their own here and now in interpreting history—on the basis of the subjective conditions prevalent in their own lifetime, which of necessity are part of a "cultural paradigm" foreign to that in force in the period under study. (I will return to the concept cultural paradigm in chapter 4.)

The degree of incompatibility between the cultural paradigm of the historian's present and that of the period under study can vary. Thus, the observing subject can be part of a cultural paradigm so far removed from the paradigm in which the object being observed is found that understanding the earlier paradigm can pose great difficulties, while another paradigm closer to the observer would enable a much more direct understanding of the subject under study. There will always be a disparity, however, between historians' present and the past era they are observing; this is an unavoidable fact of historical work, of the work of writing history.

In addition, history is also a discourse, in the usual sense of the term (i.e., not in Benveniste's sense of the term): What historians bring back to life before our eyes is not, of course, the past itself, but rather the present of this past, that is to say the present of the historian's discourse on the past. History is a discourse, in the usual sense of the term, because what historians show us, when they attempt to recreate the past on which their work is based, is not a past, but rather a present: the present of their discourse. It is not the past as past that comes to the surface in the historian's work, but rather the present of this past—the present of the historian's discourse on the past.

As many people have recently remarked, history as a discipline is not as objective as it may appear at first sight. In this sense, the social historian Georges Duby has demonstrated that historians, in the end, invent their sources: "We can see that each generation of historians makes a choice, overlooks certain traces, and exhumes others to which no one for quite some time, or ever, had paid any attention. As a result, the way we look at all this detritus is already subjective; it needs to be inquired into, to be cast in the light of certain questions."[46]

And this inquiry, these questions of interest to historians, is necessarily a product of the present of those historians. In other words, they arise out of what the social agents active in the present—and the historian is one of these agents—see as the inquiry and questions of the day. The first factor historians should take into account is thus the historicity of their own approach, of their approach to past works and acts. Historians are thus led to emphasize the distance between them and the past. Acknowledging the historicity of one's own approach is to understand that there is no fresh approach to the past and that one's perspective on the past is always, of necessity, at a distance from the object under study.

This principle, which holds that it is always a good idea for historians to emphasize the distance separating them from the past, should even serve as a guide and disabuse them of the illusion that their research can give them direct access to the past, or that, by means of patient recreation, they can bring back the past or bring it back to life.

In the end, historians ask only the questions in which they and their contemporaries are interested. This explains, precisely, the historicity of their approach to the past, as well as their necessary historical subjectivity and the equally necessary relativity of their interest in events in the past. The historicity of the historian's approach to the past resides quite simply in the fact that the nature and intensity of this approach are also part of a historical process; it too forms part of a history. Not of the history of past lives or of the objects of this past in which the historian is interested, but the history historians themselves are in the process of experiencing, even as they write their histories, even as they project onto the history of the past an analytical framework inherited from their own history—a framework that retains only those historical objects that fit this framework.

A Case Study: The Film Lecturer

If one is looking for a good example of a widespread phenomenon that nevertheless escaped notice by traditional film history, one need think only of film lecturers and their strange lot in the early part of the twentieth century. Animated pictures, we now know, were often accompanied by live commentary spoken by a "lecturer" present in the room who embellished the film screening with his live performance. Despite this service rendered and the way it benefited film shows, and despite his usefulness (he was even able in many cases to help the viewer grasp the film's narrative), the institution did not hesitate to kick this "vile" accomplice of the exhibitioner[47] out of the venues in which films were seen. Indeed, the institution would soon encourage exhibitioners to transform themselves into shrewd theater owners serving up a canned discourse prepared elsewhere by the film's "publisher" (in France, midway through the first decade of the century, companies associated with what we today would call film production began to call themselves publishers in a desire to take on some of the prestige of a book publisher). These changes foretold the beginning of the era of the producer, whose nose, and traditional cigar, was already beginning to peek through in the mid-1910s.

The lecturer's disappearance from the quite empirical and historical world of film exhibition is not the only time he disappeared last century, because it would soon be the turn of film historians to ignore him. This second disappearance a few decades later from the world of memory and history is interesting in light of my discussion here because it is a flagrant example of the way all historians of necessity select sources and facts from the historical material at their disposal.

Lecturers appear to be absent from the work of traditional film historians, but if you look closely you will find that they never truly disappeared from film history (from film historiography). Occasional mention of their performances can be found in the writings of the principal film historians, but these are usually brief and scattered allusions that are rarely based on documentary sources.[48] In this sense, I have been able to identify in Georges Sadoul's principal work six minor mentions of the lecturer.[49] Let's look at them one by one:

> Attracted by this grandiloquent handbill [for the Cinéorama], a crowd gathered in the basket of the giant hot-air balloon. . . . The voice of a lecturer barked: "Now, ladies and gentlemen, we are going to Brussels, to Marché aux Herbes Square."[50]
>
> In fairground cinemas, *lecturers* replaced the ideal *phonograph* during the films' projection.[51]
>
> *The Barber of Seville* and *Faust* are pure filmed theater without any true inventiveness. These films, when not commented on by a skilled lecturer, must have been boring.[52]
>
> "In the ten-cent halls, tickets are distributed by 'checkogramm' [*sic*]. The orchestra is a piano, a violin, and a large crate, each playing its own part out of tune with the others. From time to time an individual with a megaphone tosses out jokes."[53]
>
> What with the confusion caused by the absence of live actors, three dimensions, color, speech, and sounds, and what with the imperfection of the lighting, which did not set the characters off from the decor, Méliès had to resort to coloring, a lecturer, sounds, outlandish mimicry and the conventions of pantomime while at the same time abandoning any expression on the part of the actors.[54]
>
> Some of these films may have been made in Japan. They were commented on by lecturers, as they were in Europe. Japanese audiences developed a taste for this commentary, which became an essential part of the filmgoing experience.[55]

These are the parsimonious references to a figure whom Sadoul nevertheless acknowledges, judging from his remarks, to be of some importance. This shouldn't surprise us. What should surprise us is not that Sadoul very nearly doesn't mention the lecturer, but that he is mentioned as little as he is. Since Sadoul mentions in passing the lecturer's relative importance, he is obviously not unaware

Figure 5. A film lecturer in action. Drawing used in the publicity materials of the company Raff & Gammon. Source: GRAFICS.

of his existence. The film lecturer, as he was called back then, was an essential part of presentations of animated pictures, and for a historian not to notice this in the documents he consults must mean he is literally closing his eyes to the fact. Yet this is what Sadoul did, to a certain extent, because while he was not unaware of the lecturer's existence, he chose to ignore him—because of that fundamental parameter, that shortcoming of writing history: the historicity of the historian's approach, which guides and programs their interest toward one or another aspect of the phenomena under study. In fact, his silence on the lecturer's performances might lead us to accuse Sadoul, under the influence of his own historicity, of inflecting his own approach to early cinema. This is the fate of every historian, whether "traditional" or "new."

For Sadoul, who carried out the bulk of his research in the 1930s, '40s, and early '50s, the film lecturer, despite his widespread presence, was a negligible factor in film history. Worse than that, we might even suppose that it was in Sadoul's interest, whether he was conscious of it or not, to conceal this embarrassing figure, because he revealed the narrative shortcomings of kinematography and held back in the "realm of the fairground attraction"[56] an art form that was still trying to establish its pedigree and achieve a minimum of social recognition in the years Sadoul wrote his multivolume film history, in the 1940s and '50s. We should also add that, in Sadoul's day, this art form was still seeking its identity and, above all, its theoretical specificity, and had no interest in showing that it was incapable of narrative self-sufficiency in its early years of existence.

It must have been embarrassing, in fact, that cinema had to rely for so many years, in both towns and traveling fairs (in which it was long captive), on the support of this champion of exogenous and nonspecific discourse—an "illegitimate" forebear of what Albert Laffay, already in Sadoul's day, called the "great image-maker," which films with a narrator brought to the forefront of ideas about film narrative: "Films with a narrator may be less common today. Nevertheless, this style was the chemical developer that revealed a hidden virtual presence in all films: a kind of master of ceremonies, the great image-maker who gives photographic views their meaning, rhythm, and duration."[57] By his relative silence, Sadoul was in line with the nascent cinematic institution of the 1910s, which believed it had to keep the film lecturer at a distance from this supposedly "silent" art. This leads me to believe that early cinema was deemed "silent" retrospectively, after the arrival of talking films, out of pure denial, as if to repudiate in an overdetermined manner the verbal yet embarrassing presence of the lecturer.

The Return of the Repressed Lecturer

After the Brighton congress, the film lecturer was back in the spotlight thanks to an article by Martin Sopocy, in which he tackles the question head-on, not restricting himself to fairground cinema.[58] Sopocy does not discuss the film lecturer in an empirical manner; on the contrary, he remarks that it was through a close reading of the film catalogues issued by James Williamson, an artisanal British manufacturer of animated pictures, that he was led to surmise the necessary presence of the lecturer at film screenings, without whom Williamson's views would have been completely incomprehensible for the average viewer. Sopocy also explains in his article how it is evident from a reading of these catalogues that the company making the views advertised within them was counting on the presence of a lecturer at the screening.

In the early 1980s, scholars had to work inductively in order to trace the poorly defined outlines of the lecturer. Back then we had only a few dozen documented references from the period that unquestionably attested to his presence at film screenings. Once the "hunt" for the lecturer began, references to this essential "actor" in so-called silent cinema and to his verbal performance have been popping up everywhere.[59] The historicity of our approach is also a programmed approach: in the end, we see only what we are prepared to see.

Do not think that this historicity can be found only in the work of the so-called traditional film historians. As I mentioned above, this same bias can be found in the work of everyone who tries their hand at history. The relative hypertrophy of the lecturer in contemporary discourse on animated pictures would appear to be due to an approach whose historicity is in no way in doubt, even though this historicity is different from that found in Sadoul. The difference between these two discourses is a result, precisely, of the fact that they belong to different historical periods. Wasn't it in keeping with the mission of showing cinema's grandeur and of attempting to obtain recognition for it in intellectual circles as an art form that the widespread presence of this base mountebank, the lecturer, was well hidden in Sadoul's day? And isn't it also in keeping with the state of affairs today, when cinema's legitimacy and specificity have been widely acknowledged, that one of the hottest research topics is narratology and that there has been an inflation of discussion of this narrative helper, the lecturer?

The Revisionist Brighton School

Contrary to what we might sometimes be led to believe, the foremost task of the historian is not to re-create the past as it was at the time under study. As we will see farther on, the work of historians, whether they are conscious of this or not, always involves a balance of re-creation and interpretation. The interpretive task insidiously determines how the re-creation is carried out, because any attempt at re-creation always occurs on the basis of one interpretation or another.

The history of the period of animated pictures written by Sadoul, Jacobs, and Mitry will always remain, almost necessarily, the history that had to be written between 1940 and 1970, with all the prejudices of those years intact. And the history being written today by the "new historians" of the "revisionist Brighton school," which arose in Brighton in 1978,[60] is the history they had to write after the end of the 1960s (a decade that includes a famous month of May in 1968 in France). These new historians, to our eyes, certainly use a series of more scientific suppositions than those underlying the research of Mitry, Jacobs, and Sadoul, but they may not be seen as such by historians a few decades from now. Won't the historians of the future adopt other suppositions in their turn, ones better fitted to their ideology and era? Won't they too have to rewrite the history of animated pictures, to come up with their own history?

Any history is contingent, and yet it is also necessary.

Chapter 2

The Emergence of the Kinematograph

As I have mentioned several times already, one of the fundamental questions in any historical study of film today is the following: Can "early cinema" really be described as cinema? Would it not be preferable to establish a clear distinction between kinematography before institutionalization and the cinema that came with and after institutionalization? Are there not good reasons to believe that there was a clean and radical break between so-called "early cinema" and institutional cinema?

This situation is pretty much analogous to that which can be found with respect to what people call, mistakenly to my mind, "precinema." This unfortunate expression is an attempt to gather together under a single heading the various experimental techniques and instruments, optical toys, and other visual devices that came before cinema (at the same time as they "foretold" it to various degrees), whether the phenakistiscope, chronophotography, or the magic lantern. Isn't this another flagrant and extreme example of cutting history up after the fact in a way that does not respect the integrity of the object under study? To try to study chronophotography, say, in light of its supposed "precinematic" quality is to shackle oneself with a teleological approach. It seems to me that defining forms of visual observation that came before cinema as precinematic is a way of denying history, of taking the object under study and removing it from history. It prevents us from thinking historically. A conception such as this involves a reductive and ahistorical vision that any historian should want to reject in favor of a variety of points of view on the object under study.

To achieve this, historians must adopt a panoptical vision. They must take a panoramic perspective and assume a variety of successive observation posts that would be the envy of the most complex of Eadweard Muybridge's camera setups. These are the multiple perspectives I will endeavor to employ here. This change of approach applies not only to the relationship between film historians and "precinema," but also to their relationship with "early cinema." Both these phenomena have an essential feature that has not been sufficiently recognized until now: their fundamental diversity. Film history is too often written by historians who espouse a unified view and search among the odds and ends of early cinema or precinema for something that is not there.

The traditional distinction between precinema and early cinema supposes that there exists a break between the two periods, one located around 1890 for the partisans of Edison and around 1895 for those of Lumière. As I remarked in the Introduction, the invention of the basic apparatus is not, for me, a true moment of rupture. By postulating, mistakenly it would seem, a break between precinema and early cinema sometime in the last decade of the nineteenth century, historians are literally cutting the latter off from its deepest roots, which reach into the most distant lands of what is known as precinema. This approach reinforces teleological reflexes in historians, leading them to evaluate early cinema's place in history from a strictly forward-looking perspective and to view it above all else as an antechamber to latter-day cinema (or "second-era" cinema),[1] the logical and natural outcome of the zero era that was precinema and the initial era that was early cinema. Once historians do this, it becomes difficult for them to establish a method for recognizing the ties that would otherwise be apparent between early cinema and precinema.

In particular, this teleological reflex leads film historians, quite "naturally," to give weight to those agents, actions, and procedures in these early years that foretold the cinema yet to come, thereby (because they appear to prefigure the new paradigm) officially taking on a highly progressive aspect. At the same time, this same reflex leads historians to devalue those elements of early cinema that seem to grow directly out of so-called precinema, thereby taking on a regressive air. This, as we saw clearly in chapter 1, was one of the greatest complaints made in the 1970s and '80s against traditional film historians such as Georges Sadoul and Jean Mitry. What is needed, however, is to go beyond reproach and to radically change our approach.

Naturally, it would be difficult to argue that early cinema was not, in a sense, the antechamber of what came afterward, but it is far from that alone. So-called early cinema was not only a point of departure; it was also a point of arrival. It didn't only foretell the cinema yet to come; it also, at the same time, was the culmination of various cultural practices based on images, whether photographic or not, moving or not, illuminated or not—cultural practices, we should add, that were part of the social fabric.

This is why I lobby for a study of early kinematography that would systematically give precedence to a retrospective rather than prospective approach. There is more to be gained, at least for some time to come, in studying cinema from before 1908, say, from the point of view of its direct connection with what is commonly described as precinema. That is to say, by looking backward rather than forward, by tracing its chronology in reverse—contrary to the method employed by traditional film historians who, although they devoted a great number of pages to cinema's "pioneers" (for which we must be grateful), carried out their work from a radically forward-looking perspective and without clear awareness of the trap of teleology. In this sense, Walter Benjamin's remark about materialist historians, that they "regard it as [their] task to brush history against the grain,"[2] could be adopted here. Perhaps we should even play out the metaphor and say that the task of the materialist historian is also to brush history "against its path."

To take a retrospective approach is to make as great an effort as possible to see early cinema and institutional cinema as something other than a single block and to emphasize the enormous distance separating them. Such an approach can only promote the repatriation of early cinema to the side of "precinema" and place the two of them in a single synchronic block. We must thus persuade ourselves that the fundamental moment of rupture in film history was not the invention of moving picture cameras in the 1890s (the Kinetograph, the Cinématographe) but the constitution in the 1910s of the institution "cinema," whose primary principle could be seen as a systematic rejection of the ways and customs of early cinema, to which some might argue it no longer owed a thing (this is not an entirely false statement). From this point of view, what is required is to emphasize what I have proposed elsewhere[3] we call early cinema's alien quality.

A Troubling Alien Quality

It would be wise to bring out this alien quality of early cinema in our research into and work on the phenomenon—to highlight both the fact that it was irreducibly alien to the cinema that followed it and, just as important, the fact that early cinema (or at least the films it gave rise to) seems alien to the distant observers we are, watching it more than a century later. This recognition of the alien quality of early cinema has quite major consequences, if only in the way it facilitates an awareness of the fundamental differences in the way films such as *L'Arrivée d'un train en gare de La Ciotat* (*Train Entering a Station*, Lumière, 1897) and *Le Bourreau turc* (*The Terrible Turkish Executioner*, Méliès, 1903) are seen today and the way these same films (but are they really the same films?) were seen a hundred years ago by early cinema's spectators. Historical research must take into account the incommensurable distance separating us, and that will always separate us, from the past.

It is impossible for film historians to ensconce themselves in the mind of a viewer in the past and unthinkable that they adopt a position of internal focalization, or internal ocularization, based on what they believe to be this viewer's consciousness.[4] Unless they were to undertake highly blameworthy (blameworthy from the point of view of the paradigm "history") paraleptic contortions.

The break in continuity that can be seen between early cinema and institutional cinema is the equivalent in the arts of an epistemological rupture for the historian of science. It would seem more worthwhile, if only for heuristic reasons, to exaggerate this alien quality of early cinema with respect to institutional

Figure 6. *Le Bourreau turc* (*The Terrible Turkish Executioner*, Georges Méliès, 1903). Film still. Source: GRAFICS/Library of Congress/Georges Méliès © ADAGP, Paris, 2007.

cinema than to try to nullify it. The irreducibility of this alien quality becomes apparent when we seek to remain conscious of the extent of the break in continuity being proposed here and succeed in making its various aspects materially present. When describing early cinema, one of the techniques we could use to clearly distinguish between the two paradigms would be systematically to use the terms and expressions current in the period in question. Spelled out, this would mean saying, for example, "manufacturer of animated pictures" instead of "film producer," "kinematographer" instead of "cineaste," et cetera, in keeping with the usage of the day. The mental effort needed each time we are forced to make a lexical choice of this kind is a form of intellectual gymnastics that enables us to get a better and more tangible grasp of the alien quality of early cinema. Seeing Méliès and Porter, for example, as kinematographers (which they were) rather than as cineastes (which they were not) does not at all involve the same critical and theoretical framework.[5]

The suggestion that we use the vocabulary of the period is not without danger. We must beware of working at cross-purposes to historicism, something decried by Hans-Georg Gadamer: "This was, however, the naive assumption of historicism, namely that we must set ourselves within the spirit of the age, and think with its ideas and its thoughts, not with our own, and thus advance toward historical objectivity. In fact the important thing is to recognise the distance in time as a positive and productive possibility of understanding."[6] Let's take another look at one of Gadamer's last comments: "the important thing is to recognise the distance in time as a positive and productive possibility of understanding." The important thing about an action that brings to the surface of our discourse the lexemes of a past discourse is thus not the completely artificial closeness such a thing almost automatically creates. What is important, rather, is the distance between our minds and those lexemes that, strangely enough (when I say strange, think alien), seem not to fit their referent ("manufacture a picture" for "produce a film," but also "artificially arranged scenes" for "film shot on a set" and "film publisher" for "film producer" or "film distributor"). Or the distance between our minds and other lexemes with which we are not familiar and that, just as strangely, appear in the language of the day ("kinematograph" as a verb, etc.).

It is thus not a question of finding ways to think about early cinema using concepts from the period, or of picturing ourselves in that period. The movement we seek is not from the present to the past but rather from the past to the present—to bring into the present the fragrance of the past, a little like Marcel Proust's madeleines, if you will. In short, it is a question of bringing the past to us in a way that enables the spirit of our age (the only one we have access to), once the shock has passed, to examine (using the methods of our day) the correct objects—past objects as they existed in relation to one another in the past. In short, we must avoid examining objects outside their context. To study the work of Méliès-the-cineaste is to study an ahistorical object outside its context. It is neither more nor less than mistaking the object of study.

This lexical flashback, whose relevance I have tried here to demonstrate, enables us to make tangible the temporal distance that, in Gadamer's view, is a "positive and productive possibility" for understanding. My idea is not so much to use period concepts to take us back in time artificially, but to create true lexical contrasts. Not, to rephrase what I said in the preceding paragraph, to take us back there back then, into the spirit of that age, so that we might make that spirit our own, but rather to bring out, here and now, the difference between early cinema and institutional cinema—to grasp the distance that separates us from the past because of the intrinsically alien quality of early cinema. To think here and now, in the early part of the twenty-first century, about the reality of this cinema back there back then, at the end of the nineteenth century and the beginning of the twentieth.

This approach will also make life easier for anyone who categorically refuses to see this earlier period as an antechamber to the latter, something that has been part of the new historians' program for quite some time. It is sometimes difficult systematically to put this point of view into practice for lack of the means and methods. It seems to me, therefore, that a rejection of teleology thus involves dissociating early cinema from institutional cinema. And exacerbating the break between the two paradigms is the only viable, or valid, method to guard against any tendency to adopt, even unconsciously, teleological concepts.

With these two specific and quite separate moments, like two opposite poles (the here and now of the historian and the back there back then of the event), it becomes possible to emphasize in a fully conscious manner the distance separating us from the past and, especially, to bring out what lies between these two poles: the historian's approach. One of the essential conditions of this approach is temporal in nature, because it is from the here and now that historians apprehend the past, a past that is always and already endowed with an intrinsic historicity.

And what might the historicity of the historian's approach be? What are its effects? I would say, first of all, that they are of primary importance; for it is through them that history is built and written. The historicity of the historian's approach is the primary determinant of writing history.

Manufacturing Animated Pictures versus Producing Films

I believe we should posit early cinema's alien quality as one of the bases of our approach to its study as a way of adequately taking into account the institutionalization process cinema underwent in the 1910s. The cultural practice we are studying would thus not become film production, an expression that describes an activity that did not yet exist at the time of so-called early cinema. What did exist was the artisanal manufacture of kinematographic views, a cultural practice not subject to the conventions that would form the basis of cinema as an institution. It is not enough to remark and acknowledge that the forms of narrative found in early cinema are different from those found in institutional cinema; one must go beyond this mere fact and fully realize what underlies it. This is why I will emphasize here the need, both methodical and heuristic, to dissociate early cinema and institutional cinema and to see them as quite distinct.

The period described as early cinema gave rise to all kinds of relatively ephemeral practices—so ephemeral that they appear not to be of great importance in the long diachronic continuum that stretches from the invention of the Kinetograph and the Cinématographe to celebrations a few years ago around cinema's supposed centenary. Yet when we examine these practices using early cinema alone as our yardstick and view them against the brief diachrony of this historical period (a diachrony so brief that one might easily mistake it for a synchrony), they take on importance and become preeminent. This is because within this historical period there exist, with respect to both filmic practices and the filmic texts, specific differences that we must not erase if we wish to better understand the cultural and formal issues at stake in early cinema.

A clear distinction between the periods before and after cinema's institutionalization is especially important if we also wish to understand the role of the various agents responsible for what we might call the process of *mise en film*, to use an expression sometimes used in French in the 1910s.[7] The manufacture of animated pictures,[8] that is, their *mise en film* in the era of so-called early cinema, involved those agents that, since institutionalization, have been strictly associated with distribution and exhibition on the one hand and production on the other. Indeed it is well known that, in those days, showmen manipulated their strips of film without hesitation. This was done not only with the manufacturers' knowledge, but also with their approval and encouragement—when they didn't instigate the practice themselves. If only for this reason, we can see the distance separating the world in which animated pictures were manufactured and the world in which films are produced under the institution.

This manipulation of the film by the person showing it was often quite extensive: Not only did they choose the films for their program (quite a few films because of their very short length); they also chose the order in which they would be shown. In addition, they edited or reedited the strips of film as necessary, prepared any commentary that would accompany them, and arranged for musical accompaniment or at the very least a musician. The agents we call "exhibitors" undertook a series of operations that would later be a part of the process of production, literally appropriating the films and branding them in a sense. They were thus not mere exhibitors, and it is essential to avoid speaking of them as such. This is why, as I explained in chapter 1, I often refer to them throughout this book as "exhibitioners." The production/exhibition division is part of a dialectic that does not jibe with the practices seen in early cinema, and we must undertake to divide these functions up in a new way that takes into account the things we have learned about this period in recent years.

Institutionalization as a Point of Rupture

To state that there was a break between so-called early cinema and institutional cinema is to bring a radically new approach to early cinema studies and to finally stop trying to see what remains of it in institutional cinema. It is also to bring out the differences between these two paradigms and to show how "organic" these differences are, as a result of the fact that before cinema's institutionalization nothing was yet cast in stone with respect to film practices and the uses to which the medium was put. Between the time of the invention of the basic device (between 1890 and 1895) and the period of the institution (beginning around 1915), kinematography was a wide-open field of experimentation. This was when artisanal manufacturers of animated pictures took various initiatives, almost all of which tended to modify the initial project inscribed, so to speak, in the "genes" of the apparatus (or, if you prefer, in the various patents filed by its many inventors). The views manufactured at the time of early cinema contained a diverse range of formal devices and techniques, of unequal merit in the eyes of today's scholar. Kinematographers' initiatives gave rise to two kinds of devices and to two kinds of techniques: those that would survive in the institution and those that would not. Early cinema's trajectory was not regular, and historians have to take this into account when they describe and evaluate both the devices and techniques that survived and those that did not.

This is essential and must be followed by any researcher wishing to avoid teleology. Teleology is not simply to return ad nauseam to cinema's "firsts"; it is also to say about Méliès, for example, that he introduced trick effects, makeup, sets, et cetera into cinema. When it comes down to it, Méliès was incapable of introducing anything into cinema because cinema as such did not exist when he was making films.

Early Cinema?

Beginning in the 1960s, in French, the expression *le cinéma des premiers temps* gradually began to take the place of *cinéma primitif*, whose equivalent was less common in English and which I will discuss below. We might translate this expression as "the cinema of early times" or "the first cinema," while the expression that has been adopted in English, of course, is "early cinema." Another term used in French is *le cinéma des origines*, which we might translate as "cinema at its source."

The expression "early cinema" beguiles us with illusions and is unsuited to the reality it pretends to describe. Beginning, as we have seen, with the use of the very word "cinema" to describe this period in which the manufacture of animated pictures reigned; to describe these views as cinema seems to usurp the term. According to the position I am arguing here, cinema as such did not yet exist in the period of so-called early cinema.

Early cinema? If it is not cinema, exit, therefore, the term "cinema"!

Each of the other two components of the expression "the cinema of early times" is worthy of suspicion. Let's look, for example, at the determinative complement "early times." Here is a determination whose first shortcoming is the way it implies a completely Western sense of historical time, as Silvestra Mariniello has described;[9] she suggests that we should instead be addressing a set of issues. The term "early" gives off a whiff of ethnocentrism. It is not clear that early cinema in the United States, for example, has anything whatsoever in common with the early cinema of a country that had been unexposed to the new medium before the 1930s.

Some might say that this objection, although undeniable, is not a major one, because it is always possible to contextualize our use of this term. Be that as it may, the shoe also pinches elsewhere, and in a way that is clearly beyond remedy. To use "early" to speak of practices around the kinematograph, in the sense understood here, implies that the path taken when the kinematograph became cinema and the goal of that path had already been settled. To use the term "early" is to adopt a position completely opposed to my position here. It is to decide in advance to put on teleological glasses that oblige the observer to conclude that the phenomenon under observation is just beginning (this is what "early" means), that it isn't doing too badly for a youngster, and that it will surely make progress as the years go by. . . .

In the end, however, the cinema's "early times" are also, and perhaps most of all, the "late times" of certain other phenomena. Let me make myself clear: I am not saying that the kinematograph cannot be seen as being at the early times of such and such a phenomenon. Of course it can. But to label our object of study "early cinema" is to highlight one aspect that an inquiry such as ours has no interest in privileging, if our inquiry is fully to grasp the subject's contours. For the time of so-called early cinema borders on two worlds: the time when the kinematograph did not yet exist (before 1890–95) and the time when early cinema, having yielded its place to cinema—to institutional cinema—no longer existed (around 1915).

When we give our allegiance to what is presupposed by the expression "early cinema," we find ourselves saying, for example, that Méliès introduced this or that into the cinema. Rather, the reverse is true: what Méliès did, and most effectively, was introduce the kinematograph into theater, if only into the Robert-Houdin theater! Méliès's own explanation tends to confirm this: "The publishers of artificially arranged scenes have all more or less followed the path I laid down, and one of them, the head of the world's largest kinematographic company, known for its mass, low-cost production, told me himself: 'Thanks to you, the kinematograph has managed to sustain itself and has become an unprecedented success. By *applying animated photographs to the theater*, to its infinite variety of subjects, you prevented its decline, which would otherwise have rapidly occurred with natural scenes, whose inevitable similarities would have quickly bored the audience.'"[10]

What the "head of the world's largest kinematographic company" (probably Charles Pathé) reportedly said to Méliès was that his greatest accomplishment was to have applied animated photographs to the theater, that is to say to have introduced kinematography into the theater (i.e., into stage entertainment), not the reverse.

We have everything to gain, I believe, from looking at so-called early cinema not from the perspective of how it constituted the early times of the new cultural practice that was to become the cinema but rather in relation to the practices that adopted kinematography, in a sense, in order to carry out in a new way what was already being done by the practices in question before the new technique came along.

This inversion of things makes all the difference, because the arrival of the kinematograph in Méliès's world extended a firmly established practice. And, by situating this arrival in the extension of this previous practice, it becomes possible for us to better grasp its profound significance. Not by stating that something started with the introduction of this new technology and by making the past a blank slate. Nor, likewise, by consecrating Méliès as a "cineaste" while not mentioning his true nature (I should say his true culture) as a man of the theater and a magician.

Jacques Deslandes understood this perfectly when he wrote that "Méliès was not a pioneer of the cinema, he was the last man to work in fairy theater."[11] Méliès himself had no illusions about his true vocation when he declared that "My film career has been so tied up with my career at the Robert-Houdin theater that one can barely tell them apart."[12] Or, once again, when he said about his film studio, "In short, we have a quite faithful, small-scale likeness of a fairy theater."[13]

There thus may not have been, as Méliès himself said, a clear break between his theatrical career and his film career, in the same way that there is no clear distinction between the titles of his stage performances and the titles of his films. Indeed it would be impossible, without consulting the documentation, to discern which of Méliès's works were films and which were stage acts. This is true of the following list, which gives the impression of being a list of films, if it weren't for their production dates (given in parentheses), which confirm that they were all well and truly stage acts: *La Fée des fleurs ou le Miroir de Cagliostro* ("The Flower Fairy or Cagliostro's Mirror," 1889), *L'Enchanteur Alcofrisbas* ("Alcofrisbas the Enchanter," 1889), *Le Manoir du Diable* ("The Devil's Manor," 1890), *Les Farces de la Lune ou les Mésaventures de Nostradamus* ("The Moon's Pranks or the Misadventures of Nostradamus," 1891), *Le Charlatan fin de Siècle* ("The Turn of the Century Charlatan," 1892), and *L'Auberge du Diable* ("The Devil's Inn," 1894).[14]

To be persuaded that Méliès's filmed fairy plays are a strict outgrowth of the fairy plays of his day, we need only read the following text, published ten years before the invention of the Cinématographe and whose author we might mistake for Méliès in 1903, the year he made *Le Royaume des fées* (*Fairyland, or the Kingdom of Fairies*): "The fairy play [is] surely a delightful entertainment when it is in the hands of a true poet. It freely enters the whimsy of his imagination and can both delight the viewer's mind and enchant their eyes. . . . Audiences always show up in great numbers to any fairy play on offer, because they adore this truly magical entertainment, made constantly more fascinating by advances in mise en scène. . . . A fairy play . . . [can only] be performed in places where changes of perspective, trick effects, quick changes of characters and transformation scenes can be easily carried out."[15]

These words were written in 1885 by Arthur Pougin, in his *Dictionnaire historique et pittoresque du théâtre et des arts qui s'y rattachent*, a volume whose subtitle ("the adjacent arts") is an impressive list of attendant cultural practices (or, better yet, cultural series, to get ahead of myself a little here with respect to this concept I will define in chapter 4): "poetry, music, dance, pantomime, sets, costumes, machinery, acrobatics/activities from Ancient times, fairground entertainments, stage entertainment, public holidays, popular celebrations, carrousels, races, tournaments, etc. etc. etc."

While it applies almost absolutely to Méliès, my thesis remains valid, with a minimal degree of adaptation, for all manufacturers of animated pictures. What the Lumière brothers created, and this has often been acknowledged without all the repercussions being fully understood, was moving photographs, and their work must necessarily be seen as part of the history of photography. Lumière views belong as much if not more to the history of photographic views than to the history of cinema. It would be more productive to write the history of this work by comparing it synchronically with other work from the cultural practice from which it is derived than to study it diachronically as part of film history. For Lumière views did not take the place of the other products in the cultural practice from which they are derived; in a sense, what they did was amalgamate themselves with these products.

It is thus clear that the first experiments to which the introduction of the kinematograph gave rise belonged to practices that in no way whatsoever were in their "early" periods.

Early cinema? No, what we are concerned with here is not the mere "early" quality of the phenomenon. Exit, therefore, early!

What remains of this famous expression? Of "early cinema," nothing. But if we return to the French expression "le cinéma des premiers temps" and our translation of it as "the cinema of early times" or "the first cinema," we find a singular article, "the"—a quite singular article indeed! And so we must also critique this word that, despite its relatively small size, beguiles us with illusions just as much as the other two terms of the equation. Because this the, at bottom, is an attempt to join what can't be joined. The cultural practice "fairy play," even in its film version, had little in common with the cultural practice "magic act," even in its film version, and even when both were united somewhat artificially in a Méliès catalogue. The views screened at the Maison Dufayel cinema in Paris for children and their nannies surely had little in common with the exhibition in a traveling country fair of a film like Méliès's *Tentation de Saint-Antoine* (*The Temptation of St. Anthony*, 1898). So too did the screening in Paris of Méliès's *Raid Paris–Monte-Carlo* (*An Adventurous Automobile Trip*, 1905) have little in common with the conditions in which Henry de Grandsaignes d'Hauterives screened views in Quebec.[16] And a Pathé film's gay tale of a rake screened in New York's Lower East Side had little in common with a view screened to complement a magic lantern show organized by *La Bonne Presse* in Paris.

Before institutionalization, the various practices around the kinematograph had little in common with each other; it is film historians and theorists who have united them, artificially and idealistically, in their discourse: "the" first cinema, "the" cinema of early times. But there was not just one cinema before 1910, there were dozens, and none was truly dominant, because the cinema, precisely, had not yet been institutionalized.

The cinema of early times? Exit, therefore, the!

Some of my film studies colleagues, I presume, will be pleased at this dismemberment of the expression "early cinema." Jacques Aumont, first of all, who recently wrote, "Why replace a word [primitive], whose history after all is interesting, with the awkward and outrageously inelegant expression 'the cinema of early times' ('cinéma des premiers temps')?"[17]

In place of the expression "early cinema," or "the cinema of early times" in French, some prefer the expression "primitive cinema," which was so popular in French that it dominated discussion of film history in France for forty or fifty years. To my mind, the expression "primitive cinema" prevents historical thinking[18] about cinema just as much if not more than "early cinema." In French, references to this period since the end of the silent era have thus been divided between "primitive cinema," which took hold in the 1930s, and "early cinema," which began to be seen in the 1960s and ended up becoming dominant, rather belatedly, some fifteen or twenty years ago.[19]

A "Primitive" Cinema?

One might retort that the word "primitive" does not always have negative connotations. As an adjective, according to the *Oxford English Dictionary*, the word has no fewer than twelve accepted meanings, of which only two are clearly pejorative. The first and thereby oldest meaning given by the *OED* is "of or belonging to the first age, period, or stage; pertaining to early times; earliest, original; early, ancient" (note here the use of the adjectives "first" and "early").

But we must not forget that primitive also refers to "a group, or to persons composing such a group, whose culture, through isolation, has remained at a simple level" and to art "[e]xecuted by one who has not been trained in a formal manner." In the context of our new approaches to the history of the kinematograph's early years, what do we have to gain by adopting a label for our object of study that might equate the earliest animated pictures with crude and simple objects, the product of an undeveloped culture and founded on ignorance?

Whatever one may say, the word "primitive" always leaves a bad taste in the mouth. This is not new, if we are to believe one of the historical actors whose wide-ranging influence we study: Georges Méliès himself. In 1926, when the earliest French kinematographers (beginning with Méliès) had become fashionable in certain French intellectual circles, Méliès wrote: "A true injustice is committed when certain columnists write such things as these earliest kinematographers were 'primitives.' . . . Do they really believe that we were still primitives after twenty years of sustained work and constant perfecting of our craft? . . . Why call us 'primitives' with such an air of contempt?"[20]

But this is not all. Even in one of the nonpejorative noun forms of the word (the *OED* recognizes ten all told), "primitive" misses the mark when it comes to describing kinematographers. In artistic usage, for the *OED*, a primitive is "A painter of the early period, i.e. before the Renaissance." The French-language *Robert* dictionary goes a step further in this direction; for this dictionary, a "primitive" is "an artist from a period prior to that in which the art form in question attained its maturity." There are thus primitive Greek sculptors and primitive Dutch and Italian painters. But Georges Méliès, Edwin Porter, and Louis Lumière cannot be described as "primitive" in this sense! Rather, we should think of Charles Chaplin, Thomas Ince, Louis Feuillade, Abel Gance, and D.W. Griffith as primitive, because these were the artists of the period prior to their art form's supposed "maturity." An art cannot attain what traditional historians consider its maturity (an unpleasant and wholly teleological metaphor) the moment it is born; as François Jost has convincingly demonstrated,[21] film art was not born until the 1910s. And it would not reach so-called maturity until at least the 1920s.

To my mind, the matter is settled. While it is true, as Aumont remarks, that the history of the word primitive is interesting, we must nevertheless formulate ways of thinking about film history that require us to throw the word overboard.

A Terminological Problem

How then are we to name our object of study without getting everything askew? How, on the basis of the criticisms I have just formulated, can I avoid exposing myself to criticism in turn? What might I propose to take the place of the consecrated—and inadequate—expression "early cinema"? I might, for example, get around the problem by resorting, as I have been doing for several years, to the expression "animated pictures" ("vues animées") to speak of the films themselves. This was one of the terms used at the time of their production, but it is not suitable for describing a period or a paradigm. We might also, following the previous generation of scholars (Edgar Morin and Jacques Deslandes in particular), use the term "kinematograph" (*cinématographe*) to identify "early kinematography" (*cinématographie des premiers temps*) and contrast it with the "cinema," which would then be used for institutional cinema alone. Although this is a subtle and quite useful distinction, it is not enough, in my view, to enable us to distinguish clearly and unmistakably between the two entities. What we need for designating so-called "early cinema" is a general and all-encompassing term that ties everything together and subsumes the entire phenomenon we are attempting to put our finger on.

Initially, I thought of returning to the expression "the cinema of attractions," which has the advantage of taking into account that fundamental category, the attraction. Tom Gunning suggested this expression, and he and I introduced it into the field of "early cinema" studies in 1985.[22] But the thorny contradiction posed by the use of the word "cinema" remained. Then I thought of proposing the expression "early kinematography" (which I used a few lines back), but, as we have seen, the determinative complement early gives me cause for concern (although these concerns are fewer and less serious, because I refer to "kinematography" and not "cinema," but still . . .). I would very much have liked to have had a flash of genius and been able to blend these two expressions to come up with something like *cinématographie-attraction*, but I found that I had been beaten to the punch: in consulting Jean Giraud's indispensable *Lexique français du cinéma des origines à 1930*, I discovered that this French term already existed.[23] Its only known occurrence to date is in the writings of one of the first film historians: not just anybody because, some twenty years before publishing his history of the cinema, he had been not only a contemporary of cinémato-graphie-attraction but also one of its major figures. This early (!) historian was G.-Michel Coissac, the author in 1906 of the imposing *La théorie et la pratique des projections*, published by La Bonne Presse.[24] In his *Histoire du cinématographe* (1925), he wrote that, around 1907–08, "the large boulevards in Paris quickly became the center of cinématographie-attraction."[25]

It appears that this is the only time in Coissac's entire book that this expression is used. To my knowledge, there is no other occurrence of it in any other text by any author. It is thus, pending evidence to the contrary, a true hapax.[26] And yet the sense of the expression in Coissac's hands is not clear. He says no more about it than what I have indicated here. The complete paragraph in which it is found reads as follows:

> The large boulevards in Paris quickly became the center of cinématographie-attraction. It could not have been otherwise, because they were and remain today the meeting place not only for Parisians from every quarter but for people from the provinces in Paris on business or pleasure and for a great number of foreigners. A picturesque, cosmopolitan area with a village-fair atmosphere, with new people constantly streaming into it, its sidewalks, which extend from the Madeleine to the Place de la République, are a little like the alleyways of two worlds. There the language of silent film will soon have a better chance of being understood than French itself. We do not wish to see this day, but we are preparing ourselves for it in order to soften the blow![27]

Jean Giraud provides his own definition of this concept but does not push it very far, and particularly not in the direction I take it when I extend the term well beyond, I am aware, what Coissac meant by it. The only source for under-standing Coissac is the brief reference I have just quoted; this accounts, I be-lieve, for the poverty of Giraud's definition: "The force of attraction exerted by the cinema in the day when large cinemas were being built on Paris's boulevards. The specific interest people had in film shows as a result."[28]

Here nevertheless is an expression, *cinématographie-attraction* or, as I will henceforth describe it in English, "kine-attractography,"[29] which, in my view, has the quality of dynamically "problematizing" our object of study. It is an expression that, at the same time as it befits the gaze cast in the 1920s by a participant in the period, corresponds to the idea we have come to have of the early years of kinematography in the past few years, at the beginning of the twenty-first century.

Chapter 3

Attraction and the Kinematograph

We might suppose that a scholar such as Jacques Aumont—who has argued, as we saw in the previous chapter, that the expression "primitive cinema" be retained—would approve of the term "kine-attractography," if only because it incorporates one of the key themes—attraction—in the ideas of Sergei Eisenstein, ideas for which Aumont is one of the most accomplished heralds. In fact there is a lot to be said for the convergence of Eisensteinian attraction and the attractions of early kinematography,[1] as well as for the importance of attraction throughout the twentieth century in the cultural sphere in general.[2]

This convergence of the attraction of early kinematography and Eisensteinian attraction should not surprise us, because they share a common source. The attractional quality of kine-attractography is not merely an intellectual category devised by contemporary scholars in need of interpretive models. Attraction was a fact of life that the various protagonists of kine-attractography had to face in their daily activities, being fully aware of the fact. When, in the early 1920s, Eisenstein seized on the concept of attraction and gave it a place in his theory (and thus in film theory as a whole), the word attraction had already been on everyone's lips, or almost, for nigh on thirty years. And all that time it had the same meaning as it had, in the beginning, for Eisenstein.

In fact, Eisensteinian attraction and the attraction of early kinematography both derived directly from a common source, the culture of popular stage entertainment dating from the beginning of the twentieth century. This is something that Tom Gunning and I were completely unaware of when, in 1985, we proposed that the concept of attraction be used to better understand early kinematography.[3]

Thus, in the same year that Eisenstein published his first article on attraction, in 1923,[4] the popular French magazine *Ciné pour tous* published an anonymous two-page article entitled "Attraction in Films,"[5] which basically set out how films of the day were constructed around brief moments of attraction such as storms, explosions, and other sudden occurrences. The article praises chase films in particular for being able to exploit all the possibilities of movement. The author mentions the climactic rescue scenes in D.W. Griffith's films and does not hesitate to criticize the films of the day (the early 1920s) for indiscriminately employing a wide range of disasters as climaxes (fires, cyclones, explosions, earthquakes, etc.): "We have quickly reached the point where the attraction reigns in a sensational manner and is incorporated into films sometimes without cause in order to heighten their appeal." The author even asks whether such a great number of "high points" are necessary when they so often seem to be "perfectly useless to the logical development of the action."

The word attraction, as I remarked above, was on everyone's lips and at the tip of everyone's pen. We find it in journalism as early as 1896: "With the arrival of the warm weather, attractions in Paris are more numerous and varied every day at the kinematograph."[6] Or, as another commentator wrote about a 1906 Pathé view, "*Le Tour du monde d'un policier* (*A Policeman's World Tour*) is a magnificent kinematographic attraction."[7] We also find the term in more theoretical or at any rate more reflective texts. This is true of the following particularly penetrating judgment by Louis Delluc in 1917: "Viewers couldn't care less about attractions. They prefer a story, a good story, vivid and well told."[8] The prize for lucidity, nevertheless, goes to E.-L. Fouquet, writing in 1912:

> The kinematograph was long seen as an "attraction." It was used in café-concert, music hall, and vaudeville programs, just like a singer or an acrobat. . . . Today, this is no longer the case: kinematograph shows generally last the whole evening and the audience does not tire of them. The cinema is no longer an attraction but a standard form of entertainment. Unlike what was previously the case, now it is the kinematograph that makes use of certain attractions. . . . Moreover, what is seen as an attraction in music halls, vaudeville theaters, and circuses (tests of strength, balancing acts, magic shows, comic scenes, dances) can be kinematographed and in this way become an entertainment just as interesting as it would be in reality.[9]

As Timothy Barnard and Ada Ackerman have remarked,[10] the link between Eisensteinian attraction and the various forms of attraction that can be found in early films may not be as strong as Tom Gunning and I may have believed when we proposed in 1985 that the concept be applied to the study of early kinematography.[11] Moreover, it would be difficult to dissociate Eisenstein's very conception of attraction from ideas on montage, thereby distancing it considerably from the attractions found in early kinematography.

But what exactly is an attraction?[12] Jean Giraud describes it as the "captivating and sensational element of the program."[13] Or, as Gunning remarks, it is a moment of pure "visual display"[14] characterized by an implicit acknowledgment of the viewer's presence, a viewer who is directly confronted with an exhibitionist display. The attraction is there, before the viewer, in order to be seen. Strictly speaking, it exists only in order to display its visibility. As a rule, attractions are momentary, if not instantaneous; Gunning says that "they can be defined as an immediate presence."[15] In other words, as he comments elsewhere, an attraction is "something that appears, attracts attention, and then disappears without either developing a narrative trajectory or a coherent diegetic world."[16]

The attractions of kine-attractography are thus the peak moments of the show, the aggressive moments punctuating animated pictures. They are scattered throughout their discourse and even form the kernel of most views. This is the case of the punctiliar view (a view made up of a single "shot," a single tableau) *How It Feels to Be Run Over* (Hepworth, 1900), in which an automobile advances toward the camera and knocks it over, causing a sudden and unexpected interruption in the filming. It is also true of *L'Arrivée d'un train en gare de La Ciotat* (*Train Entering a Station*, Lumière, 1897), at the spectacular moment when the locomotive seems as if it is about to run the viewer over. And it is true, finally, of that moment of sudden action in *L'Arroseur arrosé* (*Waterer and Watered*, Lumière, 1895) when the stream of water, suddenly unblocked, sprays the poor gardener in the face.

Attractions, however, are not only the dominant principle of short, punctiliar views from the early years of kinematography. They are also present in the pluripunctiliar views (views made up of more than one shot) that began to grow in number around the turn of the century. Attractions are everywhere, for example, in chase films, which place a series of shots in a sequence that generally serves to show much more than the mere passage of the people taking part in the chase. It is rare for these films not also to outdo each other in the spectacular qualities of their events. When the shot on screen isn't showing us the commotion created by the sudden appearance of a runaway horse and carriage in an outdoor market, it is bringing us into the presence of the repeated stumbling of the pursuers over some immutable obstacle, or showing us the "accidental" fall of worthy ladies as they try to climb a fence.

Figure 7. *How It Feels to Be Run Over* (Hepworth, 1900). In this film, an automobile runs over the movie camera, forcing a sudden halt in filming. Film still. Source: GRAFICS/NFTVA.

Attraction versus Narration

Attraction is not just the dominant principle of kine-attractography. It is also in contradiction with the dominant principle of institutional cinema (and of the cinema of institutionalization): narration. Nevertheless, it is true that attraction and narration can work well together: Often, the attractions found in kine-attractography even form part of a narrative infrastructure. This is what Méliès himself remarked when he wrote the following: "We might say that in this case the script is nothing more than the thread for tying together the 'effects,' which are not closely connected, the way the announcer in a variety performance is there to link scenes that have nothing in common with each other."[17]

Conversely, narrative cinema is often riddled with attractions. Indeed these are present, often on a massive scale, in popular entertainment films, even the most recent; this is especially true of adventure films, musical comedies, suspense films, science fiction films, et cetera. What are James Bond or *Star Wars* movies if not a series of "effects" without much to connect them? (Not to mention pornographic films, which, more than any other kind of film, place the attraction front and center.) Doesn't the tour de force of the scriptwriter of such films consist precisely in tying these scenes together in not too slack a manner? Indeed, this is one of the institution's principles: to dissolve the attractions scattered throughout the film's discourse into a narrative structure, to integrate them in the most organic manner possible.

After all, the apparent contradiction between attraction and narration is only the resurgence of what we might think of as the essential contradiction of the cinema as a system, the ineluctable contradiction that weighs on the kinematograph, constantly torn between the momentary on the one hand and linear progression on the other. The momentary is the attraction, which is inevitably and constantly called into question by the contamination of narrative progression, by the folding of the momentary into progression. By definition, the kinematograph supposes a discourse that unfolds in time and is experienced in its duration. What this means is that any film, and any animated picture as well, no matter how short, is made up of a chain of signifiers lined up one after the other: momentary signifiers subjected to progression (subjected to the process of creating progression involved in the unspooling of the strip of film).

This tension between the momentary and linear progression, moreover, can be found everywhere in the categories we use to think about the cinema. Think in particular of the opposition between monstration and narration, between spectacular effects and narrative effects, the photogram and the shot, framing and editing, et cetera. In the end, the problem of cinema is always the same: to create linear progression out of the momentary. On a strictly technological level, this is even the very definition of cinema: With one photogram, we are in the realm of the momentary (this is the thesis); with a second photogram, and those that follow on, we enter the realm of linear progression (this is the antithesis). We could therefore probably put forward the idea that narration, by virtue of this very dynamic, is a sort of antithesis of attraction.

Monstrative Attractions versus Narrative Integration

An examination of these sorts of questions led Tom Gunning and me, some twenty-five years ago now, to propose that this period from the invention of the kinematograph to the institutionalization of cinema (today I would say the period from kine-attractography to institutional cinema) be seen as a series of "overarching systems," as we called them at the time. We set out to identify and define these systems in order to be able to understand individual films in a way that made it possible, as we remarked at the time, to better discern, within each of them, which elements conform to the system and which diverge from it.[18] We thus had to bring to light the various systems of rules and norms that contributed to establishing a coherent series of expectations around the way a view or film should function in any given era. The stylistic choices of kinematographers and, later, cineastes were made on the basis of these expectations.

Within the period leading up to institutional cinema, Tom Gunning and I identified two successive "modes of film practice."[19] The first of these modes dominated the very earliest period of film history, until about 1908, and the second extended its dominion until about 1915. We called the former the "system of monstrative attractions" and the latter the "system of narrative integration." Within the system of monstrative attractions, film narration was of course completely secondary. In this system, filmic monstration and the attraction reigned. The various cinematic devices we have come to call, perhaps with exaggeration, film language first made their appearance during this period (close-ups, high-angle shots, tracking shots, etc.).

Figure 8. *The Great Train Robbery* (Edison, 1903). An example of a close-up with an undeniable attractional quality. Film still. Source: Cinémathèque québécoise.

In the system of monstrative attractions, however, these devices did not necessarily have the same functions as they would have in the system that followed, that of narrative integration. Thus the close-up, for example, might in the former have a "magnifying glass" function. (The filmic monstrator's close-ups enable us to see "swollen heads," an attractional element if ever there was one.) In the system of narrative integration, however, the close-up had a more indexical and indicative function. (The filmic narrator's close-up became this agent's principal means for indicating a detail and bringing it to the fore without using a magnifying-glass effect, thereby highlighting the device's narrative function.)

In the first case, the object depicted is artificially brought closer to the viewer's eye through a kind of blowing up of the image. Our vision is stimulated by such an attraction, as for example by the highly attractional close-up of the leader of the gang of robbers shooting at the camera in *The Great Train Robbery* (Edison, 1903). In the second case, through some mysterious, unknown process, the viewer comes closer to the object being observed and not the other way around (and herein lies the "magic" of narrative cinema). An example of such a highly narrative close-up is that of the medicine bottle in Griffith's film *The Medicine Bottle* (Biograph, 1909). This shot is a narrative close-up in that, unlike the close-up in *The Great Train Robbery*, it shows a detail from the medium shot preceding it and contributes to the unfolding of the story (by making the viewer aware that the little girl is about to give her grandmother poison and not medicine).

Within the system of monstrative attractions, then, close-ups, high-angle shots, and tracking shots do not have the same function as they do in the system of narrative integration. The reason for this, in particular, is that in the former they are not strictly subjected to "narrativization." The system of narrative integration appears to be a system through which the cinema followed an integrated process of narrativization. During this period when narrative integration took hold (1908–14), filmic discourse was put in the service of the story being told. The various components of cinematic expression were thus mobilized around, and subjected to, strict narrative ends. The dominant feature of the system of narrative integration is essentially one of choosing an element of filmic signification and endowing it with an integrating role. This element is the story to be told. In this system, the goal of better recounting the story it wishes to tell prompts the agent responsible for the film's production to privilege one element of its discourse over another. Pursuit of the same goal leads it to arrange the profilmic[20] one way rather than another, to record unfolding

Figure 9. *The Medicine Bottle* (Biograph, 1909). An example of a "narrative" close-up, used to bring out an element of the story. Film still. Source: GRAFICS.

events one way rather than another. It is also with a view to the story to be told that this agent organizes its filmographic[21] interventions according to one norm and not another. The system of narrative integration also supposes that the story to be told determines how the viewer interprets the filmic discourse's various devices.

What guarantees the suturing of the film narrator and the viewer is the coherence of the process of narrativization. When the system of narrative integration was taking shape, a being was born whose existence is only theoretical but whose task is to modulate and direct cinematic discourse: the filmic narrator, whose "voice" is heard from the beginning of the film to the end. Institutional cinema is a narrative cinema and thus requires a narrator. Early kinematography needs no such narrator. To this internal and relatively invisible agent of the film, the filmic narrator, it prefers the fairground crier, the master of ceremonies in music halls, vaudeville theaters or caf'concs, and the storefront cinema barker, who add the attraction of their own performance to the attractions of kine-attractography.

The Three Paradigms of the Kinematograph

This initial attempt, in 1985, to identify the systems that may have been at work before institutionalization might benefit today from being placed alongside the periodization model I have more recently sketched out with Philippe Marion (and afterward with Frank Kessler). This model distinguishes three paradigms:[22]

1. The paradigm of capturing and restoring
2. The paradigm of monstration
3. The paradigm of narration

The first paradigm, that of capturing and restoring, supposes a minimal threshold of intervention (almost nil) on the part of the person filming: here, we are still under the sway of the fascination exerted by the new possibilities offered up by an invention for reproducing movement. There was no need to intervene in reality, or to manipulate the camera, because the mere recording of reality was quite sufficient to distract and satisfy the viewer. The capturing/restoring paradigm was thus refractory to any manipulation. It contained no profilmic "ar-

Figure 10. *Shooting the Chutes at Coney Island* (Edison, 1896). An animated picture that required minimal intervention on the part of the person behind the camera. Film still. Source: Charles Musser.

Figure 11. *Place Bellecour* (Lumière view no. 129, 1896). Another example of a shoot requiring minimal intervention on the part of the person behind the camera. Source: Association frères Lumière.

tificially arranged scenes"[23] or any direction of the actors. On the filmographic level (the sum of all kinematographic techniques), there were no interruptions, fragmentation, or cuts. The ideal form of this paradigm was the punctiliar view shot on the fly. This was the case, for example, with some Edison strips (such as *Shooting the Chutes at Coney Island*, 1896)[24] and Lumière views (such as *Place Bellecour*, 1896),[25] in which no action was carried out on the thing being filmed[26] or on the filmic.[27]

The kinematographer's job at the time was thus limited simply to supervising the recording of the event he wanted to capture on film. His task involved no manipulation beyond the simple taking of an impression; apart from the choice of the field of vision, the kinematographer's role was practically nonexistent. In this paradigm, what was at stake was only ensuring the optimal recording of a profilmic event whose unfolding the kinematographer had no hand in. Here, the kinematograph employed something of an inborn narrativity, a kind of narrativity that is an intrinsic quality of the cinema's machinery. If kinematographers ventured into the realm of narrative, it was only by way of their "passive" recording of an event that itself, on the profilmic level, was narrative (in the way that what a surveillance camera captures is always narrative).

Thus, the person filming, when subjected to this paradigm, tended to preserve the autonomy of the object being depicted by showing it in its absolute temporal integrity and by attempting to reveal its properly attractional quality. He did not submit his instrument, which is an instrument for capturing and restoring, to the intentionality and discursive goals that define monstration and narration. When a narrative effect was produced by the filmic utterance, therefore, it was not because of but rather almost in spite of the medium.

This proposed model of three paradigms should not be taken as a taxonomy under which every view made in this period can unequivocally and exclusively be filed away. Rather, they are categories constructed on the basis of various intentionalities (the word intentionality should of course be understood here in its pragmatic sense). In the case of the first paradigm, what matters is that emphasis was placed on capturing and restoring to enable emphasis to be placed on the machine's possibilities and not on what was shown as such. From this perspective, we might see the paradigm of capturing as a sort of horizon category, a zero degree of filming, without in the process asserting, historically speaking, that such an activity ever existed in a pure state.

Once the person filming assumed the right to intervene in the profilmic and create complicity among the subjects being filmed (when mise en scène is present), we enter headfirst into the paradigm of monstration (on the profilmic level). Similarly, when the person filming intervenes in the filmic (or the filmographic, to be more precise)—when the kinematographer, while shooting, suspends filming by using the stop-camera technique[28]—we also find ourselves in the realm of monstration, but this time on the filmographic level. This second paradigm, monstration, thus rests on the willingness of the kinematographer to fiddle with what is being shown or to act upon its representation, unlike what is produced under the paradigm of capturing and restoring. By means of this twofold paradigm of monstration, the cinema puts its singular ability to tell a story to the test (an ability that will reach its zenith under the third paradigm, that of narration).

In the monstration paradigm, kinematographers began to distance themselves from the basic proposition of merely capturing and restoring and gave themselves over to manipulating the profilmic—mise en scène came to play an increasing role—and began to manipulate the film's kinematographic elements. Several forms coexisted within this paradigm:

a. clearly punctiliar views—what, with Frank Kessler, I have described as "complete punctiliarity"—which show a necessarily staged action without any chopping up of the strip of film (such as *L'Arroseur arrosé* [*Waterer and Watered*, Lumière, 1895])

b. views taken on the fly without any intervention in the profilmic on the part of the kinematographer but which are the product of some sort of fragmentation or assemblage of the strip of film. The strip can remain within the limits of "apparent punctiliarity," the product of camera stoppages alone (such as *Paris: Les Souverains russes et le président de la République aux Champs-Élysées* ["Paris: The Russian Sovereigns and the President of the Republic on the Champs Élysées," Lumière, 1896]),[29] or can belong to what we have called "reiterated punctiliarity," wherein the view is the result of an amalgam of segments creating an accretion of tableaux rather than a concatenation of shots (such as Lumière view no. 1299, shot in 1900, whose "subtitle" is *Épisodes du voyage du président de la République à Lyon* ["Episodes from the President of the Republic's Trip to Lyon"] and which is made up of three segments)[30]

c. views, finally, which combine these two kinds of intervention and use mise en scène—the profilmic—and manipulation of the strip of film—the filmographic. This kind of view can belong either to the category of apparent punctiliarity (such as *L'Homme orchestre* [*The One-Man Band*, Méliès, 1900])[31] or to the category of reiterated punctiliarity (such as *Uncle Tom's Cabin* [Edison, 1903]).[32]

In the third paradigm, in which narration rules, kinematographers (who were on the verge, in a sense, of becoming cineastes) gave themselves over by definition to the manipulation of profilmic elements in addition to, practically by definition also, the manipulation of the filmographic. The rise of certain procedures, however, especially editing, gave to filmographic manipulations a quality previously unseen under the monstration paradigm alone. Here, the mere aggregation of tableaux gave way to the creation of closer links between fragments. To mise en scène was now added *mise en chaîne*, or putting in sequence: the creation of a chain of fragments, giving rise to a decisive move away from the punctiliar to the pluripunctiliar. It seems to me that it is only with the emergence of this paradigm that it becomes appropriate to speak of "shots," the concepts "view" and "tableau" being more apt at rendering the true nature of the various cinematic utterances in the two punctiliar paradigms. Fragments and shots now enter into a relationship of greater concatenation among themselves and become more closely connected.

The systems monstrative attractions and narrative integration, in the first model proposed in 1985, reappear in the second, three-paradigm model as two elements of this model's second paradigm: in the monstration paradigm, when

Figure 12. *Le Locataire diabolique* ("Diabolic Tenant," Georges Méliès, 1909). A film squarely on the side of monstrative attractions. Source: Cinémathèque Méliès/ Georges Méliès © ADAGP, Paris, 2007.

Figure 13. *A Drunkard's Reformation* (Biograph, 1909). A film squarely on the side of narrative integration. Source: GRAFICS.

what is being chopped up is the profilmic or the filmographic (or both), we are in the realm either of monstrative attraction or of narrative integration (when the narrational element holds sway over the attractional).

We find ourselves in the realm of monstrative attraction when the element of attraction holds sway over the element of narration, for example in Méliès's *Locataire diabolique* ("Diabolic Tenant," 1909), and in the realm of narrative integration in a film such as Griffith's *Drunkard's Reformation* (Biograph, 1909), to take as our example a film made in the same year as the Méliès film just mentioned. These two well-known films make clear to which paradigm they belong: the latter film is a pure product of narrativization and the former a worthy representative, as late as 1909, of kine-attractography.

Chapter 4

Intermediality and the Kinematograph

One of the advantages of the term kine-attractography is that its very formulation makes it possible to contextualize the phenomenon we are trying to observe. First of all, it allows for a vertical understanding of the phenomenon, if you will, as it itself was: This new apparatus, with a quite attractional novelty aspect, was used to convey new attractions or old attractions served up with a new sauce. At the same time, the term also allows for a rather more horizontal understanding, a flattening of the phenomenon, that reminds us, in its very formulation (this is why it has a hyphen), that it is an attraction among attractions, a phenomenon among other phenomena of the same kind. Over the past few years, this diversity of phenomena has been one focus of the study of early kinematography, as scholars try to address it with greater precision than before. Expressions such as "early cinema" or "primitive cinema" (and in French we also say "le cinéma des origines" or "cinema at its source"), on the contrary, isolate the phenomenon by cutting it off from its context. These expressions remain hopelessly turned toward the future: this "cinema" is said to be early in relation to what came later; this "cinema" is said to be at the source of what was yet to come; this "cinema" is said to be primitive because it was less advanced than the cinema that would develop out of it, et cetera. These rather unfortunate expressions are all, to some degree, part of a clearly diachronic approach, one constantly threatened by the traps laid by teleology. "Kine-attractography," on the other hand, resituates the phenomenon in its synchrony and invites us to decipher the conjuncture and context in which the new invention was used: to decipher, in particular, the media context in which the phenomenon appeared— its intermedial context, I should say.

In addition, when we relate the expression "kine-attractography" to the expression "institutional cinema," we come up with an antagonistic pair of successively dominant paradigms clearly opposed to one another. The contrast between these two paradigms has hermeneutic, pedagogical, and heuristic virtues that cannot be overlooked, if only because they make it possible to apply principles for exclusion from one paradigm or the other and to observe what distinguishes them (in particular what makes them alien to each other, for example).

The question of the kinematograph's "multiple personality" has been the subject of research in the field for some time now.[1] We are becoming increasingly aware of the importance of writing a history of cinema that pays close attention, at least for the first years of this history, to the way the new apparatus was "subordinated" to other media and other cultural spaces. The question of the cinema's institutionalization is a crucial one, and the best way to distinguish it within the artistic indistinctness that reigned in the period preceding this process of institutionalization is, precisely, to look at it from an intermedial and transdisciplinary perspective.

Before the cinema ended up becoming a relatively autonomous medium, kinematography was not merely subjected to the influence of the other media and cultural spaces in vogue at the beginning of the twentieth century. It truly was at one and the same time magic lantern show, fairy play, magic act, and music hall or vaudeville act. At the beginning of the twentieth century, intermedial meshing was so fertile in the world of kinematography that a great number of animated pictures paid tribute to other media or media spaces, if only in the topic they were addressing.

As I argued at various points in the preceding chapters, there is indeed good reason to cease looking at early kinematography merely from the vantage point of cinema. Rather, it would be preferable to look at it from the perspective of the other media and cultural spaces that initially welcomed the new technology into their orbit and to develop an approach founded on the very principle of intermediality. In return, we hope, our object of study will enable us to analyze this principle of intermediality itself in its historical depth. Intermediality will have then contributed to defining the conceptual framework of a developing field of study. This detour through the kinematograph's intermedial relations in the first years of its existence is essential for anyone wishing to understand how it came into the world and how it ended up giving birth to a relatively autonomous media institution: cinema.

Cultural Paradigm, Cultural Series

In order to understand kine-attractography and the complex relations it had with other media of the day, we must study it in light of the cultural and media context in which it was immersed. To do so, we need different conceptual tools than those that traditional historiography has accustomed us to use. In recent years I have proposed that we use two concepts from the same family that, while not completely new, introduce new elements, I believe, in the way I have defined them, refined them, and found for them a field of application. To my knowledge, these concepts or their equivalents have never been introduced into historical writing about film. I believe that we have much to gain from granting them an important role in the way we approach the topic. These concepts are "cultural paradigm" and "cultural series."

I have borrowed the idea of the former concept and my formulation of the latter from the Quebec scholar Louis Francœur, who uses semiotics to identify a hierarchical system made up of a "polysystem" to which "various forms of signification (literature, painting, art, popular tradition, etc.) . . . are subordinated as subsystems."[2] Francœur describes this polysystem as a "cultural series," and I take the liberty of rebaptizing the polysystem in question "cultural paradigm"—an expression not found anywhere, if I am not mistaken, in Francœur's work—so as to reserve the expression "cultural series" for the subsystems or forms of signification that make up the larger system, the cultural paradigm.

In the present case, the cultural paradigm could be, for example, late-nineteenth-century stage entertainment. This cultural paradigm would be made up of "various forms of signification": music hall, shadow plays, magic sketches, fairy plays, circus arts, variety shows, pantomime, et cetera. Each of these forms of signification is a cultural series, and their overlapping creates a context in which kine-attractography attempted to carve a space, often from within these same cultural series.

The cultural paradigm institutional cinema, therefore, did not yet exist during the period when, to take a particularly well-known and significant example, Georges Méliès created his œuvre. Méliès was thus not a cineaste (and this is not a shortcoming!), and the art he practiced was not cinematic art, which did not yet exist in his day. What Méliès did was to use a new machine—the Cinématographe (or one of its equivalents)—within a cultural paradigm, the stage show, whose identity had nothing or very little in common with what we call today the cinema. Jacques Deslandes understood this well when he wrote: "Beginning in 1897, Georges Méliès stopped staging great 'tricks' in his theater-salon, because he was doing the exact same thing on film in his film theater. He then projected these images on the screen of the Robert-Houdin theater instead of performing the usual illusion."[3]

While we may be able to postulate, as I propose, a break in the history of cinema with the arrival of institutional cinema, we might not be able to say the same for the intrusion of the Cinématographe Lumière (or similar devices) in the professional life of Méliès, Cecil Hepworth, or Ferdinand Zecca. The arrival of the Cinématographe in Méliès's professional life was for him, of course, a moment of transition. In my view, however, it was not a real moment of rupture. Méliès's magic "views" were an extension of his fantastic stage performances and belong to the same cultural series as his stage activity. This is why, in the end, a film such as *Le Royaume des fées* (*Fairyland, or the Kingdom of Fairies*, 1903) is as much a part of the history of the fairy play as it is the history of cinema. The fairy play (whether on stage or screen) and the cinema (by this I mean institutional cinema) are two different cultural practices that are part of two different cultural paradigms and merit the attention of the scholar or historian in equal measure.

On the other hand, most Lumière views belong to the cultural series photography, while a good number of other products of kine-attractography belong to the series music hall (this was the case of the first Gaumont chronophones) and others still belonged to the series vaudeville (this was the case of Edison's filmed stage performances).

The use of the concept "cultural series" appears to me to be fundamental, in the sense that it subsumes the more current expression "cultural practice." Practices are observable facts about social, cultural, and historical reality. They are a division from without imposed by the scholar in question (historians, cultural sociologists, etc.). The fact that the cinema, today, is a particular cultural practice, and that this practice is distinguished in an almost irreconcilable way from other cultural practices (such as the theater), owes nothing to the perspective of the historian or to historical discourse. On the contrary, the concept "cultural series" supposes that the scholar (whether a historian or not) has divided the object of study up and taken on the task of constructing, by him or herself, story events, factual events, and cultural series, whose ties to each other he or she then undertakes to explain.

Institutionalization

What I am suggesting here is that, in order fully to understand the first images produced by the kinematograph, it would be better to connect films from the early days to a noncinematic cultural series than it would to cinema itself. I am also suggesting that, in order to understand the meaning of kine-attractography, we must render it autonomous of institutional cinema and posit a break between the two. What does it mean, therefore, to claim historical autonomy for kine-attractography with respect to the institution cinema? What, in other words, is the status of kine-attractography with respect to the institution cinema?

In order to answer this question, we must first define the very concept "institution." Over the past few years, general agreement appears to have been reached on this point in the field of cinema studies. The "classic" definition of the institution is derived from the semio-pragmatic theories of Roger Odin.[4] For this French theorist, the institution is, above all, "a structure linking a range of determinations."[5] This somewhat laconic definition benefits from being read alongside that of Alain Berrendonner, quoted by Odin in his article[6] and whose ideas are essential to the present discussion: for Berrendonner, an institution is "a normative power subjecting individuals to certain practices, on pain of sanction."[7] In other words, an institution regulates and sanctions.

For fields such as cinema, in which there is supposed to exist a form of "communication" among various agents, the institution tells the agents responsible

Figure 14. *Le Royaume des fées* (*Fairyland, or the Kingdom of Fairies*, Georges Méliès, 1903). A film that is as much a part of the history of fairy plays as it is of kinematography. Source: Cinémathèque française/Georges Méliès © ADAGP, Paris, 2007.

for producing utterances how to express themselves in order to "address" the other, while telling the agents receiving these utterances how to read them. Odin explains: "Thus, in the end, communication can occur because the Subjects producing meaning (the filmmaker or viewer) are not free to produce the discourse they would like. They can only express themselves by conforming to the constraints of the 'discursive practice' of their time and milieu."[8]

As Lucie Robert suggests, an institution is a "normalization 'system'" which is structured in order to "produce, in its area of influence, certain particular forms of behavior."[9] In other words, as Clément Moisan puts it, an institution is made up of "a set of codified practices."[10] Clearly normalization and codification, in the case of the cinema, did not appear the day the Cinématographe or Kinetograph appeared on the scene. Time was required, a minimum amount of time, for production codes and norms—and thus interpretive codes and norms—to appear or, if you prefer, to be instituted. It is also quite clear, moreover, that from this perspective, the institution "cinema" appeared only after rules, which are the corollary of production codes and norms, took on the force of law, if only relatively.

The reason for this is, precisely, the fact that the institution "cinema" did not yet exist at the time of kine-attractography: We can postulate, as I have done above, that in some sense early "cinema" was not yet cinema. Part of this "cinema" belonged fully, as we have just seen, to stage entertainment, while another part belonged to photography and yet another to fairground attractions, et cetera. If kine-attractography is not really cinema, it is because, when we speak of cinema today, what we have in mind is not simply the technological and mechanical act of projecting moving photographic images on a screen, accompanied or not by recorded sound. What we are clearly referring to, even if only implicitly, is the institution that cinema became, with its rules, constraints, exclusions, and procedures.

What Lumière, James Williamson, and Méliès did was "simply" to use a new device, the kinematograph, within other cultural series (photography for the first, magic lanterns for the second, and magic sketches, among other things, for the third). Each of them was already working in these domains in their own identifiable way. At this time, cinema had not yet become an autonomous medium, and the kinematograph was neither more nor less than an instrument, a tool, that made available to anyone cultural practices and genres in vogue at the close of the nineteenth century, when there had been considerable research into the reproduction of movement. This instrument was thus located on the margins of this "range of determinations" (Odin)—the various legitimate and institutionalized media and genres that were already known at the time of the advent of this instrument. The kinematograph therefore underwent a kind of integration into other practices, in keeping with known social and cultural uses, at a given time and for a given community. The question of the autonomy of the new medium and the "specificity" of its language had not yet been posed. At best, these were visible on the horizon. The new possibilities of the medium thus remained in a state of complementarity, dependence, or continuity with respect to older, well-established generic or media practices. Only through gradual shifts and modifications in the use of the new medium, through socioeconomic changes, et cetera, would it come to reveal some of its expressive specificities (communicative, aesthetic, generic, etc.).[11]

Kine-attractography's Intermedial Meshing

From this we can conclude that, as long it was not institutionalized, as "cinema" developed it was subjected, through kine-attractography practices, to the constraints of other institutions: Kine-attractography was a sort of hodgepodge of institutions, to borrow René Lourau's term (he was referring to the ego).[12] This idea of a hodgepodge of media must be in the air, because we also find it in an article by Éric de Kuyper describing kinematographic phenomena of the beginning of the twentieth century. His argument is entirely compatible with what I am proposing here, because he emphasizes what I have described above as "intermedial meshing," out of which animated views arise:

> These borrowings, which were many in number and often unconscious, or only slightly conscious, drew on diverse models used most often in arts without official status, such as variety performances, illustration, journalism, or other artistic practices parallel or marginal to artistic practices that enjoyed full status as such. . . . [W]hat took place was the redeployment of an established technique, an entire artistic heritage, whether it enjoyed full status as an art or not, major as well as minor or marginal (it would be better to call it a hodgepodge than a cultural heritage!), but in a brand-new medium: the kinematograph.[13]

We find the same idea in the work of Rick Altman, whose proposals with respect to intermediality are entirely in keeping with mine:

> [I]n the strong sense of the term, intermediality, to my mind, should describe a historical stage, a transitional state in the course of which a form in the process of becoming a full-fledged medium finds itself still torn between various existing media, to the extent that its own identity is not yet resolved.

Until around 1910, what we today call cinema found itself in this thoroughly intermedial situation. Torn between several media, all of them wishing to appropriate its technological novelty, cinema emerged from intermediality only after having been definitively separated from all these other media.[14]

The cultural practice animated pictures—kine-attractography—thus developed within other cultural practices, whether recognized or not as art forms, before becoming defined as a practice, achieving a degree of autonomy and becoming a true institution in its own right.

Let's turn our attention now to institutionalization as a process. Lucie Robert explains the birth of the law in a passage that could practically be applied wholesale to a description of the fundamental shift experienced by animated pictures when cinema was in the process of being institutionalized: "[T]he law was not born out of some sort of primordial void. It was designed to normalize the conflicts that arise out of new social relations and to enable these relations to develop. It develops with or against a certain number of other institutional forms, which it absorbs, destroys, or marginalizes."[15]

Couldn't we adopt, almost word for word, what Robert says here about the law and use the various semenes of her discourse to enable us to better grasp the cinema's movement toward institutionalization? The cinema, as an institution, was also not born out of a sort of primordial void. It arose out of conflicts deriving from the new intermedial relations engendered by the advent and development of the kinematograph. It developed with or against a certain number of other institutional forms (genres, cultural series, etc.) that it absorbed, destroyed, or marginalized. Institutional forms that, we should recall, began by trying to absorb it and which could just as easily have destroyed or marginalized it.

The period from 1895 to 1915 was thus the scene of two complementary but somewhat contradictory movements, movements in some way different: On the one hand, the kinematograph had a social existence because of its integration into diverse institutions, while on the other this subordination daily paved the way to the detachment that would lead it to a fundamental insubordination, its own institutionalization.

Genres as Institutions

How then was the subordination of the kinematograph to those institutions that took it under their wing as a valiant "instrument of reproduction" carried out? First and foremost, it was carried out through genres. Basically, genres are the intramedia equivalents of what I have described as cultural series. Isn't a genre, in truth, a cultural series? Doesn't this description reveal some of the most fundamental qualities of genres that the word genre alone obscures? Let me put the question again: Aren't genres true cultural series that transcend cultural practices and violate their borders? This, in any event, is how the matter appears to have been seen, quite consciously by the way, by certain manufacturers of animated pictures—some of the largest, in fact, because they included Pathé, which went to some lengths in its statements to link specific animated pictures, through a reference to their genre (or rather, to the institution genre), to one cultural institution or another by deliberately and clearly adopting a representational model derived from that cultural institution.

This can be seen in the following excerpt from the 1902 Pathé catalogue: "Until now, almost every subject has been employed. . . . There remained, however, a genre that no manufacturer dared attempt: Drama. Why? Does this mean that it wouldn't be as successful as the rest? We believe otherwise. Don't audiences, popular audiences especially, run to the theater the moment a fine Drama is announced?"[16]

In the interpretive system I am proposing, there is on the one hand, therefore, the cultural paradigm, which I defined earlier, and on the other the cultural series, which is born out of—necessarily born out of—its materialization in one medium or another. This gives us the following schema:

Cultural paradigm→ medium→ genre (genre as a cultural series)

Both a medium and a cultural series can be seen as institutions, but in a different sense. A medium is an institution in the sense, to adopt a definition Roger Odin has more recently proposed, refining the one I gave above, that it is "a range of determinations that regulate the production of meaning by selecting, hierarchizing, and structuring the modes of producing meaning to be employed."[17] For its part, the genre (the genre as cultural series) is an institution in the sense that it is a "regulatory convention," to borrow Jean-Marie Schaeffer's expression.[18] The genre is an institution in the sense that it is an institutional model for producing meaning,[19] in keeping with the definition given by Berrendonner I quoted above: "a normative power subjecting individuals to certain practices, on pain of sanction."

Various particularly enlightened comments in this vein can also be found in the work of Christian Metz. The following remark can be found in his book *Lan-*

guage and Cinema: "Certain *genres* . . . have a clear existence: their homogeneity, already felt in the simple viewing of the films, is confirmed by historical facts: we know that, in the cinema of Hollywood of its 'golden era,' genres were in some sort institutions (and not only textual ensembles). Each genre had its regular script-writers, sometimes on yearly contract, its directors, its craftsmen, its studios, its partially autonomous financial circuits, etc."[20]

That genres are institutions is already taken for granted, moreover, in literary studies, if we are to take Tzvetan Todorov at his word: "It is because genres exist as institutions that they operate as 'horizons of expectation' for readers and as 'writing models' for authors."[21] Incidentally, can't the "genrification," if you will allow me this neologism, of animated views be seen as a step in the direction of institutionalization? Is it not, quite simply, a process for normalizing films, of subjecting films to noncinematic institutional norms? Is it not also a dual phenomenon, both subscribing to and inscribed in a given institution, while at the same time surreptitiously appropriating a cultural series, which it absorbs and adopts?

For each genre system there is a corresponding function. Such and such a genre system seeks to classify, while another seeks to normalize. To which system did the publishers of animated views subscribe? The genre system they offer in their catalogues makes abundantly clear that, for them, genres are institutional frameworks developed earlier by the various companies manufacturing animated views—"institutions" on another level and in another sense. These artisanal manufacturers themselves are a part of the maze of sociocultural institutions that enabled the kinematograph to find its niche before succeeding in finding its own path to institutionalization.

Kinematographers and Cineastes

In thinking about the topic the way we have been here, the excesses of some commentators (excessive and yet fairly widespread and commonly accepted) become apparent. To these people, kinematographers such as Edwin S. Porter, Louis Lumière, and Georges Méliès are the first cineastes. I believe it would be a mistake to adopt this view, however, despite the regularity with which it is done.[22] This choice of words is going to extremes, and tendentious, not only because the word *cinéaste* did not exist at the time, but also because the signifier *cinéaste* denotes and connotes signifieds that could never be applied, strictly speaking, to the various agents responsible for the work of "putting into film" during the period of kine-attractography. It is significant, moreover, that no term or expression was used exclusively to describe the agent responsible for the work of putting into film during the kine-attractography period. This period's lack of institutionalization, which is the basis of its "alien quality," enabled the various agents to shift function as they sought specificity and an exclusive definition of their tasks.

The term that returns most often to describe the agent responsible for the work of "putting into film," at the very beginning at least (that is, before the turn of the century), was "operator." This word refers without a doubt and quite directly to the agent responsible for "putting on film."[23] During the very first years, this term, which by the way is present in every period of film history, was used to describe not only the agent responsible for the putting on film, but also (out of necessity, we might say) the agent responsible for the putting into film. Thus the Lumière views, to take just one example, were generally punctiliar (made up of only one shot), very brief (the film was 17 meters long, giving a duration of about 50 seconds), and, most often, showed more or less live action. In this way, they did not usually demand much effort on the level of what we call "profilmic manipulation" and were thus, most often, the work of a single person, the camera operator.

Nevertheless, films rapidly became more complex and, over the years, longer as well. "Artificially arranged scenes" (the term used at the time, corresponding to the French *vues composées*) began to take precedence over live-action views (what Méliès called "natural views"—*vues de plein air*)[24] and became pluripunctiliar, made up of more than one tableau or shot. The operations involved in manufacturing a view became more numerous, and thus more people were involved in making them. In French, the term *metteur en scène*, inherited directly from the theater (ah, my beloved intermediality), began to appear at this time and gradually imposed itself as the dominant expression. Not as a way of describing the "supreme" agent of the work of putting into film (because this role did not yet exist, at least for people at the time) but to describe the acolyte of the operator, the agent responsible for what we would call today, more or less, art direction (the decor) and, at the same time, directing the actors.

In French, the term *metteur en scène* has also survived throughout every period of film history, probably because it is anchored in a cultural series other than cinema alone. (No equivalent term in English exists; it refers to the person who carries out the mise en scène and literally means the "putter on stage"; here I will refer to this agent as the "putter in place." A highly prosaic term, the reader may protest, but one that reflects the prosaic nature of the task in those days.) At first, since it came from the theater, the expression "metteur en scène" had a relatively limited meaning. With respect to kinematography, "mise en scène" seems exclusively to have described, at the very beginning at least, the work of directing the action to be filmed. (It would soon also come to describe, but in a somewhat secondary way, managing the entire "set" and arranging the decor.) Over the years, the expression came to take on a larger sense, if we are to believe Jean Giraud: "As in the theater, it involves not only 'the art of directing the on-stage action in every respect' . . . but also directing the actors and the filming."[25] In other words, "directing" the film as a whole (the "filming [*prise de vues*]," Giraud says) fell to the agent that, in the beginning, had been responsible above all for organizing and arranging the profilmic.

In any event, in the age of kine-attractography it is easy to imagine that mise en scène found its greatest expression in the films of Méliès. For Méliès directed not only the actors (after having taken care of the decor, the scenario, etc.) but also the filming, despite the seeming impossibility of accomplishing this latter task. It is difficult to imagine how, captive as he was to the role he was playing—recall that Méliès appeared as an actor in most of his "artificially arranged scenes"—he would have been truly able to direct the filming. But this would not be taking the fellow's ingenuity into account. He was obliged to foresee the tiniest detail of his camera tricks and the movements of his actors before giving the camera its first turn of the crank.

We can even imagine that Méliès gave instructions to the camera operator and actors while the film was being shot. (It would be hard, at the distance at which his films were shot, for us to see his lips moving.) We might also presume that he took advantage of the intermittence that is almost inherent in the type of shooting he preferred (with its numerous stoppages of the camera) to give instructions and advice. In the case of a film such as *Le Diable noir* (*The Black Imp*, Méliès, 1905), which required some sixty stoppages of the camera[26] in order to carry out its trick effects, it is easy to imagine that Méliès took advantage of these pauses to carry out himself the various adjustments required and to give any number of instructions to his collaborators, considering that he was a metteur en scène who was all over the map. This, in his case, is what is meant by "directing the filming."

Despite its fairly common use at the time, the expression "metteur en scène" seemingly did not satisfy the various people working in kine-attractography as the term to describe the agent more or less responsible for the putting into film.

A symptom of this state of affairs is the incredible number of terms that were suggested, in French at least, in an attempt to describe this agent. In addition to *cinématographiste* (which I translate here as the "kinematographer")[27] and *metteur en scène*, the following terms appeared (with the year of their first known use and English translation in parentheses):[28] *cinégraphiste* ("cinegraphist," 1912), *compositeur de films* ("film composer," 1917), *filmeur* ("filmer," 1917), *réalisateur* ("director," 1917), and *directeur de films* ("film director," 1918).[29] We must note, moreover, that it was only at a very late date—in the 1930s, if we go by what Giraud tells us—that the term *cinéaste*, which had been proposed by Louis Delluc around 1920 (the exact date is unclear), became common.[30]

Reading Méliès's article "Les Vues cinématographiques," published in 1907 and reproduced in translation in the present volume, we see very well how the idea was taking shape in Méliès's mind that it was necessary to identify one of the many people who work on a film as more "important" than and directing the others, a sort of foreshadowing of the "film director" and, to a certain extent, the "cineaste." This is what Méliès has to say on the topic:

> The actors, hurried along by the assistants, go down to the stage. There, the metteur en scène, who is usually the author, first explains the overall scene to be performed and then has the actors partially rehearse the various parts of the action: the principal action first and then the secondary episodes. He directs their movements and the positioning of the extras and must act out each character's part in order to indicate their gestures, entrances, exits, and position on the stage.[31]

And again:

> The mise en scène is also prepared in advance, as are the movements of the extras and the positions of the workers. It is exactly like preparing a play for the theater, with the exception that the author must know how to work everything out on paper by himself. As a result, he must be the author, metteur en scène, set designer, and often an actor if he wants to obtain a unified whole.[32]

It is not surprising to find such ideas in the mouth of Méliès, because the essential problem of coordinating the various agents involved in the manufacture of animated views is posed to a greater extent in his films than in any others. His films were generally more complex than those of his competitors, and they generally required a greater number of people in their manufacture. The magician from Montreuil even ended up, as we saw above, using the word "author" to describe the agent responsible, no more and no less, for the "putting into film," taking his own case as an implicit example ("the author must know how to work everything out"). What Méliès is saying, in the end, is that it is in the interests of the author of the scenario (and Méliès uses the word "scénario"),[33] the person who initiates the view being made, to take on the job of directing the action to be filmed, in addition to being the designer and even an actor. He doesn't go so far as to give a name to this major player, who is both author of the scenario and the putter in place (in addition to being the designer and an actor), but it is quite apparent that the individual is a real one-man band,[34] responsible in the end for what we could call today the filmic utterance. This one-man band plays an equivalent role to the orchestra conductor in music and is charged with ensuring that "perfect agreement" and "cooperation" reign among the various agents involved in the manufacture of a view: the putter in place, technicians, actors, and camera operator.

Méliès even goes so far as to state clearly the role of the film director, without however naming this agent:

> When it is cloudy, and damnably dark cumulus clouds delight in constantly cross-ing in front of the sun, the photographer's friend, exasperation is quickly seen in the person who directs the operators, assistants, stagehands, actors, and extras. You must be patient throughout all kinds of ordeals; sometimes it is better to wait for daylight to return and at other times it is better to close the shutters if there is too much light or open them if there is not enough. All this must be done without losing sight of a thousand details inhering in the work at hand.[35]

When he speaks of "the person who directs the operator, assistants, stage-hands, actors, and extras," Méliès establishes the existence and precedence of a figure in kinematographic practice who is in some sense fundamentally responsible for all the operations that go into the work of putting into film. The ideas Méliès expounds on a practical level foreshadow Riciotto Canudo's wish, in a text written a few years later, in 1911, although this time from a more aesthetic perspective:

> The kinematograph, like life, shows a succession of gestures, attitudes, and representations. It transports painting, immobile and durable, from the space in which it lay and forces us, in the time in which it shows itself and is trans-formed, to imagine what might be if a *truly superior guiding idea* were to con-tain, in an ideal and profoundly meaningful line, a central and aesthetic idea of the tableaux unfolding in it. We might view this as the creation of a *Moving Visual Art, a sixth art*.[36]

What Canudo wants is for the kinematograph to leave the task of raising the kinematographic view to the level of art to the incipient cineaste or film director (this is the underlying sense of the "superior guiding idea" he calls for). This notion, as the saying goes, was in the air back then. We even find it expressed, almost word for word, in a book published three years before Canudo's article (and a few short months before Méliès's)—a book written, not by aesthetes like Canudo, but by lawyers. In their 1908 book, Émile Maugras and Maurice Guégan took a pioneering step by writing what might be seen as the first treatise on film art, *Le Cinématographe devant le droit*.[37] This quite amazing work made the claim in particular that "the [device] doesn't choose the landscape, it doesn't appreciate the lighting effects or judge the decor or the composition of the shot" and that we must, as a result, postulate the existence of a "*'guiding spirit'* which feels, tastes, and determines."[38]

Thus we have, on the one hand (Canudo in 1911), the "guiding idea," while on the other (Maugras and Guégan in 1908) the "guiding spirit." The coincidence is nothing less than stunning. What's more, the goal of our two lawyers is clear. They want to prove—and remember, this is 1908—that kinematography is an art and that "the film's author, who prepares the stage, places the characters in their positions, and arranges the decor, is an artist."[39]

For the moment, however, a fig for art, a fig for the "cineaste"! Make room, instead, for the "ci-ne-ma-to-graph-ist," a term used—in French, at least—into the teens and, to a lesser extent, even into the 1920s. Later it fell into disuse and oblivion. The term first appeared at a fairly early date, as early as 1896 ("Mr. Lumière, the *cinématographiste* en route to millions")[40] and 1897 ("Our *cinématographistes* have little desire to put an idea suggested to us into practice").[41]

Derived directly from the moving picture camera of the same name (or least from the most popular of these machines, that of the Lumière brothers), the word *cinématographiste* was initially and exclusively used to describe the camera operator. This seems normal because, in the very first years at least, filming was most often the responsibility of a single person, the operator. Over the years, however, the term came to be applied to other situations. This is clearly visible in Méliès's 1907 article. Once (the term is used only twice in the entire article), Méliès uses it with reference to the camera operator alone and is clearly thinking of the work of recording the images on film—the putting on film (he talks about lighting, handling the camera, the film stock, the emulsion, etc.):

Apart from the obstacles related to the execution of such scenes mentioned above, others still can hinder kinematography. These include varying light conditions, clouds passing in front of the sun, accidents involving the camera, the film jamming in the camera, film tearing when it is too thin, emulsion that is not adequately light-sensitive, stains or dots on some film after development, making them unusable, and imperceptible holes that become great boulders when enlarged and projected.[42]

Elsewhere—the sole other occurrence of the term in this article—Méliès is thinking, rather, of the *metteur en scène*, the person responsible for putting into film, as we can see:

> This will suffice to explain why, after having thrown themselves into this new genre, the majority of photographers have abandoned it. You have to be more than a mere operator for all this. While kinematographers are a dime a dozen, the ones who have succeeded in doing something different than the others are far less common. There is no more than one per country, if that, since every country in the world depends on French manufacturers for artistic views.[43]

When we consider that Méliès did not operate the film camera himself (except during the very first years, when he shot live-action films; but once he began to act in the films himself, he was obliged to turn the camera crank over to an acolyte), we have to conclude that he couldn't view himself as a kinematographer in the strict sense of the word (as a camera operator). When Méliès says, moreover, that there appears to have been only one kinematographer per country to have succeeded in "doing something different from the others," and when we consider that it is hard to imagine the French kinematographer he has in mind being anyone other than himself, we have to conclude that a kinematographer may, in his mind, be someone other than the person who turns the camera crank!

Méliès's contemporary Émile Cohl, when signing his correspondence, described himself into the 1910s as a *cinématographiste* (see the reproduction opposite of the first page of one of Cohl's notebooks).[44] And in 1913 Léonce Perret made for Gaumont a film entitled *Léonce cinématographiste*.[45] During the period of kine-attractography, and in the early years of institutional cinema,[46] the cineaste was thus always lurking in the background. This appears normal, once we take a closer look at the relative complexity of "putting into film." The exact nature of the task of putting into film went through a number of changes in the first years of the kinematograph's appearance. The fact that the term *metteur en scène* appeared quite quickly, around the turn of the century, already speaks long about the process underway, even as the word "operator" never fell into disuse. Because the first metteurs en scène, of course, didn't replace the operator, who was essential. The two worked together. For the art of putting into film involves a great number of activities of a highly varied nature, unlike, say, writing or painting.

The Fields of Cineastic Activity

To make a film, you must not only record the images but also, first of all, prepare and direct the action that is going to be captured by the camera. Once the images have been taken, it is necessary to reorganize the various fragments taken during the shoot. I have described these operations elsewhere as the "fields of cineastic activity"[47] and they involve three levels of activity: putting in place (basically the organization of the profilmic), putting in frame (basically the shooting), and putting in sequence (basically the editing).

It is thus possible to see, going by the preponderant use of the term "operator" in the very early years, say between 1895 and 1900, that putting into film

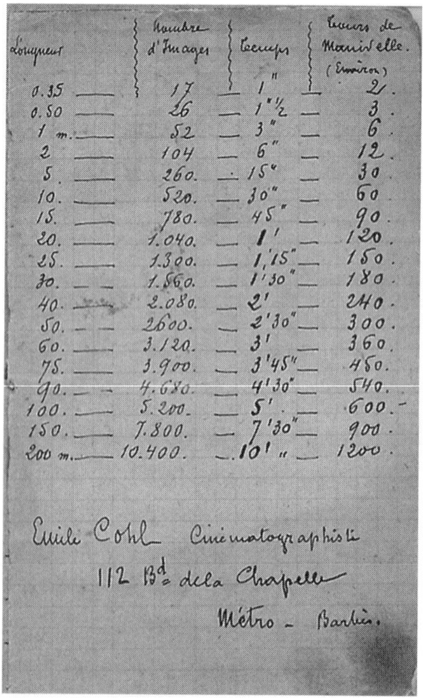

Longueur	Nombre d'Images	Temps	Tours de Manivelle. (Environ)
0.35	17	1"	2.
0.50	26	1"½	3.
1 m.	52	3"	6.
2	104	6"	12.
5.	260.	15"	30.
10.	520.	30"	60.
15.	780.	45"	90.
20.	1.040.	1'	120.
25.	1.300.	1,15"	150.
30.	1.560.	1'30"	180.
40.	2.080.	2'	240.
50.	2600.	2'30"	300.
60.	3.120.	3'	360.
75.	3.900.	3'45"	450.
90.	4.680.	4'30"	540.
100.	5.200.	5'.	600.
150.	7.800.	7'30"	900.
200 m.	10.400.	10' "	1200.

Emile Cohl Cinématographiste
112 Bd de la Chapelle
Métro - Barbès.

Figure 15. Notebook kept by Émile Cohl dating from 1910 or 1911. Note that Cohl gives his profession as "kinematographer" (*cinématographiste*). Source: Pierre Courtet-Cohl.

in those years relied largely on the properly cinematic (and filmographic, in the sense I use the term) activity of putting in frame. By later privileging the expression *metteur en scène*, around the turn of the century in France, emphasis was henceforth, and temporarily, placed on an activity that was not specifically cinematic but was derived from the profilmic rather than the filmographic sphere: putting in place. As for the third operation, putting in sequence, hardly any attention is paid to it: at the beginning of the twentieth century there was still very little awareness of its importance, and no one claimed any special status for it. It was still a responsibility shared by the kinematographer and the exhibitioner of animated views and would become the sole responsibility of the manufacturers of views only around 1907–8, when the sale of films was abandoned in favor of renting them and intervention in the syntagmatic structure of the films by exhibitors began to be proscribed. Nevertheless, the putting in sequence operation lost nothing by waiting: an era soon began in which it came to be employed to such an extent that it eclipsed the other two operations.

The very term "kinematographer" seems to me to reflect the imprecision in the difference between putting in frame (the task of the operator) and putting in place (the task of the metteur en scène). This imprecision was due, precisely, to the seeming lack of specificity, during the kine-attractography period, of this new activity, "putting into film." Normally, this activity transcends the two operations putting in frame and putting in place. These two operations remained autonomous and independent and would become truly subsumed by the putting into film only once institutionalization got underway. It is as if, at the time, there was no word to describe the relatively abstract activity of the *metteur en film*, the putter into film: that agent—theoretical or empirical—that directed the work of both the putting in frame (the work of the operator) and the putting in place (the work of the metteur en scène). It's as if a synthesis between the profilmic and the filmographic had not yet been achieved and the two were seen to contrast. This is all the more true in that, in the era of kine-attractography, it was often, empirically, the same person who was both operator and metteur en scène (in this case, Méliès was the exception).

Cinematic Art and Art in the Cinema

It shouldn't come as a surprise, then, that people had difficulty viewing the cinema as an art form during the kine-attractography period. Naturally, the metteur en scène's activity can be seen as an art but, because of its lack of specificity, it was an art outside the cinema. On the other hand, the activity of the operator, because it lacked legitimacy, had difficulty raising itself to the level of an art: It seemed to boil down to operating a machine designed to produce, "mechanically," animated photographs. This supposed artist's hand was used only to turn the crank of the picture box.

It is therefore quite easy to deny explicitly any suggestion that operating the camera alone was a form of artistic labor. This is what a Lubin company representative blithely did in 1902 in testimony (biased and interested of course) during legal proceedings brought by the Edison company against Lubin for duping their films. According to this Lubin employee, merely shooting the images has, in itself, no artistic value: "These photographs are purely the results of the functions of cameras, and a dozen different photographs with a dozen different cameras from the same general location would necessarily have obtained the same results."[48]

This opinion was contradicted by the plaintiff, as seen in this testimony by an Edison employee: "In taking moving pictures photographically, great artistic skill may be used. . . . [A]rtistic skill is required in placing the camera in such a position that the lights and shades of the picture when taken, shall have proper values, and the grouping of the figures and the background shall constitute an [sic] harmonious whole and have a graceful composition."[49]

Because they lacked an institution they could call their own—because of the lack of a cinematic institution, in fact—the various agents involved in making animated views were thus obliged, as we have just seen, to turn to the courts to decide where the necessary artistic legitimacy was to be found. The interested parties didn't know where to look for it in the stages of making a film: did it lie before the camera? around the camera? in the camera? The question they posed at the time is essentially the following: Who among all those who participate in the putting into film can legitimately pride him or herself on being an artist? the operator? the metteur en scène? Wasn't art simply the product of contributions external to the process of putting into film: those of the costume designer, the set designer, the laboratory assistant, the colorist?

Given this flagrant lack of legitimacy, a turn-of-the-century exhibitioner even went so far as to attribute cinema's art to the simple but hardworking female employees of Mme. Thullier, graduates of the School of Fine Arts: "Naturally the sets were painted in black and white and special artists, graduates of the School of Fine Arts, undertook a special study of these photographs' backgrounds and, through a judicious arrangement of colors, have achieved the most beautiful and highly delicate photographic reproductions."[50]

Figure 16. Pathé coloring studio on the rue du Bois de Vincennes in Paris, 1907, where female employees colored each print of a film by hand, frame by frame. Source: Fondation Jérôme Seydoux collection, Pathé.

A journalist made the same claim in 1905: "The scenes are all in natural colors and each of them contains thousands of little paintings, all of them hand-painted by French artists."[51] What the art of putting into film lacked was recognition—social recognition, cultural recognition, and institutional recognition. What was needed, as François Jost has written, was for parafilmic discourses of all kinds to join the cause and recognize the artistic intentions of the metteur en film: "[I]f all the efforts made tend to create the social conditions that transform the film into a work of art, it is still necessary that the film be put together as an artistic statement and not as a purely anonymous recording."[52]

The artist had to move forward and, in a sense, "sign" the work. This may also be why in France, home to theories of authorship and the *politique des auteurs* (the "auteur theory" or "authorship approach"), early cinema has long been seen as a vulgar, primitive cinema. This may also be why many French film scholars are unbearably indifferent to films from the kine-attractography period, before cinema's institutionalization. Why should a film that did not deserve to be signed deserve to be analyzed? Or, in other words: Why sign analyses of films that themselves are not signed?

The question is thus not "Is the cinema an art?" or "When did cinema become an art?" but rather "Was kine-attractography an art?" Apparently not.

I arrive at this conclusion because, in particular, kine-attractography is not institutionally recognized and because it therefore does not have "specific artistic legitimacy." The star of the period of animated views, moreover, the only agent recognized to any extent, was not the actor, or the film (the "view"), or its author, but rather its "second-tier author," if I can use that term: the exhibitioner, who showed his audiences the program he concocted of which he, more or less, was the author. An author, yes, but of a practice that was in no way artistic (or at least one that was never socially recognized as such). This, by the way, should not deprive him of any credit.

Chapter 5

A Problematic Institutional Space

For cinema to be admitted to the realm of art, its problematic institutional space had to acquire, as Denis Simard has suggested,[1] stability, specificity, and legitimacy. All these things would gradually be gained throughout the long process I will describe here as institutionalization. We mustn't imagine that the institution "cinema" appeared as if by magic, as the result of some event, however major that event might have been. The institutionalization of a medium is the product of a slow process. It is an evolutionary and diachronic process that supposes the regulation, regularization, and consolidation of the relationship between those who work in it (stability); the choice of practices that are proper to the medium in question, thereby distinguishing it from other media (specificity); and the setting up of discourses and mechanisms that sanction those relationships and practices (legitimacy). As we have already seen, the first form of the institution cinema dates from 1914–15, but it is possible to understand the process leading up to it as having begun around 1907 or 1908. These two years, I believe, were crucial, setting in motion the process I am describing here.

It was during these years, for example, that trade journals devoted to the film industry alone were founded (*Moving Picture World* in the United States and *Bioscope* in England in 1907; *Ciné-Journal* in France in 1908). Before these dates, film was covered in trade journals devoted to heterogeneous cultural series, such as the *Optical Magic Lantern Journal and Photographic Enlarger*[2] and the *Industriel Forain*. It was also during those years that the crucial transition from the sale of films to film rental took place. This was a condition essential to film manufacturers taking control, not only of what left their production studios but of the final product itself, as it was seen by viewers. It was also during these years that various national and international umbrella organizations were founded, such as the Motion Picture Patents Company in the United States and the Congrès international des producteurs de films in France, thereby facilitating consistency and standardization.

Within the various groups at work in the period under discussion, there thus existed actions and attitudes in keeping with a process of institutionalization and others that were not. We might also suppose that it was only beginning in 1907–8 that the former group of actions and attitudes were greater in number than the latter group or, in any event, that they had a greater influence on the milieu. The rupture between kine-attractography and the institution cinema is a conceptual tool that the historian needs in order to think historically. In practice, however—in the everyday realm of kinematographers—there was of course no such open break.

Of all those at work in the world of kinematography, some companies, less clearly identified with the tradition of extra-kinematographic cultural series, were more susceptible to creating what we might call "aesthetic propositions" of a new kind. This was the case at the turn of the century, for example, with the Pathé company, which came to dominate the kinematography business until as late as the early 1910s. Because of its worldwide dominance, Pathé's new aesthetic propositions gave rise in a sense to a new order, or at the very least paved the way for this new order. This new order was not yet, of course, the institutional order "cinema," but it was in a sense the antechamber to that order, and for this reason we are justified in describing it as "proto-institutional."[3]

The First Subjective Condition

The establishment of what I call cinema's institutional order required the fulfillment of "objective" conditions such as those mentioned above. But it also involved the fulfillment of a number of subjective conditions. In this sense, for cinema to attain the realm of art, it had to wait for the various agents at work in it to cast off the purely instrumental vision of the film camera that they had shared since the moment this new form of technology had made its appearance. For a long time, the kinematograph was seen by its first users as a simple "reproduction" device, one capable not of producing things, but of reproducing them as they are, as products of preexisting cultural series. The kinematograph was used to record vaudeville numbers, magic acts, everyday scenes, living portraits, stage acts, fairy plays, and the like. The subordination of kinematography to other institutions is founded in particular on such a conception.

The kinematograph became part of preexisting cultural series by virtue of its identity as the direct descendant of photography. It was because of this lineage that it was immediately seen as a device for recording a preexisting object. The most important thing was its ability to relay, on a strip of film, a visible and tangible trace of the reality in front of which it had been placed. In other words, a visible and tangible trace of what, since the work of Étienne Souriau, we have called the profilmic. Hence the profusion in the age of kine-attractography of semantic isotopies around the reproductive abilities of the camera:

> Of all the tricks capable of being *reproduced* by kinematography, none is unfamiliar to us. We demonstrate this daily, with the variety of scenes we produce.[4]
>
> Boxing contest between Young Griffo and Charley Barnett. A *reproduction* of the Four-Round Contest (Life Size).[5]
>
> At the Battle of Nuits (côte d'or [*sic*]) in 1870 a partial battle took place on the railroad embankment. A *reproduction* of this bloody scene.[6]
>
> The course taken by one of our special operators is the exact *reproduction* of that taken when running bulls in Spain.[7]

We find the same thing, in even more inspired prose, in a text that appears to date from 1906 and was written by a certain "Georges Ménard," although it was visibly influenced and likely written by Georges Méliès himself.[8] This text appeared in an undated program of the Robert-Houdin theater:

> For some people, [the kinematograph] is used to reproduce natural scenes . . . these people are photographers who have simply replaced their old camera with a new and better one. . . . For others, the kinematograph is used as an accessory, to record *Personal Compositions*. Mr. Méliès belongs to this latter category. . . . After producing several so-called natural views, like the device's inventor, he had the idea of using the new invention for a quite special purpose: to photograph his fantastic theatrical compositions, enabling him to project them simultaneously in countless theaters.[9]

What Méliès has the supposed author of this text say is this: first there was Lumière, the inventor and first user of the device, who set out to "reproduce natural scenes," and then there came others, the second-generation users (including Méliès), who began to employ the device to "record their personal compositions." One of these second-generation users (a fellow named Méliès) then set himself off from the rest by using the device to "photograph his fantastic theatrical compositions."

Méliès couldn't have been clearer: The kinematograph is first and foremost a

device for recording, an accessory for photographing scenes in order to reproduce them. As long as we remain under the dominion of the capturing/restor-
ing paradigm, the kinematograph will be seen in a purely instrumental manner. According to this conception, what counts most of all is the ability of the
"picture-making machine" to record and re-create on screen in a literal manner
the visual properties of the profilmic, somewhat like a gramophone did with
real sounds. The kinematograph's destiny was thus predetermined: It was made
merely to record, no more and no less, a spectacle of some sort, whether this
spectacle was a "natural scene" (as was the case with "documentary" genres such
as actualities) or a "personal composition" (as was the case with artificially arranged scenes).

Film Production versus Kinematographic Reproduction

Ultimately, the reason the expression "film production" belongs to a different
paradigm than that under which kinematographers worked is that what they
carried out was not film production but rather kinematographic reproduction.
It is hardly surprising that in a context such as this, a conception of cinema as
art was slow in making its appearance. In the era of kine-attractography, what
was placed before the camera may or may not have had some artistic value, but
not the way in which it was photographed, recorded, and reproduced. A recording device is not likely to add a sense of artistry to the (natural or arranged)
reality in front of which it is placed. We wouldn't say that recording an opera
on wax cylinders, for example, imparts to the original work any additional artistry whatsoever.

The recording device captures whatever is placed in front of it and the value
of what it shows depends, in the end, on—what it shows! "Kinematographic-
ity" certainly adds a kind of value to what is shown, but this value is merely
added to the fundamental value that is always-already in the profilmic; it comes
on top of and after this value and is purely instrumental. The only actors and
performers singled out in catalogues of animated pictures are from outside the
field of kinematography, from theater or the stage: Dranem, Little Tich, Sarah
Bernhardt, and so on. The only authors singled out and worthy of mention also
come from another field (for the most part literature): Shakespeare, Zola, Dick-
ens, and so forth.

These actors and authors, then, come from other institutions, other cultural
series. Actors and authors from within kinematography had not yet made their

mark. What was of foremost importance, then, was how literal the photographic record was—kinematography's ability to convey the literal content of the scene captured on film. Herein lay the importance, in French, of the expression *metteur en scène*, the person who stages the events recorded by the camera and who is more or less responsible for the view. Most of all, this person is responsible for the way the profilmic elements are "arranged," whose variations the camera operator records. Moreover, isn't the meaning of the word "operator" symptomatic of what I am trying to convey here? How can there be art in a function such as "taking" pictures and recording them on the strip of film when this function is carried out by an "operator," someone who, according to the *Oxford English Dictionary*, "performs the practical or mechanical operations belonging to any process"?

It is thus not surprising that, at first, the kinematograph was seen as a means of transmitting, as a device for recording images, stage routines, vaudeville numbers, theater, magic sketches, fairy plays, and the rest. These were pure attractions, which were reproduced before the camera so that it could record them with complete literalness—what the *OED* defines as "with exact fidelity of representation." Isn't this all that could be expected of the kinematograph, which at first was no more than a passive recording device? Literalness was the complete extent of the value of this instrument without a signature of its own, one seen purely as a relay for an extra-kinematographic reality. We might add that this value rested on a thoroughly instrumental conception of the kinematograph and condemned the cultural series "animated pictures" to the role of mere transmitter, like radio, television, or even a fax machine.

The Second Subjective Condition

There is another important subjective condition that can affect the establishment of an institutional system: the degree to which the first two generations of practitioners are attached to their own cultural series. While Edison's "kinetography" continued from chronophotography, Lumière's kinematography was a continuation of photography, and Méliès worked in what we might call the institution of stage entertainment. Each preexisting cultural series (in the case of chronophotography we should speak instead of scientific series) has its rules and conventions, which Edison, the Lumières,[10] and Méliès submitted to in some degree. As Edison became more involved in kinetography (and eventually, after 1896, in kinematography) he ended up distancing himself from chronophotography, to which he initially adhered. (Think, for example, of the black backdrop of his recording studio, the Black Maria, which came right out of Étienne-Jules Marey and Eadweard Muybridge's systems.)

Edison's attachment to the series "chronophotography," however, was less strong than the Lumières' or Méliès's to their own series. The reason the Lumières submitted to the institution photography and Méliès to the institution stage entertainment seems obvious because, when you think about it, the Lumières and Méliès had already been a part of these institutions for many years and came up with their aesthetic systems and approach to kinematographic discourse from within them. In addition, the Lumières on the one hand and Méliès on the other did not have the strength, or the will in a sense, to free themselves from their original institutions, to break loose from them completely. Laurent Creton says pretty much the same thing when he remarks that "For the Lumières and for Méliès, the kinematograph was a form of diversification developed by extending their primary profession and intended to make it more complete and flourish more. The original profession remained the fundamental reference and the new activity neither replaced it nor did away with it. . . . [I]t remained part of the initial activity, which did not cease to be the guiding light behind the development of their work."[11]

The path chosen by the Pathé brothers, on the other hand, was completely different from that of Méliès and the Lumières. They arrived in the world of kinematography with a clean slate as far as institutionalized cultural practices are concerned (apart from their initial and introductory involvement with the phonograph, alongside which they initially developed and marketed the kinematograph, particularly in itinerant fairs). Not merely individual choices are at issue here: It is clear that individual destiny is involved. In any event, the hypothesis I would like to put forward is the following: Since the Pathés, as practitioners, had no strong ties to any cultural series and since they appeared to have no precise aesthetic program, no canon to respect (apart from those of the cultural institutions they would have encountered merely as members of society—as spectators, for example), they were able, for these very reasons, to put in place a sort of experimental laboratory, the Pathé "studio," where the seeds of the institution were able to sprout more freely than elsewhere.

According to this hypothesis, the Pathés' relative detachment from any preexisting cultural series would explain, at least in part, the appearance in their wake of new aesthetic approaches to the medium. Because they had no master, apart from financial gain, the Pathé brothers were freer to create a space in which their inquiring minds—the likes of Ferdinand Zecca, Gaston Velle, and Lucien Nonguet, who came out of cultural institutions contemporary with kinematography but were not immersed in them to the extent of Méliès or the Lumières[12] and did not own the company they worked for—set off hesitatingly in search of new representational strategies that took into account the constraints to which the new technology was subjected.

According to this new hypothesis, it was for this very reason that the Pathé studio blindly followed the others' lead during its initial years. Having no attachments, and thus no program, Pathé's employees initially had to try their hand at making, in their own fashion, the same things being made by other manufacturers of animated pictures. The Pathé brothers thus proceeded by gauging

Figure 17. À la conquête du Pôle (Conquest of the Pole, Georges Méliès/Pathé, 1911). A worthy representative of kine-attractography, as late as 1911. Source: Cinémathèque Méliès/ Georges Méliès ADAGP, Paris, 2007/ © Renn Pathé Catalogue.

which way the wind was blowing—until the day when, freer than the others to behave as they saw fit, they began to develop their own ideas.

Pathé, of course, was not the only place or the only "actor" where we can find aesthetic ideas that foretell or confirm the arrival of a new order. More in-depth research should make it possible to find similar ideas at work in other companies and among other kinematographers.[13] One thing is certain, however: Manufacturers of animated pictures and kinematographers were not all headed in the same direction. It would not be revealing a secret to remark that Méliès's "film manufactory" was not the nerve center of institutionalization (any more than the Lumière company, which folded and gave up the fight in 1905). The films Méliès made after 1907–8 were still completely tied up with kine-attractography. This was the case in particular with one of his final films, *À la conquête du Pôle* (*Conquest of the Pole*), a worthy representative of kine-attractography (even if, ironically, it was produced by Pathé), despite the fact that it was made in 1911, the same year that D.W. Griffith made *The Lonedale Operator* along more narrative lines.

Throughout the proto-institutional period (roughly 1908–14), Méliès attempted to adapt to the new reality, of course, strictly in order to survive, but he did

Figure 18. *The Lonedale Operator* (Biograph, 1911). A pure product of narrativity. Source: Cinémathèque québécoise.

not succeed. He remained faithful to the cultural series to which he "belonged," we might say, and he simply could not—did not want to—free himself from their grasp. Institutional (future) cinema was not his thing. Méliès was first and foremost a magician, a conjurer, a creator of magic sketches, and someone who staged fairy plays. He ended up becoming a kinematographer because he used the kinematograph to reproduce his acts on film. He was a kinematographer, and a kinematographer he remained. He would never be a cineaste the way we understand the term today. And, as owner of his own brand, Star Film, he was also a manufacturer of animated pictures, and a manufacturer of animated pictures he remained. He would never be a film producer.

If you'll pardon the expression, one might say that there was no hope for Méliès. Unlike Pathé, he was of another generation, part of another paradigm. He was located elsewhere. He was unlike, also, the few British, French, and Americans who succeeded in bridging the two paradigms, who moved without difficulty from kine-attractography to institutional cinema.[14] Unlike, in particular, Alice Guy, to mention one especially obvious example, who initially worked in kine-attractography for Léon Gaumont before the turn of the century and then, after 1907, took time off to start a family and change her name before returning, under the name Alice Guy-Blaché, to kinematography in the United States in 1910. There, she would soon be called upon to change from a kinematographer to a cineaste and, especially, a film producer: an exemplary case of an individual destiny (that of a woman, moreover) following the same course as the evolution of kinematography, moving from one continent to another in the process. This was the individual destiny of a key figure in kine-attractography who succeeded, seemingly without difficulty, in migrating from one continent to another, from one culture to another, and from one paradigm to another.

The Genealogy of Film Form

The new aesthetic ideas advanced by Pathé and other companies of the same stamp covered various aspects of filmmaking: what I call putting in place (mise en scène), putting in frame, and putting in sequence. With respect to this final stage, putting in sequence, the talents of what we might call the Pathé studio were considerable. Recent research has made it possible to identify Pathé as the laboratory where a prototype of the institutional form of crosscutting was developed (see in particular *Le Médecin du château* [*A Narrow Escape*, 1908]). We see this device used in Pathé films in various ways, and pretty much uniquely at the time, as early as 1906, in the remarkable and unjustly forgotten *Je vais chercher du pain* (*I Fetch the Bread*), for example,[15] long before it appeared in the films of Griffith.[16]

What is needed, if we are to be able to produce one day a "genealogy" of cinematic forms, is a history of these new aesthetic ideas and forms of film language during this period when kine-attractography still reigned for a little while. To achieve this, we must continue to investigate the various qualities of kine-attractography in order to better define it and better grasp its varied forms. We would thus be able to understand why some of its features persisted, often on a large scale, in certain bodies of work. This is the case, for example, of the films of André Deed (who came out of Pathé, where, until 1908, he had shot the *Boireau* series of films). Deed's Italian films (beginning in 1909 with the famous series based on the character Cretinetti, a character known in France as Gribouille and in English-speaking countries as Foolshead) reveal an unusual degree of some of the fundamental features of kine-attractography that were normally absent from films at this late date. To give just one example, there is his film *Come fu che l'ingordigia rovinò il Natale di Cretinetti* (*Foolshead's Christmas,* Italia Film, 1910), which, like the other films in the series, includes in particular a plethora of direct addresses

Figure 19. *Le Médecin du château* (*A Narrow Escape,* Pathé, 1908). A relatively early example of crosscutting. Source: GRAFICS/ Renn Pathé Catalogue.

to the viewer (true, one still sees this in many slapstick films in the early 1910s) and a few occurrences (at least two quite obvious ones) of long, repetitive editing sequences of the action (as people pass through a doorway—the gate to heaven, which Cretinetti causes to fall down as he passes through it).[17]

Repetitive editing of the action was fairly frequent between 1902 and 1905, when characters or the camera moved between two adjacent locations separated by a wall, but had pretty much disappeared by 1910. The reason it persisted in Deed's work is not immediately apparent, and if we wish to have a better understanding of certain phenomena we would do well to find an explanation for the relatively widespread presence of the style of editing in this unique body of work.

We must also focus on the paratext of kine-attractography by continuing to go through the trade journals of the period, which might suggest what some of the period's agents thought of what I call kine-attractography and how they conceived it. We must also continue to examine announcements of forthcoming works in the catalogues of film manufacturers and publishers. In this sense, to give a final example to conclude (for the moment)[18] the present volume, I quote here once again the Pathé catalogue, whose declaration of the company's

Figure 20. *Come fu che l'ingordigia rovinò il Natale di Cretinetti* (*Foolshead's Christmas*, Italia Film, 1910). In the background, the door that will be entered to create temporal overlapping. Source: Turin film museum.

future intentions seems to me particularly symptomatic, emblematic even, of this company's symbolic place in the field of kinematography at the beginning of the twentieth century and the leadership role it played within it:

> Until now, almost every subject has been employed. Natural views, town squares, military processions, comic scenes, transformation scenes, fairy plays, and so on have been its subject matter.
>
> There remained, however, a genre that no manufacturer dared attempt: Drama. Why? Does this mean that it wouldn't be as successful as the rest? We believe otherwise.
>
> Don't audiences, popular audiences especially, run to the theater the moment a fine Drama is announced? The success of films such as *La Porteuse de pain*, *Roger la Honte*, and *Les Deux Gosses*, to mention just those three, provides an answer to our question. . . .
>
> This is why we now submit a Drama for the approval of our many customers
> . . .
>
> This film will in addition have an advantage, and it is to this especially that we draw our customers' attention: it has a real drawing card, a sensational title that will draw in the audience, keen on strong emotion. This title is:
>
> L'HISTOIRE D'UN CRIME ("The Story of a Crime")[19]

If we read this catalogue description with the least bit of attention, in light of present-day knowledge about kine-attractography, we cannot help but notice that there is something more than a base and common business motive behind a remark such as the following: "Until now, almost every subject has been employed. . . . There remained, however, a genre that no manufacturer dared attempt: Drama. Why? Does this mean that it wouldn't be as successful as the rest? We believe otherwise."

Who is this "we" who, as early as 1901, when the kinematograph had barely appeared in fairground booths, could claim with a straight face that drama, the prototype par excellence of the dramatic film, which would soon be the mainstay of the cinematic institution, could find success in kinematography, in the anemic and straitjacketed cultural practice, monumental jumble, and lawless land that was kine-attractography?

In order to assert, as early as 1901, that drama had a chance of success in the cinema, one must have believed, it seems to me, that the kinematograph was going to be capable of quitting the realm of the mountebank. And one surely required a degree of prescience, no doubt of a fairly simple variety, and a fair bit of nerve, to make a statement such as this as early as 1901. In any event

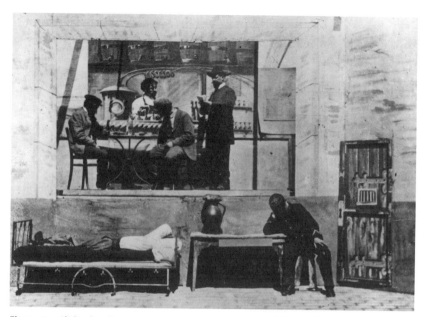

Figure 21. *L'Histoire d'un crime* (*The Story of a Crime*, Pathé, 1901). "A sensational title that will draw in the audience, keen on strong emotion"—Catalogue Pathé, 1901. Source: Cinémathèque française.

one must have believed in the kinematograph's growth potential, that it could be something other than photography and a form of stage entertainment, and that it was here to stay, to grow and discover new directions. One had to take seriously the future of the kinematograph, to believe in it at least, something that even one of the first film historians was not prepared to do as late as 1908. I refer to G.-Michel Coissac, to whom I owe the expression "kine-attractography": "The kinematograph will remain in the realm of the fairground. For the lecturer, it will be an extra reward for his audience, an extraordinary but ephemeral aspect of his success. It is not and will never be more than that."[20]

Because of the date of Pathé's remarks, they may have had a profound impact on the kinematograph milieu, insofar as its argument met with approval and the films it made as a result met with success. We know too that *L'Histoire d'un crime* was, precisely, a key work of the time. Because it was accompanied by an unequivocal declaration by Pathé, this film is not just one example among many others. What is now needed is to analyze the company's statements, particularly in its catalogues,[21] to see whether the trend suggested here is truly sustained. We might thus be able, one day, to evaluate with more precision whether it is legitimate to see this declaration about *L'Histoire d'un crime* as a break, as the point of entry into a new paradigm.

It remains the case, nevertheless, that Pathé's filmmakers, despite their relative freedom from the cultural series in vogue at the time of kine-attractography, were subjected to certain influences we can associate with these series. Thus *L'Histoire d'un crime* was directly inspired by a series of wax-figure tableaux.[22] From my point of view, however, it is one thing to import into kinematography a few elements from one cultural series or another (a well-known practice similar to an adaptation) and another thing entirely to create something kinematographically out of another cultural series, which is, it seems to me, what Lumière and Méliès did. I imagine that a formal comparison of Pathé's fairy-play films with those of Méliès[23] carried out in light of the principles I have outlined here would make it possible to gauge the distance that may have existed between adopting the camera to film fairy plays to be shown on the stage of the Robert-Houdin theater and adapting fairy plays to film.[24] Closer analysis might make it possible to see whether a particular kinematographer, in light especially of his professional past, was more in thrall than his peers at Pathé to the principles of one cultural series or another.

The Cultural Series "Theater" Is Incorporated into Film

After this "freeze frame" on *L'Histoire d'un crime*, we are in a position to ask ourselves whether the cultural series with the greatest influence on Pathé was not, despite Zecca's later denials,[25] the theater (not to be confused, of course, with stage entertainment). Or, if you wish, with drama, in a very broad sense. To say this about the Pathé studio of 1901 can only bring to mind the approach this same studio would take later, during the *film d'art* period, in this case with respect to bourgeois theater and not melodrama. In this respect, let's take another look at what the Pathé catalogue has to say about *L'Histoire d'un crime*:

> There remained, however, a genre that no manufacturer dared attempt: Drama. Why? Does this mean that it wouldn't be as successful as the rest? We believe otherwise. Don't audiences, popular audiences especially, run to the theater the moment a fine Drama is announced?

Compare this to another of Pathé's declarations, from a catalogue of 1902:

> When the kinematograph appeared, its only goal was to demonstrate the progress of science and human wisdom, which is to say to bring photography to life. The

least everyday event sufficed. The same is no longer true today, when exhibitors have raised it to the level of theater.[26]

Was Pathé moving in the opposite direction to that of other manufacturers of animated pictures, who placed the kinematograph once and for all time within one or more other cultural series foreign to cinema? Could we not see a declaration such as this as one of the first appearances of a discourse that would soon become that of the institution? Can we not see the ideas underlying Pathé's declaration as the first blush of the discourse of a medium in the process of taking form (one that would soon begin a process of institutionalization and become a cultural series in its own right)? Are we not in the presence here of a new phenomenon—that of a new medium, which would soon become known as cinema, beginning to incorporate, into its own sphere of action and according to its own rules (even if these have been only partly sketched out) and conditions, a cultural series inherently foreign to it—the theater? The theater that, as I have attempted to demonstrate elswehere,[27] had been only an illusory and fleeting model for kinematographers, a model that would soon be relegated to the dustbin in order to pass over to the "age of the cineaste," basing its discourse this time on that of literary narration. Thus it came to pass that literariness, thanks to the cinema's institutionalization, took precedence over theatricality.

Conclusion

It shouldn't be necessary to point out that there are no such things as continuities and discontinuities in history, only in historical explanation. So my broad temporalizing is not in the interest of a "true history," or of restoring to the record "what actually happened." The stakes are quite different: how one periodizes and where one locates ruptures or derives them are all political choices that determine the construction of the present.

—Jonathan Crary,
Techniques of the Observer

For more than thirty years now, research into so-called early cinema has been growing at an amazing rate. In the late 1970s, a new generation of scholars took up the task of reexamining the phenomenon from top to bottom, causing convulsions in the young discipline of "cinema studies," which had just gained admittance to university and was still far from having acquired complete legitimacy. In addition, the increasingly insistent and visible presence of this inquiry into the past was certainly a factor in the remarkable reversal in the discipline in the 1980s, when historical questions resumed their place alongside theoretical ones after the latter had been the only questions to find favor among the leading "institutional" scholars of the 1960s and '70s. We might even say that research into "early cinema" was an essential factor in this transformation, which went so far as to facilitate a veritable alliance between history and theory. This first significant encounter between synchrony and diachrony on the ground also had lasting repercussions for the discipline, whose effects are still being felt today. It would be impossible to carry out a prolonged organic alliance between theory and history without having an effect on both theoretical and historical studies.

A Starting Point: The 1978 Brighton Congress

The Brighton congress was of immense importance to this development, because it crystallized a process of rediscovery begun some time before. Most of the scholars who attended it were there precisely because they had already become involved, to various degrees, in research in the field. This crystallization had far-reaching effects and made possible, over a period of nearly twenty years, the publication of a number of books that contributed to establishing a new way of examining and understanding our topic. The rupture brought about by Brighton thus enabled a new generation of scholars to break away from the essentialist and normative film history practiced by their elders. After the congress, which remains a symbol of the collaboration between archivists and scholars, the latter finally had more accessible archives at their disposal, enabling them to call into question a large number of received ideas about the early years of kinematography. Not only were these new historians ready to examine this past through a different lens than that used in the writings of their predecessors, they were also called upon to observe new artifacts that these predecessors had never had access to, even in their old-fashioned manner.

If this conjuncture did not have a catalytic effect, one might well wonder what possibly could have. . . .

In this sense, the development of an institution such as the International Federation of Film Archives (FIAF) played a fundamental role in providing access to works from film's past. The leadership demonstrated by some members of this organization, more at the forefront of the field than some others, made it possible to penetrate the age-old cult of archival secrets that had hitherto severely hampered research. The institutional culture of film archive circles has been sharply and broadly transformed over the past twenty or thirty years, to the extent that today we can say that the historical film research currently being carried out is the fruit of an alliance between the archival and scholarly milieus.

The subterranean force of early kinematography in film studies is, I believe, far from exhausted, contrary to what some naysayers maintain—that the interest in early cinema is just a flash in the pan that will soon peter out. How many times has it been said, in fact, that after the supposed centenary of cinema the interest in early kinematography would lose steam? More than fifteen years have passed since the centenary, and nothing of the sort has occurred.

A Point of Arrival: Calling Outmoded Concepts into Question

If traditional film historians had had concerns similar to those of Jonathan Crary in the passage quoted as an epigraph to this Conclusion, many of the questions formulated in their day would have quickly been deemed inadmissible and a number of historical misunderstandings could have been avoided. It is quite normal, however, for the history produced by each generation to meet the needs of that generation. The research and inquiries of traditional film historians from the 1940s to the 1970s responded to their concerns and to those of their contemporaries. Among these concerns when they wrote their histories, the most agonizing was that of historical truth. From the vantage point of the twenty-first century, this period of seeking historical truth seems quite distant, but for film historians this transcendental truth was of primordial importance. Because we are more inclined today to make a distinction between historical fact and historical interpretation (or discourse), we are less concerned with mastering the past than in understanding it. For it has now become clear to most of us that, in the end, to write history is to take up at the same time past and present: the past in question and the questioning present. For the simple reason that, when we set out to write history, we must, as Hans-Georg Gadamer remarks, accept the idea that its preferred object, the historical object, is and will remain in a sense inaccessible: "There can be no such thing as a direct approach to the historical object that would objectively reveal its historical value."[1]

The reasons for this are many, but among them is the fact that the object exists, always-already, for a subject, and that it is the relationship between the object and the subject that gives the object meaning. We can discover "historical" objects as much as we like (the way we do for films of bygone days); what remains of history for us is the relationship between yesterday's objects and the subjects of today, not yesterday's objects and the subjects of yesterday, who gave it meaning and for whom it had meaning. Accepting this reality is to accept the reality of history as a discipline able to re-create not just the past, but an always-already presentified past, which is and will always inevitably remain at a distance from what we might call the "past-past." In the same way, this past-past is and will always be at a remove from those "distant observers"[2] we are and will always remain.

Historians thus have every interest in comprehending, as Pierre Sorlin has so aptly remarked, that "even completely immersed in their archives, even isolated in the year 2,000 BC, they always respond only to the questions of their contemporaries."[3] This is because historians, as I remarked in chapter 1, must always be aware of the constraints of their approach to the past and must also take into account the temporal distance between themselves and this past. In short, they must always be conscious of the fact that their task consists not in re-creating a bygone era but in re-creating a past taking shape in their present-day interpretation.

If it is true that this distance separating the contemporary observer from the past object is irreducible, we must conclude that this past is always alien to whoever is observing it. From our contemporary observation post, we cannot aspire to hold the past in our arms. All we can aspire to do is to understand it, which is already quite a lot. In order to do so, we naturally need new historical (and empirical) research, but we also need new concepts, new ways of approaching the historical phenomenon, new conceptual tools. These are the points I have dwelt upon here.

New Conceptual Tools

The underlying principle of the endeavors that led to the present book is that we must attempt to find the theoretical means to better understand the empirical data that historical research makes it possible to gather. My basic idea is that we must continue to seek out the means for giving new impetus to studies of early kinematography, of kine-attractography. This new impetus, I believe, would be more theoretical than historical in nature (film theory or the theory of film history more than historiography). It is in this sense that the hypotheses I have presented here are an attempt at a kind of theoretical model with the aim of carrying out (in fact redoing) a history of early kinematography and conceivably of cinema. These hypotheses are "theoretical" in another sense, because they are the result of a mental construction. In any event, they are the product of a mind trying to convey, one way or another, a complex phenomenon such as a nascent medium, one inextricably linked to other, already-existing media at the time it came into the world.

In addition, as we have seen, intermediality is the point of view or approach to adopt more than any other if we wish to thoroughly revise our notion of the emergence of cinema and develop new ways of thinking about how this emergence fits into media history and cultural history alike. For its part, the concept "cultural series," an extension of the intermedial approach, is the base upon which the model I am proposing rests. To my mind, it remains the interpretative key through which it becomes possible to see the emergence of cinema in a different light from that in which it has previously been seen. This, in any event, is what I have tried to demonstrate here. The concept "cultural series," properly handled, enables us to understand and explain not only early kinematography (what I describe as kine-attractography), but also—and this is no small feat, you must admit—to understand where cinema came from in a much more enlightened and enlightening manner than what we have traditionally been provided. I sketched out this question of the emergence of the kinematograph (and thereupon of cinema) early on in this book with reference to the distinct projects undertaken by Edison and Lumière. I returned to this topic in chapter 5 and widened our perspective through the use, in particular, of the concept "cultural series." I will return to this question once more in the present conclusion, if only to demonstrate how a scholar's work can change tack and take a new direction when he or she adapts new concepts to their object of study.

As I have attempted to demonstrate in these pages, the cinema and, equally so, the kinematograph were inextricably tied up with the most diverse cultural series. Nevertheless, we might think of the very first "impression,"[4] so to speak, as being made by two cultural series that served more or less as models to the original designers of the new recording device, with Edison and Lumière[5] in the lead: I refer to chronophotography and photography.

Edison, as we saw earlier, falls more to the side of the cultural series chronophotography: like Marey, Muybridge, and Anschütz, what was important for Edison (or rather for his team) was to control the objects placed in front of the Kinetograph to record their movement. Thus Edison began by shooting in a real laboratory, the famous Edison Laboratory, before building in 1892–93 the film studio the Black Maria (see figure 1 in the Introduction), a close relative of the "physiological (and chronophotographic) station" that Marey built in the Parc des Princes, with its black background, rails for moving the camera, et cetera. Edison's studio, however, was an enclosed space (or rather semienclosed, if we take into account its retractable roof, which made it possible to flood the scene to be "kinetographed" with light), while "classical" chronophotography took place out of doors. Edison, like Marey, most of the time introduced real-world "specimens" (or phenomena)[6] into his "station" in order to capture their movements with the Kinetograph.

The Lumière brothers, for their part, extended the cultural series "photography." They adopted, at least initially, the photographer's reflex (for which their father's factory produced its famous "blue label" photographic plates), turning their camera on their family, garden, and factory (and later on their city, country, and finally the entire world). What the Lumière Cinématographe recorded was bits and pieces of the world. And it was precisely in combining Edison's specimens of the world and the Lumières' bits and pieces of the world that the kinematograph (in the broadest sense, including "cinema") traveled from one end of the twentieth century to another.[7]

This is true of both the invention of the device and the initial culture it gave rise to. Nevertheless, a number of other cultural series left an impression, not on the design of the device, but on its use, with respect to both the production of views and their reception. Indeed, on the level of what we today would call the phenomenon's syntagmatic aspect, we might say that the cultural series that left the greatest impression on kine-attractography was the magic lantern. This is also true with respect to the attractional quality of certain techniques, such as the close-up (the depiction of "swollen heads"). We might also ask ourselves what impression on kinematography was left by the cultural series we might describe as the light show, a model Edison chose not to follow for his Kinetograph but which joins, in a single "line," the magic lantern, optical theater (Reynaud), and the Lumière Cinématographe.

It is thus apparent that we must think of cultural series in the plural. Indeed, the concept can be employed beneficially only if we carry out a constant comparison and systematic juxtaposition of the various impressions left on the kinematograph by each of these series. Thus, after publication of the present volume, I hope to carry out in the near future an in-depth study of the relative importance of the cultural series that left their mark on the new invention.

A Series of Cultural Series

I believe that the approach I have taken in the present volume, founded on the kinematograph's simultaneous belonging to a series of cultural series, enables us to think about the history of the emergence of cinema differently. It may also help us resolve certain problems raised by early kinematography's relationship with the cultural practices of the day. This is the case of the seemingly aporetic problem raised a few years ago by François Jost in an inspired article that set out to sum up the achievements of research into early cinema:

> Cinema and the other arts, cinema and live entertainment, cinema and theater: we might almost say that cinema's connection to something else was the childhood illness of early cinema. Reading histories of this period can be a dizzying experience: postcards, fairground attractions, mime; there seems to be a con-

nection to everything. Are some more relevant than others? Without a doubt. We must admit, however, that a great liberalism is at work. It is rare at an academic conference to see someone stand up and complain about an abusive connection being made. And it is true that most of these are persuasive. . . . The parallels and comparisons between early cinema and every conceivable kind of cultural manifestation are not always (in truth quite rarely) based on a solid connection between them.[8]

"There seems to be a connection to everything," Jost writes with a touch of irony, distrustful of the parallels and comparisons between early cinema and "every conceivable kind of cultural manifestation." "The 'demon of analogy' (Mallarmé), guided by a comparativist fervor, sometimes neglects to start out by considering the status of the two objects being compared," he adds.[9] The problem arises, in my view, in the case of the scholars Jost has in his sights, and of Jost himself, when they reduce this question to a simple matter of connections, parallels, comparisons, and analogies. Instead, what the very concept of "cultural series" enables us to do, precisely, is to avoid such a snag (and this, in my opinion, is what it is). This concept forces us to shift our perspective, rendering Jost's reservations and fears moot. The blind spot in his argument is that it does not observe the rule that we compare like things. Theater, other forms of stage entertainment, postcards, fairground attractions, and mime (but also fairy plays, magic sketches, photography, magic lanterns, etc.) were well-established cultural practices with their own history—and even, in some cases, recognized art forms—that enjoyed a degree of legitimacy and stability. In practical terms, they were "institutions," even when, in the case of some of them, they did not have a very broad social following.

This is not the case with early "cinema," or "kinematography" if you like, which was neither an established cultural practice, nor a recognized art form, nor an institution, and which enjoyed neither legitimacy nor stability—at least in the preliminary period of its history.

We may be justified in comparing theater and mime, because these two practices each had their own identity, even if this identity could be shifting and unstable, and because they were, by virtue of this very fact, comparable. But we cannot compare "nascent" (or rather, emerging) kinematography and mime, or emerging kinematography and theater, or emerging kinematography and magic lantern shows. For the very simple reason that kinematography, practically speaking, did not yet have its own identity. It belonged to a variety of cultural series (while it was still emerging in any event), and it took time, a fair length of time, for it to attain the status of an autonomous cultural series. In the early years, kinematographers were content, as I have mentioned on several occasions in this volume, to continue doing what they did "before" (or what was done "before"). Before what? Before the invention of the kinematograph (and its availability). Thus early kinematography (or at least very early kinematography) cannot be compared with contemporaneous cultural series because it was a part of those series. This, one must admit, changes things considerably.

A New Way of Writing History

In the end, what I am proposing here is that we write the history of the emergence of kinematography in a manner completely different from that to which traditional historians have accustomed us. But also, if I may say so, from the manner in which we too have become accustomed to writing this history since Brighton. We are still far from having a perfect grasp of all the ins and outs of kine-attractography, and still far from having a perfect grasp of the ways in which cinema was institutionalized. Only more in-depth empirical and reflexive research will make possible new advances in the field. And we know how desirable such advances are.

They were in any event highly desired by François Albera in an article written in 2006, with respect to France in particular, in *1895*,[10] the journal of the Association française de recherche sur l'histoire du cinéma. In an article with a strong editorial slant and in the form of a frustrated summing-up of the situation in France, Albera laments the fact that recent advances in film history have not been acknowledged:

> After the epistemological break carried out by those who promulgated an Althus-serian Marxism in the early 1970s (in the pages of *Cinéthique* and especially the incomplete series of articles under the title "Technique et idéologie" by Jean-Louis Comolli) and later the reflexive and methodological sequence of the 1980s and 90s, when the work of Allen and Gomery on the one hand and Michèle Lagny on the other appeared, we have seen in France the theory of film history and even the history of film history come to a halt.[11]

In his article, Albera also demonstrates how film history has been denigrated in French institutions, especially in universities, where it has quite simply not succeeded in being recognized as an "academic discipline," contrary to what has occurred in other countries. In such a context it is not surprising, in Albera's view, that film history has ended up being "watered down" into history plain and simple, cultural history, and, at the same time, into a broadened art history, one that includes the general history of representation, thereby losing in the process its specificity and relevance.

The prime culprit for this situation, in Albera's view, is the "somewhat unhealthy hegemony of *critical discourse* in the French cultural sphere."[12] This hegemony troubles the scholar in him, especially since the critical discourse in question (we are speaking of film criticism, of course) is guarded around and keeps its distance from all scholarly research. This discourse even flouts the concept "research," at least in the sense it is used in a university setting:

> This kind of attack on knowledge . . . is a way of privileging the "sentient" over the "intelligible," "the love of cinema" (I don't dare write "cinephilia") over analysis. We have seen this in the case of filmology in 1947 and in the semiology of Metz and of Pasolini (the Pesaro debates): it is a topos. The deprecatory language remains the same and scholarly work is equated with "flattening" (before, the term "vivisection" was used). . . . *This break between criticism and research*, its autonomy and arrogance . . . this privileging of the singularity of the sentient: is it not the same as claiming oneself to be "deaf and blind," no matter what kind of row it produces?[13]

Whether by chance or epistemological necessity, similar remarks were also recently made, this time not with respect to film history but rather film theory, by Roger Odin, who identifies the same culprits: film criticism and, lurking in the background, *cinephilia* (never named but whose presence we sense). In an article with editorial overtones similar to Albera's, an introduction to a thematic issue of the scholarly journal *Cinémas*, published at the Université de Montréal, which he edited and which addresses the topic "the crisis in theory," Odin starts out with a remark just as "sad" (the term he uses in his text) as Albera's:[14]

> At the origin of this issue [of the journal] there lies my sadness, even annoyance: film theory, although it had been one of the major sites of modern thought . . . is hardly visible today in the space in which I work, cinema and audiovisual studies at the university level in France. . . . Today the fashion is for a discussion of intangibles, of that "je ne sais quoi." But I thought universities should teach rigorous thinking—I was going to say epistemological rigor, but that has become a word one no longer uses in polite company.
>
> It is quite clear what lies behind this "je ne sais quoi": teaching cinema has come to mean shaping students' tastes. Shaping taste: Here we can recognize the "mission" that some film critics have taken on. But universities and criti-

cism are two different things. If critics want to try to get people to share their tastes, fine. But teaching taste at university? That might (perhaps) be something done in high school, an institution midway between teaching and shaping, but we would still have to define our objectives, because *shaping taste* is too often reduced to merely *transmitting "legitimate taste"* (Bourdieu). In a university, however, we are dealing with adults, and this idea has always seemed to me an incredible pretension. We can accept that university professors place themselves above students in terms of skills, but in terms of taste? By what right?[15]

Reading these two contemporaneous "editorials" by two leading lights of French academia, one focused more on history and the other on theory, it would appear that the French film research community is in the midst of a crisis and that the state of affairs is troubling to some. True, the French case is rather unique, when we consider that there reigns there a truly "indigenous" cinephilia without equivalent anywhere else in the world and which, it seems to me, is the primary determinant of the approach to cinema cultivated and propagated by various cultural and scholarly figures in the film community, whoever they are and wherever they are found. The presence of this decisive factor changes the situation completely; it is almost as if the French scale of values with respect to cinema could not be the same as places where cinephilia does not predetermine, regulate, and configure in an almost physiological manner a person's approach, in a manner somewhat like religion. It is often said that the "Langlois affair" could have taken place only in France; that no other place could have contributed to the fantastic growth and acceptance of the famous *politique des auteurs*; that nowhere else could aesthetics play such a large role; et cetera. Is it not possible to see, in these peculiarities of the French situation, a kind of "collateral damage" caused by the reign of cinephilia, which sometimes takes the form of a dogma?

I can't help recall, to turn this discussion back to early kinematography, that I had come to the same sort of conclusion in 1993 in a conference paper (prepared in collaboration with Denis Simard) for a symposium at the Sorbonne. Our paper was entitled "The Alien Quality of Early Cinema: Where Things Stand and Research Prospects."[16] In it, we discussed the way the French were "strangely behind the times" with respect to research into early cinema that, at the time, was in full swing in Canada (in Quebec especially), the United States, Great Britain, and Italy in particular. We remarked how early cinema, "as a privileged research field," had not, "since Brighton, created any real interest on the part of any university-level scholar in France."[17] We explained that the decisive factor in this disaffection was probably early films themselves, which functioned as a kind of foil to cinephilia, which could surely not accommodate films as "unkempt" as these.[18]

That was the case then and it remains the case today; let's hope that it will not be the case in the future. I hope that the present volume, which is intended to contribute to the development of both the theory and the history of film history, can help resolve as well, if only to the tiniest extent, the crises of history and theory in cinema studies. May the present volume, which straddles these two disciplines, contribute to this discussion and give a small measure of hope to those who struggle against the distortions (let's not be afraid of words) of a certain form of obscurantism.

A Discussion between the Author
and the Editors of the Journal *1895*

François Albera, Alain Boillat,
Alain Carou, and Laurent Le Forestier

This exchange between André Gaudreault and members of the French film history journal *1895, Revue de l'association française de recherche sur l'histoire du cinéma* (no. 57, April 2009; part of the exchange was inadvertently omitted from this issue and was published in a subsequent issue, no. 60 [Spring 2010]), after the release of the French edition of the present volume, is included here for the additional light it throws on the ideas discussed in the preceding chapters.

. . . .

André Gaudreault, whose name is bound up with the "new history" movement born in 1978 at the International Federation of Film Archives (FIAF) congress in Brighton, has just published with CNRS a volume whose title is *Cinéma et attraction*. The book's subtitle, however, *Pour une nouvelle histoire du cinématographe* ("For a New History of Kinematography"), better expresses the volume's ambition: to overhaul the theoretical underpinnings of film history using a methodology whose theoretical tools are called "paradigm" and "cultural series" and whose references to narratology and semiology give it the status of a new historiographical perspective posited on a radical break between what was once called "primitive cinema" and then "early cinema"—between a phase marked by technological inventions and modes of discourse involving monstration and attraction and a second phase that in reality is the first phase of "cinema" after its institutionalization around 1906–10, upon which classical cinema would be built.

This subtitle has the ring of a manifesto, of a foundational text, and the theses the book develops, which are openly located on the level of theory and epistemology and not on the concrete study of a period, a group of films, or an aspect of film history, appear to us to represent an event in the discipline of film history. We discuss with the author here, in a question-and-answer format, some of the directions and prospects of writing film history and the problems it raises—its historiography, in the sense Michel de Certeau used the word.

Our thanks to André Gaudreault for replying to the written questions we submitted to him. Not often in our discipline do discussions like this take place. We hope, moreover, that this exchange, as lively and free of concessions as it was on either side, will give rise to others like it.

André Gaudreault: My thanks first of all to my colleagues at *1895* for giving me this opportunity to develop a little some of the hypotheses found in my book, which are somewhat isolated and confined there (given the limitations of the medium and the genre, a book will always constrain and restrain to some degree the author's ideas).[1] I raise my hat to them, even though I believe their interpretation to be based on a number of misunderstandings, which I will point out as we go along. Nevertheless, they have brought to light a few weak links in the argument I build throughout my book, and in my responses to the five questions they ask I will attempt to supply satisfactory responses. Because these questions, for the most part, touch on sensitive matters for me (and in my work), they are not unfamiliar to me (nor do they appear strange) and I feel relatively well prepared to reply to them. This exercise should prove useful, if only by allowing me to formulate new hypotheses, or to begin to do so, and to float them by the reader like trial balloons. This will be one benefit of the exercise. It will also enable me to fill my interlocutors in on a few details, since they have not, by all appearances, always understood the implications of some of the theses I propose. I will thus be able to put forward a few roughly sketched hypotheses that, because of their unfinished nature, I would not have dared include in a finished book, and to begin a public dialogue on these questions. I will preface my series of answers with a question about the preliminary text furnished by *1895*. These remarks present the new historical point of view found in my book as being based on a radical break between two phases ("between what was once called 'primitive cinema' and then 'early cinema'"). They see the first phase as "marked by technological inventions and modes of discourse involving monstration and attraction" and a second phase "that in reality is the first phase of 'cinema,'" or institutional cinema. The problem I would like to raise here (no one should be surprised by this) has to do with vocabulary and, by extension, a certain way of seeing the world. Can we continue to see historical development as development in phases? Much has already been said about this and I have no definitive answer. All I can say is that I am constantly beset by doubt whenever this question is raised. So much so that I avoid this word like the plague in my book. In any event, I feel the need to raise this here at the start in order not to sow confusion about the way I divide up history. The new historical perspective I propose is based on a break so radical between the period[2] of what I call kinematography and that of cinema properly speaking that it behooves us not even to speak of the first period as a phase giving rise to a second phase, for the simple reason that it seems to me important, primordial even, not to highlight the fact that the second period came out of the first. For me, placing what I call kine-attractography and institutional cinema back to back is irreducible. I will go so far as to state here that there can be phases only within a phenomenon or a relatively homogeneous group, such as the phases one might wish to identify within kine-attractography, or within institutional cinema.

Naturally, one can object that in the empirical and "historical" world there is no clean break between the two phenomena, between the sets kine-attractography and institutional cinema, and that their "systems" coexisted for a relatively long time. This is true, but the break I argue belongs to the world of historical understanding and not the world of historical phenomena themselves.

1. Breaks and Paradigms

1895: The subtitle of the French edition of your book *Cinéma et attraction* is *Pour une nouvelle histoire du cinématographe* ("Cinema and Attraction: For a New History of Kinematography"). Here can be seen a number of methodological proposals and theses on film history and theory. We would like to come back to the hypothesis that a new history has been founded and to the tools that will enable it to be carried out. This "new history" has been established out of a break between what should henceforth be called "kinematography" and what succeeded it without proceeding directly out of it (except for the technology it inherited from it), and certainly without being its development: "cinema." In other words, you propose to replace the "periods" that have been perceived and discussed from the beginning, or almost—that of invention, when technology dominated, and that of expression, or art—with a series of discontinuities, each belonging to a different paradigm. Various features of these discontinuities are described in order to define them: capturing/restoring; monstration and, later, attraction; and heterogeneity on the one hand and narration, institutionalization, art, and specificity on the other. Most of these features relate to narrativity and determine the paradigmatic "ruptures" and changes described without reference to criteria of a different order (economic, legal, etc.), which could produce different markers of discontinuity. From this point of view, doesn't the "alien quality" of "early cinema" run the risk of shifting from an epistemological position to an essentialist one once you try to contain it within a closed set of phenomena?

In addition, isn't the logic of the succession of paradigms a way of insisting on the many differences between them to the point of multiplying the number of paradigms willy-nilly? Moreover, in your book we go from one paradigmatic shift to a description of three paradigms (p. 56)—but why stop there, under the logic you have adopted? As factual research develops and is placed within the narratological-taxonomic perspective you propose, won't the identification of differences lead to greater numbers of paradigms that will define kinds of historical monads?

Various related questions arise, in particular the question of the connection between "new paradigm" and "break" and between "paradigm" and "cultural series." Doesn't the paradigm "recording," therefore, because of its division, its "cutting up," appear to be simplified in your text, if not impoverished, perhaps because of your desire to bring out its difference with the paradigm "narration"? (You state that "kinematography was a wide-open field of experimentation" [p. 39].) Doesn't this "radicalization" of differences strip Lumière views, for example, of the complexity of the manipulations that lie behind them on the level of their composition or abutting? (It must also be said that you examine a very limited number of kinds of such views.) The same could be said of the comparison between the kinematograph and the phonograph as "recording" machines that merely re-create ("We wouldn't say that recording an opera on wax cylinders, for example, gives the original work any additional artistry whatsoever" [p. 86]), which takes no account of comments on this topic by authors such as Alan Williams, Rick Altman, James Lastra, and Friedrich Kittler. In your formulation, there is no indication of the role necessarily played by representation in any reproduction, however mechanical it may be. Your use of the term "literal" ("re-create on screen in a literal manner the visual properties of the profilmic"; "how literal the photographic record was" [pp. 86–87]) may be taken as emblematic of this sometimes reductive tendency in your book.

André Gaudreault: Judging from my interlocutors' first question, they do not share with me a number of suppositions that I believe to be essential, if only to be able to understand one another. Or perhaps a number of misunderstandings have crept in between me and them? The first misunderstanding I encounter is in the meaning (or rather meanings) of the word "paradigm". This word is now part of common usage and is increasingly served up in all sorts of ways. It seems to me that it has been a long time since it has had the almost exclusive meaning that some people still appear to want to ascribe to it (in particular when one brandishes reference to Thomas Kuhn,[3] who from my point of view is just one reference among many and has usefulness only within a quite precise framework). It is common knowledge that the philosophy of science is not the only place the term is used (to identify, to put it simply, an intellectual model in an academic discipline), because we find it in linguistics, sociology, computer programming, and history. Naturally, there is also the paradigm of the average reader—without overlooking the fact that in cinema we must also address the "paradigm of syntagmas" that is Christian Metz's "Grand Syntagma." In short, let's say that the word "paradigm" has a brilliant future ahead of it, and that it would be vain to try to rein in and tame it. This is the open and multifaceted context in which I use the word. True enough, this may lead to confusion in the mind of anyone for whom the epistemological sense of the word takes precedence over all others.

No one would object if I were to say of film history that it was witness to an encounter or a crossing of a series—a succession—of cultural series (here I deliberately use the word "series" in two different ways). There are thus series and series. There are also paradigms and paradigms. What I call the "paradigm of kine-attractography,"[4] therefore, is not for me a paradigm on the same scale as what Philippe Marion and I have defined as "the three paradigms of kine-matography" (the paradigms of capturing/restoring, monstration, and narration [p. 56]). If one had to categorize these two kinds of paradigms with respect to each other (something I don't do in my book), I would say that the second kind is narrower than the first (we might say that the first type of paradigm—the "epistemological" paradigm—encompasses the three paradigms of the second type, which are more "representational" paradigms).[5] All of which is to say that these three representational paradigms are categories of the great epistemological paradigm kine-attractography, just as, moreover, they are categories of the great epistemological paradigm institutional cinema. What's more, in addition to these epistemological and representational paradigms is the "cultural paradigm" (for example, late-nineteenth-century stage entertainment), made up, as I describe it, of "various forms of signification" (music hall, shadow plays, magic sketches, fairy plays, circus arts, variety shows, pantomime, etc.).

From this perspective, as long as I am not using the term in its epistemological sense, I don't quite see why it would be detrimental to have an increasing number of paradigms. These, like series, could be sets of things scholars themselves construct at will to better enable them to apprehend reality. This is what I have done in my book. As for the succession of discontinuities, each of which belongs to a different paradigm (capturing/restoring, monstration, attraction, and heterogeneity on the one hand and narration, institutionalization, art, and specificity on the other), I agree with my interlocutors that, in my book, I don't take into account economic, legal, or other factors, at least when it comes to setting out paradigms. Why not? The answer is quite simple: the two great epistemic paradigms I define (kine-attractography and institutional cinema) are necessarily in phase with economic, legal, cultural, and every other kind of aspect! It could not be otherwise, in that these two great paradigms have fuzzy dating and, in any event, they are not monads, despite what the question appears to suggest. Quite the contrary! Thus, as I demonstrate in this volume, kine-attractography is still quite alive as a system in the late work of Méliès (as late as 1911 in the film *À la conquête du Pôle* [*The Conquest of the Pole*] in particular), while institutional cinema has deep roots in the early years of the twentieth century (in Pathé films, for example). Naturally, if we are discussing paradigms of a more representational nature, the question of them being out of phase with the criteria of other orders may indeed come into play. Moreover, my questioners have in mind more "representational" paradigms when they state that most of the defining features of my paradigms "relate to narrativity" (which is too hasty a conclusion, in my view).

I don't understand, moreover, how one can state that my expression "alien quality" can be seen as delineating a closed set. The reason it seems to me too important to dwell on this aspect of kine-attractography, if only for maieutic reasons, is that I believe it to be the best means at our disposal to avoid being lulled by the siren song of the analogy between early cinema and cinema plain and simple. If this is a closed set, it is so only on the conceptual level (in the world of ideas, we might say). At first glance, the two phenomena before us, kine-attractography and institutional cinema, bear a strange resemblance. In particular, they use the same technology and same equipment, and the fundamental differences between their respective agents were quickly effaced (seeing cineastes where only kinematographers existed), especially in the minds of those who subscribe to the idea that it must be demonstrated that the former phenomenon is well and truly the antechamber to the latter. And this is what traditional historians of former times used to do. And it is what "traditional" historians (there are many more than you might think) continue to do today.

The method I develop and define (a method with pedagogical aims) introduces a degree of voluntarism into our relationship with historical objects, even if it means deliberately forcing our depiction of them. The idea is to say: let's begin with the *idée-force* that this phenomenon was completely alien, believe in it firmly for a while (why not for a generation?), and gather the results of such a credo and analyze them. It appears to me, moreover, that this method has already demonstrated its worth. If only by enabling us to bring out the distance separating the two phenomena (in my case, in any event, as soon as I hear the words "the cineaste Méliès" a chasm of incongruity opens before me and I clearly see the antinomy of using these words together, and I don't think I'm the only one—at least I hope not).

With respect to the simplification or impoverishment of which the recording paradigm is alleged to be my victim ("perhaps because of your desire to bring out its difference with the paradigm 'narration'?" my interlocutors remark), I would say this: My interlocutors have misread (or my text is miswritten). The representational paradigms capturing/restoring, monstration, and narration do not succeed each other in a strictly chronological way. Thus narration, the third, is present from the beginning in Lumière films, in particular in a work such as *L'Arroseur arrosé* (*Waterer and Watered*)—and there are many more such examples; thus monstration, the second, is the first paradigm to be widely present as early as 1894 in the work of makers of Edison Kinetoscope views that, by virtue of the fact that they imported already preconstrained attractional packages (circus or stage routines, for example in *Sandow* [Edison, 1894] or *Buffalo Dance* [Edison, 1894]), are even less hesitant than Lumière films to blithely manipulate the profilmic; thus the first paradigm, recording, is by definition consubstantial with the cinematic and runs throughout the entire first century of film history. On a historical level, it is true that the paradigm of narration is a phenomenon that became widespread only at a relatively late date compared to the other two paradigms, but it was at least present right from the beginning (and even before: think of the almost euphoric narrativity of Reynaud's *Autour d'une cabine*, an 1893 strip of hand-drawn images for his optical theater). To return to the Lumière views, these are undoubtedly complex, but I had no intention of suggesting that they pertained to the recording paradigm alone. On the contrary! The abutting found in these films (of which I have sung the praises elsewhere, but see also pp. 58–59 of my book, where I discuss in some detail the stop-camera technique in Lumière films) puts Lumière films on the side of monstration, as I define it here, because it involves manipulation on the filmographic level, which is one of the conditions of monstration. My idea behind projecting a series of paradigms onto the history of the early years of kinematography is not to section off film history and to line up in single file a litany of determining factors each more obscure than the last. Rather, it is a question of understanding this history and the various issues at stake in it. It's no small task to unravel the tangled threads of the meshing found in a medium as complex as the cinema, and a concept as linear and simplifying as "period" is of no great help when attempting to write that medium's history. The notion "paradigm" has the advantage of flexibility. It also makes possible various overlappings and superimpositions, as Philippe Marion and I argued in a text in which we also maintain that the use of the concept "paradigms of representational systems" enables us to see capturing/restoring, monstration, and narration not as mutually exclusive entities but as practices that can overlap.[6]

To conclude this long answer to an equally long question, I would like to return to an idea I propose in my book with respect to "recording" and provide a few supplementary comments on it. It is quite clear (for reasons already—always already, I'm tempted to say—well known) that pure transparency does not exist. As a corollary of this, it is equally understood that transferring the visual or sound qualities or properties of a living phenomenon onto a fixed medium can never be literally literal, if the reader will permit me the expression. And that every reproduction is, by necessity, in some degree representational. It is fundamentally a question, therefore, of degrees. Degrees that are spread across a spectrum ranging from thundering utterance (see, for example, the maximum degree of intervention that was standard practice in the era when montage held sway) to what we call, quite inadequately and somewhat idealistically—but not on account of me, I swear!—transparency (about which it must be said that it is a horizon beyond reach). This transparency presupposes a minimal number of interventions and comes close to what we might call the "zero degree of recording." Kinematography in some ways went beyond merely "putting on record" more quickly and more radically than other "recording machines" more or less in competition with it. In so doing, a new art was created (the seventh art, we say in French). The sound recording of an opera, no matter how much "artistry" is put into it, remains and will always remain "the sound recording of an opera" (and, moreover, of a particular performance, in a particular venue, at a given date in the historical continuum). The same is true of certain kinds of animated pictures. The visual recording of a performance by Sandow in 1894 in Edison's studio in West Orange, New Jersey, remains and will always remain "the visual recording of a body-builder's performance" somewhere in New Jersey that year. The device used in this recording was a reproduction device employed to record profilmic events. But the visual and sound recording of Ingrid Bergman and Humphrey Bogart included a few months after it was made in the final version of a film called *Casablanca*, at the point in the story when Ilsa leaves Rick on the tarmac of the airport, remains "the visual and sound recording of the performance of Ingrid Bergman and Humphrey Bogart" only in an exceptional sense, only in certain respects, and under certain conditions. There is a "tiny" little thing that transcends the putting on record carried out by the camera and takes us to another level. "Somebody" (or rather somebodies) has gone beyond the discourse of the putting on record and given it not simply a human element but also an artistic one, and affixed to this initial level of discourse a discourse of another order that relegates the putting on record, if not to oblivion, at least to an in-between state. A good recording (whether sound or visual or both at the same time) can certainly impart a human element to the thing recorded, but it does not necessarily give it an artistic element. The artistic element comes in when it is decided to take the basic recording and work it in such a way that it ends up saying something other than what the original event said (or what its mere putting on record would say). The artistic element comes in when the "thing recorded" is the raw material out of which one succeeds in secreting another world than the world of the recorded alone by means of a new discursive layer that is "affixed" to the world recorded.

What happened is that kinematography developed in such a way that a new category of artists (cineastes) began to superimpose a new layer of meaning, which they try to control completely and is something like an added value on top of the layer of primary meaning, the "mere" putting on record. Today we are witnessing a similar process at work with the exhibition, live or at a later date, of operas and ballets in movie theaters. This is occurring in North America in particular, but the phenomenon is beginning to spread. The question on everyone's lips is how to transmit these performances. For the initial idea was above all simply to transmit them, and to transmit them simply. Here again it is a matter of degrees. Maximum transparency would be within reach of the first crank-turner on the scene, if he or she was content to transmit the entire performance using a single camera showing the stage in a medium-long shot from the point of view of a gentleman in the stalls (as Sadoul said about Méliès) in a single long take. Yet it appears that no such thing exists. On the contrary, we see a relatively high degree of intervention, something that does not please every critic,[7] with a battery of cameras and a host of shots and camera angles. We are undoubtedly in the presence, in this new "cultural series" of filmed operas, of the early stages of the "birth" of a new art, one responsible for adding a supplementary layer of meaning to a preexisting art, to a cultural series already in place. A new speaker is thus interposed between the viewer/listener and the director of the opera (who in turn is interposed between the viewer/listener and the author of the opera). We might imagine that this new kind of artist will soon be demanding that his or her name appear on the poster and that they will one day list their occupation on a national census form as something to the effect of "filmed opera image maker," "director of artistic recordings of operas," or something along such lines.

2. Cultural Series

1895: The concept "cultural series" is one of the very productive theoretical ideas set out in your book. It makes it possible to assert that films of the period have much less in common with each other than with other, noncinematic cultural forms such as fairy plays, postcards, et cetera. The application of these ideas, however, is less convincing. People have almost always seen a link between Méliès and the fairy play, but is there a historian of "kine-attractography" with sufficient knowledge of fairy plays, well before the appearance of kinematography, who can truly offer a fresh perspective on the topic the way Thierry Lefebvre did with a specific case, Méliès's film *Voyage dans la lune* (*A Trip to the Moon*)?[8] In the case of the series "theater," the principal framework for the output of the Pathé studio, you demonstrate, using the film *L'Histoire d'un crime* (*The Story of a Crime*, 1901), that there is a slippage from "theater" to "drama in the broad sense." But what is the "cultural series" "drama"? How is it constructed? The series "theater" takes on an indeterminate, protean form, shifting from "melodrama" to "bourgeois theater." One idea runs through your discussion: that Pathé, in this somewhat shifting relationship to theater, defined the early forms of cinema's institutionalization (we will return to this point). But the very conditions of institutionalization, of the passage from a cultural series to a norm, are the blind spot of this argument. How can it be problematized? Couldn't we, at the opposite end of insular specification, seek out points of friction between different "cultural series"? For example, staged cinema enters the field of copyright with its own specific features because of its twofold assimilation to engravings and theater. Or, to take another example, writers working for Film d'art attempted to extract from kinematography what they could not obtain with theater, by conceiving of their projects as theater and natural views alike, or theater and "trick" photography, et cetera. The cultural series "photography," precisely, is not mentioned again in your book after the period of the Lumière brothers. This was the longest-lasting series, and yet it's the one people most often tend to minimize and neglect. Méliès's discourse, or that of Émile Maugras and Maurice Guégan on the almost "auctorial" function of the person who directs and composes the view, derive directly from an idea, already well rooted, of the artistic contribution of the camera operator.

André Gaudreault: The first true question in this second point is the following: "Is there a historian of 'kine-attractography' with sufficient knowledge of fairy plays, well before the appearance of kinematography, who can truly offer a fresh perspective on the topic?" On this score, I bear good news. There may not have been until quite recently, but there will be soon! And let's hope that they don't go too far in the direction taken by Thierry Lefebvre, who is certainly engaged in new research on *A Trip to the Moon*, but who is doing it the old-fashioned way, if you will. For Lefebvre, it's not a question of seeing how Méliès's film was part of one or more already existing cultural series, but of looking for "the model that inspired Méliès" (Lefebvre, p. 174), of "discussing the possible sources of Méliès's film" (p. 177), of finding earlier works of which the film was an "adaptation" (p. 180), of seeing how "the operetta influenced Méliès's masterpiece" (p. 181), et cetera, et cetera. When you look at an artist's inspiration, at a film's possible sources and the influences its author was exposed to, we find ourselves squarely in another paradigm (oops!) than that on the basis of which I set out the proposals underlying the present volume. It is not surprising in this context that Lefebvre speaks of Méliès as a cineaste here and there throughout his article, and that in his own paradigm, Abel Gance, Marcel L'Herbier, and François Truffaut would be artisans of the same stripe as Méliès who in the end can be seen as practicing the same profession.

Please don't misunderstand me. I'm not saying that Lefebvre's article is not innovative, or that it's not useful. One learns a lot reading it and it is the fruit of impressive documentary research. It could even serve as a model of its kind. But if the journal *1895* sees in it a model of profound thought on the topic of bringing new ideas to our conception of film history, we are far from being out of the woods.

More good news: first of all, the recent publication of a book of the highest importance, finally, on the history of fairy plays before kinematography: Roxane Martin's *La Féerie romantique sur les scènes parisiennes: 1791–1864*. Second, there exists at least one historian (or budding historian, at the very least) in the process of acquiring sufficient knowledge of the history of the fairy play to bring new ideas to it. I'm speaking of Stéphane Tralongo, a doctoral candidate working under my supervision at the Université de Montréal (in a joint program with Université Lyon 2 under Martin Barnier), whose project is to look at kine-attractography from the point of view of stage shows and more precisely to determine, synchronically within the cultural series "fairy play," the various forms of intermedial subjugation animated pictures entered into with the theater. As the reader can surmise, this is a very promising project.

The second question of this second point concerns the rather protean cultural series "theater" and how we should go about constructing it. I have no good news on this score but suspect that Tralongo's work will supply us with a number of interesting avenues of approach. Kine-attractography lies within a great number of cultural series (photography, postcards, fairy plays, magic sketches, caricature, theater, magic lantern shows, pantomime, illustrated songs, café-concert, shadow plays, the circus, variety shows, pantomime, magic acts, fairground attractions, stage routines, music hall, and so on and so on). And one can't specialize in everything. Research into each of these cultural series is not very advanced. It's unfortunate, but that's the way it is. All we can hope for is that the "model" I'm proposing inspires others to take up the torch. Researchers must construct each of these series according to rules yet to be decreed. For my part, I have limited myself to proposing a new way of approaching the phenomenon of cultural series and have ventured only very prudently and timorously into any one of them. Each of these series merits a study of its own, which is the only way we will have a sense of the impact it had on kinematography. As for the conditions of institutionalization and the passage from a cultural series to a norm, I don't see how these will remain blind spots for much longer.

With respect to the points of friction between competing cultural series, I would point out that Philippe Marion and I see any medium, all media, as a temporary federation of cultural series, and that frictions between series are, precisely, one of the reasons for the temporary nature of this federation. Our research has also led us to study various questions about copyright, in particular in the case of friction between writers (or rights holders) and those working for the Film d'art company, in an article[9] in which we take up the historiographical arguments made by one of the editors of *1895*, Alain Carou, concerning the work of writers in French cinema.[10] Allow me to conclude by saying, despite the fact that Méliès, as well as Maugras and Guégan, speaks of the almost "auctorial" role that the person directing and composing the view may have, that the artistic contribution being referred to by them is not the same as that of the "cineastic" agent as such and that the art in question is not, strictly speaking, film art. I have discussed this topic elsewhere, in a text I cowrote with Roger Odin, to which I refer the reader here in order not to repeat myself needlessly.[11]

3. Vocabulary and the Relationship
of Historians to Their Sources

1895: One of the book's methodological arguments is to use "period" terms in order not to impose contemporary meanings. The advantage of this is to create distance between us and the object of study—to establish its alien quality, in short. But what is the connection between this imperative and your statement that one only ever writes from within one's own era, that historians are indebted to their times and the questions posed therein? With respect to this position, two kinds of questions arise.

The first has to do with sources: Period texts—in particular, the text by Méliès published here as an appendix and to which you refer throughout the book— appear to bear witness to a period and not to the relationship that an author establishes with the subject of his or her discussion. While it is true that Méliès published this text at a time, in 1907, of a break that marginalized him, as your book indicates, isn't it just as indicative of the distance between him and the cinema being made at the time? How is it possible, in more general terms, to discern a way of thinking in a text, and a way of working with the words of this text (because your book rests on lexical choices and draws conclusions from them)? This brings us back to the "primary" vision of the kinematograph as a "mere reproduction device": Is this true only for people of the time or do you as author share this vision?

Next, on the theoretical level: The question of vocabulary seems to be essential in order to mark the break between the two "paradigms." But what are we to think of these terms in relation to this break: Do they anticipate it or follow it? Can we use period vocabulary to define aesthetic systems? Here again vocabulary is part of a way of thinking and not necessarily of how things were done. And shouldn't historians make these "words" and "ways of thinking" an object of study rather than a way to advance their theories?

There is a passage in your book that is problematic in this respect. It has already been mentioned here—your discussion of the film *The Story of a Crime* (where it might have been particularly relevant to explore the question of "series"). In wanting to see a "proto-institutional" aspect of Pathé's choice of presenting a drama, aren't you mistaken in your interpretation of the extract from the Pathé catalogue you quote on two occasions (pp. 84 and 90)? You draw attention to "drama" because of its rarity at the time, but it was a subject like any other, including those mentioned at the beginning of the quotation. In order to create a link with the institution because it is the "prototype par excellence of the dramatic film, which would soon be the mainstay of the cinematic institution," it would have to have a precise status in 1901–04. In addition, in order to argue Pathé's foresight (you see the company as being on the threshold of "cinema," which is to say the later phase), you compare this text, an excerpt from the Pathé catalogue, with a statement by G.-Michel Coissac, who "was not prepared to do as late as 1908" what Pathé did seven years earlier. But shouldn't you take into more specific account Coissac's discourse at the time on the practice of lecturing, which in his *Manuel pratique du conférencier-projectionniste* was more associated by far with the magic lantern and exhorted lecturers to use still images rather than with moving images, the latter being viewed as less well suited to verbal accompaniment with educational aims? At that point, is this really the same "cultural series" as that in question at Pathé?

André Gaudreault: Period vocabulary enables us to approach (and only to approach) the ways in which reality is divided up at a given moment in history. The nineteenth-century color chimney-sweep brown[12] can help us identify some of the realities of the time (about heating, clothing customs, the importance of chimney sweeps, etc). Knowing today that the color in question was a part of the paradigm (oops!) of colors for speakers of the day is of immense importance to historians who wish to understand peoples' relationship to chimney sweeps. If chimney sweeps today wore green clothing, there is absolutely no chance that the expression chimney-sweep green would take hold in the twenty-first century. In film, it is essential that historians know that what we call "movie theater owners" did not exist at the beginning of the twentieth century (especially because there were no movie theaters) and we have to avoid having the average reader, trying to understand and explain kine-attractography, feel that they are obliged to use vocabulary that in no way applies to the historical situation they are observing. Luckily, texts such as the one by Méliès show us, in documentary fashion, that the most frequently used expression in French during this period to describe the person who showed animated pictures was *exhibiteur* ("exhibitioner"). This new piece of information tells us many things about the alien quality of kine-attractography. It also tells us that there was a time when the agent responsible for film shows was closer to the films themselves (the "exhibitioner of views") than to the venue ("movie-theater owner"). It also enables us to suppose that the introduction of dedicated cinemas, beginning in 1905–6, did not necessarily transform the exhibitioner of views into a mere movie theater owner. It also enables us to say that one day we will have to write the history of this mutation.

Naturally, it is important to place Méliès's text in context and to take into account what my interlocutors say about his marginalization at the time it was written. At that stage of his career, Méliès must surely have begun to feel that the ground was beginning to slip beneath his feet. He had already been out of phase for some time with film production of the day, and Pathé now called the shots. The times had overtaken him and things were undoubtedly developing too quickly for him; in the strict sense of the term, he was a conservative. But because of the role he alone played, and the fact that he represented a tendency that until recently had been dominant, his article is a fine testimonial of the era, even if it is marked by the limitations of the genre. (Historians well know that a testimonial is not necessarily completely candid.) At the same time, Méliès's remarks are of great importance for us, in the sense that they appear, shall we say, to be "filtered" by his roots in cultural series other than kinematography and because they tell us a lot about his relationship with certain things. It is quite true that a period text like this speaks most of all about the relationship of its author to the topic of his discussion. At the same time, however, whether Méliès intended it to or not, it speaks no less about its era: Positively and definitively, this text is an artifact of the era in question and is part of what that era has "secreted" (Méliès's relationship with the objects of his discourse being, of necessity, one such period object; nevertheless, I agree that we should exercise caution here, because it is a discourse). We can use this text without any risk whatsoever to discern the vocabulary of the day and draw consequences from it. Especially if we corroborate the vocabulary in question by means of other, more "objective" period documents—newspaper articles, advertising inserts, correspondence, et cetera. This has been done, to give just one example, with the word *exhibiteur*.

As for the question about the "primary" conception of the kinematograph as a "mere reproduction device" and whether this was the view of people of the day (and whether I share it), I'm somewhat stunned that it has been posed. My book cries from the rooftops and thunders at every opportunity that the "basic apparatus" was seen most of all as what it most essentially is: a mere recording device. Not only is this obvious, it is self-evident. This idea is present from the very moment the Lumière Cinématographe was launched: "This device, invented by Auguste and Louis Lumière, makes it possible to capture, using a series of snapshots, every movement that unfolds in front of the camera lens during a given time, and then to reproduce these movements by projecting their images life size onto a screen before a whole room full of people."[13]

Moreover, I don't see why any particularly illuminated person around 1900 would see this device as anything other than that![14] As for whether I share this view, how can one even ask me such a question? The movie camera is a device that records images of the world placed before it or before which it is placed, period! It was like that in 1900 and it is like that in 2009! (I suspect there is a misunderstanding: I can't imagine anyone would ask me if I share the view that people of the time had of the device, because that is my thesis.)

I leave it up to the reader of my book to judge whether, in my "historical" work as a film theorist, I make these words and ways of thinking a subject of study rather than putting them to use to bolster my theory. It is not for me to say. I will conclude by saying that the part of the book where I discuss *The History of a Crime* poses no particular problem for me. I certainly don't agree with my interlocutors when they argue that drama, which the Pathé catalogue vaunts, "was a subject like any other, including those mentioned at the beginning of the quotation." The reason for this is that the "subjects" mentioned are not mere subjects, they are genres:

> Until now, almost every *subject* has been employed. Natural views, town squares, military processions, comic scenes, transformation scenes, fairy plays, and so on have been its subject matter. There remained, however, a *genre* that no manufacturer dared attempt: Drama. Why? Does this mean that it wouldn't be as successful as the rest? We believe otherwise. Don't audiences, popular audiences especially, run to the *theater* the moment a fine Drama is announced?[15] (My emphasis)

What this text says about Pathé's avowed intentions (naturally, it is a text with a purpose in mind) shows that film people back then thought, as early as 1901, that the anemic and limited cultural use of kine-attractography might soon be able to leave the realm of the mountebank. That's all I say. And I'll repeat myself here: it is instructive and truly worthwhile to place this quotation from 1901 alongside the statement by Coissac, a major figure of the period. Seven years later (that's right, seven), he declared: "the kinematograph will remain in the realm of the fairground attraction." It's true, Coissac was speaking from the perspective of another cultural series, that of the magic lantern lecture, and he was surely motivated by a prejudice against animated pictures, preferring still images. But still!

4. Epistemology

1895: By applying the term "epistemological break" to the phenomenon itself (the transition from monstration to narration) and not to the knowledge of it you propose, are you not spreading confusion with respect to the historian's purpose? By writing "the term kine-attractography . . . allows for . . . a vertical understanding of the phenomenon . . . as it itself was" (p. 62), aren't you working at a remove from Jonathan Crary's conviction you adopted earlier, to the effect that "there are no such things as continuities and discontinuities in history, only in historical explanation" (p. 20)?

Can this break apply to a change in the discursive mode at the same time as its "epistemological" dimension—see the work of Gaston Bachelard in particular—shows that it marks the passage from a "tissue of positive, tenacious, and entwined errors" to a science? Shouldn't an epistemological break apply to this "new history," to historical analysis, rather than to what it is studying?

For its part, the concept of the paradigm borrowed from Thomas Kuhn implies the collapse of the preceding paradigm, here too in the realm of science, which is difficult to transpose to our object of study (which your book acknowledges is one of hybridity and the gradual domination of one paradigm over another). In other words, are the terms dominant and paradigm compatible?

In the same vein, you assert that those who write film history must make a shift that can only come from theory—the theory of history and film theory. In the case of film theory, however, there appears to be general agreement, with no further proof required, that media narratology and semiology (taxonomy) serve this function.

Thus the explanation of your three paradigms (pp. 56ff) rests on a certain conception of narrativity, as the following sentence makes clear: "When a narrative effect was produced by the filmic utterance, therefore, it was not because of but rather almost in spite of the medium" (p. 58). "Effect" refers here more to reception than to the "intention" of the producing agent you emphasize. In addition, one gets the impression in cases such as this that stories are "in the world," bringing us back to Albert Laffay's brilliant formulation in 1947 to the effect that there is tension between these two opposing terms, the world (what would later be called "analogy") and the story: The world doesn't tell stories; only the act of putting it into discourse can (and thus never independently of the medium, contrary to what the sentence quoted above suggests). Doesn't your "in spite of" refer rather to the anthropomorphized agent responsible for enunciating the film rather than to the medium proper (which, moreover, is not singular, because it is located at the intersection of several series)? It appears that the anthropocentric tendency of the theory of enunciation developed in your book *From Plato to Lumière* is reinforced here: not only do you isolate "agents" (rather than levels); you occupy these places with individuals.

André Gaudreault: Right off the bat, an initial correction: One of the two "epistemological breaks" I speak of does not take place in "the transition from monstration to narration" but in the transition from kine-attractography to institutional cinema (what is at stake here are not representational paradigms, but epistemological ones). This is a nuance, yes, but it is an important one. Second correction: It is impossible to state that "By applying the term epistemological break to the phenomenon itself . . . and not to the knowledge of it [I] propose" that I am "spreading confusion with respect to the historian's purpose," for the following two reasons:

1. In my book I clearly establish that I am applying the concept of "epistemological break" to scientific knowledge itself: "The three conditions that made possible the recent recognition of early cinema as a specific field of study . . . have influenced research in the field to the point of introducing a break it would not be exaggerated to describe as epistemological. As we have seen, the new historians were opposed to traditional film history and the very basis of its approach; their attempt to define their project was based on this opposition and borrowed, consciously or not, from Comolli's shaking up of official history" (p. 16).
2. I also state, just as clearly, that I am speaking metaphorically when I transplant a term from the history of science into the arts: "The break in continuity that can be seen between early cinema and institutional cinema is the equivalent in the arts of an epistemological rupture for the historian of science" (p. 35). I would be the first to agree with my interlocutors that, once this metaphor has been considered and properly evaluated, we must quickly bring analogy to an end and proclaim far and wide that the application of an epistemological rule to a change in a mode of discourse most certainly has its limits.

As for the rest, I have already given a partial reply to the questions asked here (see part one above, "Breaks and Paradigms"). Because the conception of paradigms upon which my work rests owes nothing to the work of Kuhn, there is no need for the previous paradigm to "collapse." It should thus be understood that whenever I openly use the word "paradigm" there is no incompatibility between "dominant" and "paradigm" (in the expression "representational paradigm" in particular).

At the same time, I sincerely don't see where I state (and if I did, I would be the first to denounce such ineptitude!) that "media narratology and semiology" should be the only models of film theory capable of coming to history's assistance (to help it shift gears). Did I misspeak? Was I misread?

To conclude my response to this question, I prefer not to accept the invitation to enter into a detailed narratological discussion here. My strictly historical replies have already gone on long enough for what were supposed to be brief replies. We will have to discuss narratology another time!

5. Which film history? A summing up or a point of view?

1895: One of the "lessons" of the school of film historiography that studies "early cinema" has been to make us discover two things: first, the fundamental heterogeneity of the medium (the variety of films included the "scientific film," the documentary view, the comic sketch, animation, "Passion Plays," tableaux vivants, pedagogical illustration, et cetera, and varieties of discourse included direct address to the audience, the lecturer, the autonomous tableau, etc.); and second, the extent to which "attraction" has been productive as an independent concept. These two dimensions have constantly been brought into play right up to our own day. Isn't there a possibility that these two contributions, which we might describe as external and internal in a sense, disappear in the break brought about by "institutional" cinema when it creates a "representational narrative" model that takes no account of or marginalizes these two aspects of the "kinematography" era?

The initial assertion of the Brighton congress, which was epistemological in nature, consisted in saying that the principal concepts underlying cinema beginning in the years 1915–20 were not the same as those of the preceding period. Today, however, we might wonder whether the principal task of historians of early cinema—or the "newest" task in any event—is to test their hypotheses and concepts on the period of so-called "classical" cinema, perhaps to render this break relative after having served its purpose in its day. Your book, on the contrary, proposes to restrict the field of study. Substituting the expression "kine-attractography" for "early cinema" does not just represent the search for a less equivocal expression to name the phenomenon under study; it also derives from a temporal narrowing, with the distinction that it functions between an initial period, which is seen as the "heart" of kine-attractography, and a second period that is already "proto-institutional." Our impression is that the history produced by the Brighton school has won a certain number of battles, but at the cost of a sometimes savage appropriation of the concepts involved (with "attraction" foremost among them).

At the same time, isn't it strange, and paradoxical in a book whose title asks us to think historically, to read that this new history will come from theory, and not empirical research? A number of theoretical explorations would require considerable primary research that, reciprocally, would most often remain sterile without theoretical support (for example, local studies, which would benefit from replacing film shows in the cultural landscape of the region being studied). This leads to the question of the historiography of the period properly speaking. Throughout the first part of your book you refer fairly explicitly to what had already been written in the book *Pathé 1900*, published in 1993. Does this mean that nothing new has arisen on the historiographical level since then? At least two generations of scholars have appeared since Brighton, but their work is basically absent from your book—quoted occasionally, but not a part of your overall ideas. Isn't your book, which is presented as evidence of a movement (with its subtitle in French "Pour une nouvelle histoire du cinématographe"—"For a New History of Kinematography"), more of a summing up of twenty years of research?

At the same time, doesn't your book neglect some of your own work, such as your seemingly revolutionary research into "editing" in Lumière and Edison films or your work on the film lecturer? Instead, in the case of the lecturer, you deplore the "relative hypertrophy of the lecturer in contemporary discourse on animated pictures" and the "inflation of discussion around this narrative helper" (p. 31). And yet research into the lecturer has shifted, from narrativity to orality in particular.

In the end, shouldn't we be breaking down borders, in the "good sense" this time, meaning not to return to a reading of the past (the early years of kinematography) through the eyes of the future ("classical" cinema)—a teleological approach, in other words—but by seeing the remnants of early cinema in later cinema. A number of studies in this vein have already appeared, such as Ben Singer's work on the way the serial film forms a part of the cultural series "melodrama." But much remains to be said, in cinema from 1910 to the 1950s, on the ways in which attraction and narration intermingle, on the hybridism of genres, on the performative aspect of film screenings, et cetera. Thus the break posited between the "exhibitioner" of kine-attractography and the "movie theater owner" of institutional cinema does not stand up from a temporal point of view: All through the silent period, the exhibitor had a very active role in producing the film show. (See, for example, Christophe Trebuil's work on the way serial films were repackaged toward the end of their life.) Wasn't it, instead, the transition to talking cinema (that is how things such as projection speed became fixed) that determined the change in paradigm?

André Gaudreault: Should we be concerned that my insistence on kine-attractography's alien quality will prevent us from applying some of the Brighton school's achievements to institutional cinema? I don't think so (and am tempted to invoke the old cliché, "A victory without danger is a triumph without glory"). In fact I believe the opposite. The two things that Brighton led us to discover, to sum up my interlocutors' remarks, are intermediality ("the fundamental heterogeneity of the medium") and attraction. It seems to me that these concepts, each in its own productive way, are continuing on their path despite my preaching in favor of the alien quality of "early cinema" for more than fifteen years (since 1993).[16] The former concept is one that is gaining greater and greater strength and acceptance, despite most often having nothing at all to do with "early cinema," and it is the focus of several university research centers.[17] As for attraction, one need only examine the recent volume edited by Wanda Strauven[18] to see that there are many people singing its praises who are in no way lackeys in the pay of research into "early cinema"!

Clearly separating kine-attractography and institutional cinema in no way prevents us, it seems to me, from using "classical" cinema to test the concepts forged and advanced by historians of early cinema. In fact, what might happen (and I hope this would be the case) is that by applying to the great paradigm "institutional cinema" the historical principles that I employ in my book we will one day be able to divide up correctly this much-too-large paradigm. I won't be saying anything new (especially since the popular expression "grasp all, lose all" is well known) by pointing out that institutional cinema during the "silent" period is not the same as institutional talking cinema. Any more than the institutional cinema of the Hollywood studio system is not the same as the institutional cinema of Italian neo-realism.

In fact, I am pleased to announce to my interlocutors that I am not at all ashamed to repeat here that new ideas will come from theory, not from empirical research. I don't see the paradox. I'm not familiar with many unenlightened empirical studies that have advanced matters, first of all because the empirical is like historical traces: It is constructed by the historian! Empiricism per se does not exist, and every historian has his or her own little corner of it. If a historian is blind to the meaning of his or her work (only theory can enlighten them about the merit and validity of their actions) that historian will produce facts (catalogues of facts) but will not know why or how to rank them. Without theory there is no model (apart from the sometimes unconscious model of tradition). We need not only catalogues; we need *catalogues raisonnés*.[19] What purpose is there, for example, in looking for cineastes in a period when that entity makes no sense? We must combine theoretical reflection and working with primary documents. This is the model I propose in my book, and which I put into practice in my day-to-day research. And while it is true that my book sums up twenty years of research, I don't see how I could have incorporated into such a small volume the research carried out by two generations of scholars, even if I restricted myself to those I found of value.

As for having given short shrift to my own research on editing in Lumière and Edison films and on the film lecturer, I said above what I think about editing/abutting and stop-camera work. As for the lecturer, I don't "deplore" anything. Once again, I have been misunderstood or I have explained myself poorly. I speak of hypertrophy and verbal inflation out of empathy with the traditional historian. There is an element of antiphrasis in this remark and it would be ungracious of me to think this way of this figure, whose importance I pride myself on having been one of the first to discover more than twenty years ago now and who became so popular in our field.

Finally, with respect to my interlocutors' last remark about breaking down borders, in a different sense this time ("by seeing the remnants of early cinema in later cinema"), the reader can see that for me it is an entirely appropriate program.

Figure 22. *Une scène cinématographique. Établissements Méliès* ("A Kinematograph Stage. Méliès & Co."). Photograph and caption appearing on the flyleaf of the original edition of Méliès's text. Source: Cinémathèque Méliès/Georges Méliès © ADAGP, Paris, 2007.

Figure 23. Cover page of the original edition of Méliès's text. Source: Cinémathèque Méliès/Georges Méliès © ADAGP, Paris, 2007.

"Kinematographic Views" (1907) by Georges Méliès

Edited, with an introduction and
annotations, by Jacques Malthête
Translated by Stuart Liebman
and Timothy Barnard

Introduction

This text by Georges Méliès (1861–1938), entitled "Les Vues cinématographiques"
("Kinematographic Views"), is reproduced here as close as possible to its original version as published in the Annuaire général et international de la photographie.[1]

To the best of my knowledge, "Kinematographic Views" has been republished,
in varying degrees of completeness, at least thirteen times in the following books
or periodicals (the letters serve as means of cross-referring in the following):

(A) *La Revue du cinéma* 4 (Paris: Libraire Gallimard, 15 October 1929): 21–31.
   (Only the following sections were included, with a few modifications: "Artifi-
   cially Arranged Scenes," "So-called Transformation Views," "The Acting Studio,"
   "Composing and Preparing Scenes," "Sets," "Actors and Extras," and "Trick Effects.")
(B) Marcel L'Herbier, ed., *Intelligence du cinématographe* (Paris: Corrêa, 1946), 179–
   87 [a selection taken from *La Revue du cinéma* (ref. A)].
(C) Marcel Lapierre, ed., *Anthologie du cinéma* (Paris: Nouvelle Édition, 1946),
   39–45 (excerpts).
(D) Georges Sadoul, *Histoire générale du cinéma*, vol. 2, "Les Pionniers du cinéma
   (de Méliès à Pathé), 1897–1909," 3rd edition (Paris: Denoël, 1978 [1947]), 43,
   44, 55, 83–88, 143–48, 223, 224 (extensive excerpts).
(E) *Catalogue de l'exposition commémorative du centenaire de Georges Méliès*, exhibition organized by the Cinémathèque française, the Musée du Cinéma, and the
   Union centrale des arts décoratifs at the Musée des Arts décoratifs (Paris: Cinémathèque française, 1961), 52–66. (This was the first complete republication
   of the text, with a few typographical modifications and omissions.)
(F) Georges Sadoul, *Georges Méliès* ("Cinéma d'aujourd'hui" series [no. 1], series

editor Pierre Lherminier) (Paris: Seghers, 1961), 87–112; second edition 1970, 89–115. (This was the second complete republication of the text, with a few typographical modifications and omissions.)

(G) André Gaudreault, Jacques Malthête, and Madeleine Malthête-Méliès, eds., *Les Dossiers de la cinémathèque* 10 ("Georges Méliès: Propos sur les vues animées") (Montreal: Cinémathèque québécoise, 1982), 7–16. (This was the third republication of the text, with imperfections.)

(H) Georges Sadoul, *Lumière et Méliès* ("Le Cinéma et ses hommes" series) (Paris: Lherminier, 1985), 203–18. This volume, which combined two monographs by Sadoul previously published by Seghers (the "Cinéma d'aujourd'hui" series, series editor Pierre Lherminier), one devoted to *Louis Lumière* (1964, no. 29) and the other to *Georges Méliès* (1961, no. 1, ref. F), constituted a fourth complete republication of Méliès's text, very carefully established by Bernard Eisenschitz with respect to the three editions that preceded it (refs. E, F, and G).

(I) *Théâtre et cinéma, textes inédits*, Quatrièmes rencontres cinématographiques (Dunkirk: Studio 43, 1990), 97–109. (This was the fifth republication of the text, with a few omissions.) Méliès's text is followed by an article by Anne-Marie Quévrain-Malthête ("Artificially Arranged Scenes: Le Cinéma selon Georges Méliès," 111–17).

English Translations:

(J) Stuart Liebman, *October* 29 (Summer 1984): 23–31 (translation of the abridged version published in *La Revue du cinéma* [ref. A]).

(K) Stuart Liebman (a more complete translation, close to a full version) in Richard Abel, ed., *French Film Theory and Criticism: A History/Anthology*, vol. 1, 1907–1929 (Princeton, N.J.: Princeton University Press, 1988), 35–47.

German Translation:

(L) Herbert Birett, "Georges Méliès," *Filmstudio* (Frankfurt: 1963): 59–77. Translation of the complete version, reprinted in Frank Kessler, Sabine Lenk, and Martin Loiperdinger, eds., "Georges Méliès—Magier der Filmkunst," *KINtop* 2 (Basel/Frankfurt: Stroemfeld/Roter Stern, 1993): 12–30.

Italian Translation:

(M) Riccardo Redi, ed., *Verso il centenario: Méliès* (*Collana di testi e studi sul cinema* 8, series editor Lino Miccichè) (Rome/Di Giacomo: Mostra internazionale del Nuovo Cinema, Roma, 1987), 83–97. This Italian translation of the complete version, in which the author's name is not explicitly mentioned, was revised by Viva Paci and reprinted in André Gaudreault, *Il cinema delle origini: O della "cinematografia-attrazione"* (series "Le Dighe") (Milan: Il Castoro, 2004), 138–59.

The 1907 *Annuaire* was made up of five parts.

First part: Revue photographique de l'année (1. Optique et chimie photographiques; 2. Applications scientifiques, artistiques et industrielles de la photographie; 3. Mouvement photographique de l'année 1906). Second part: Variétés.
Third part: Recettes, documents, formules (optique photographique, chimie photographique, renseignements divers, formulaire photographique). Fourth part:
Sociétés photographiques (France, étranger). Fifth part: Commerce et industrie
photographiques.

In 1907, kinematography was still almost completely absent from a volume such
as the *Annuaire*, which was aimed at professional and amateur photographers.
Only two articles were devoted to it: a description of the amateur kinematograph
camera "Kino" by G. Mareschal in the first part (p. 227), and the text by Méliès.
At the beginning of his description of the dual camera-projector device manufactured by the firm Ernemann, G. Mareschal makes reference to the article by
Méliès: "There have been and no doubt will be few other examples of a scientific
discovery spreading as quickly and becoming as popular as the kinematograph;
the industry that sprang up after the first kinematographic exhibitions took on
an importance from the beginning that has continued to grow, an idea of which
will be given in the article devoted specially to this topic in the second part of
the *Annuaire*."

"Kinematographic Views" was published in the second part, devoted to "Variétés," after the articles "La Transmission à distance de la vision et des impressions
photographiques" by Arth. Da Cunha, "Le Portrait des astres" by L. Rudaux, and
"La Houillère" by G. Marissiaux and J. Bouy, and before "La Photographie noc-
turne dans Paris" by É. Sainte-Claire-Deville and "Procédés artistiques" ("L'ozo-
drome et le procédé Rawlins" by Ch. Sollet and "La phototégie" by E. Coustet).

According to Georges Sadoul, Méliès wrote his article in the summer of 1906
(ref. D, p. 42). A footnote in the third edition of his *Histoire générale du cinéma*
(ref. D, p. 154) extends this hypothesis by stating that the 1907 *Annuaire* was
printed in October 1906; another note (ref. H, p. 203) specifies that the volume bore a printing date of that month and year. I have carefully examined a
copy of the publication, however, without being able to find the printing date
indicated in the latter note. In fact, the publication makes explicit reference to
an article published in the January 1907 issue of *La Photographie des couleurs*
(*Annuaire*, 1907, p. 212, note 1) and to another article published in the 30 December 2006 issue of *Photo-Revue* (*Annuaire*, 1907, p. 247, note 1). In addition,
of the 41 photographs used to illustrate Méliès's article, three were taken during
the shooting of *Deux cents milles sous les mers* (*Under the Seas*, pp. 369 and 379;

the film is extant) and a fourth during the shooting of *Le Tunnel sous la Manche ou le Cauchemar anglo-français* (*Tunneling the English Channel*, p. 377; the film is extant). The former film, 265 meters in length (nos. 912–924 in the Méliès catalogue), was registered for copyright on 18 March 1907 and the latter, 305 meters in length (nos. 936–950), on 5 July 1907 at the Library of Congress in Washington, D.C. In consideration of these objective facts and the time required to receive the text, prepare the illustrations, do the layout, and proofread the article, it would appear more reasonable to conclude that the 1907 *Annuaire* was printed in the spring of 1907 and to deduce from this that Méliès finished his text (at the proofreading stage) in May or even June 1907.

Kinematographic Views: A Discussion by George Méliès

In this chat, I propose to explain as best I can the thousand and one difficulties that professionals must surmount in order to produce the artistic, amusing, strange, or simply natural subjects that have made the kinematograph so popular around the world.

Volumes would be needed for old hands like me to write down without omitting anything all I have learned by the seat of my pants during long years of constant labor, and the space I have at my disposal is unfortunately very limited.

Consequently, my intention is primarily to examine unknown aspects of how kinematographic views[2] are made, in particular the difficulties audiences are unaware of but which are encountered at every step of executing works that appear quite simple and natural.

I have often heard the most absurd remarks in exhibition halls, unquestionably proving that a large number of viewers are miles away from imagining how much work goes into the views they were watching. Some of them, understanding nothing of "how it's done," simply and naively say "It's only a trick!" Or "They must have taken those in a theater!" And, satisfied by their explanation, they conclude with: "It doesn't matter, it's well made all the same."

Obviously, one can have reflected only for a minute to express such an opinion. Some of the reasons it is impossible, or almost, to make these views in a theater include the absence of daylight there; the impossibility of properly illuminating the stage and sets in a steady and constant manner using magnesium arc lights; the very particular kind of miming used in kinematographic views, so different from that in the theater, as we will see later on; and the very limited length of the reels. When filmed, even the way in which the theatrical sets are painted gives a woefully bad effect, as I will explain in the chapter about sets. Some people have very little interest in these matters and are not concerned by them at all.

But there is a group of spectators who will not be annoyed but rather delighted to obtain some information to satisfy their curiosity, which is, moreover, quite justifiable and natural in intelligent people who always seek to know the explanations behind what they are looking at.

This is the category of spectator, certainly the most numerous, that I will try to satisfy.

I will start with a few words about the kinematograph camera itself.

The Kinematograph Camera

Today, everyone understands the principle of the kinematograph camera, so it will not be necessary to describe it in detail. It is sufficient to recall that the camera is built to photograph moving objects or people by fixing the different phases of movement onto a strip of film passing behind a lens, in a series of sequential images taken at extremely short intervals. Generally, the images are taken at a speed of 12, 16, or 18 per second, depending on the situation, i.e., depending on the speed of the object being photographed. The camera is worked with a crank, which is turned at varying speeds to obtain a greater or lesser number of images per second. If the object being filmed is almost motionless, a slow speed is sufficient. But if, on the contrary, what is being filmed are people or animals crossing the frame at great speed, it is necessary to turn the crank more quickly to obtain a greater number of images and thereby avoid streaking and out-of-focus images, which would otherwise inevitably be produced in the photograph. If the object crossing the frame is very close to the camera, you have to crank even faster. This is all a matter of practice. The light-sensitive film unspools by way of a special mechanism from a hermetically sealed canister on top of the camera and passes behind a small rectangular window located behind the lens. The film doesn't unspool in a constant motion, but rather by a series of jerks. It stops and starts up again 12 to 18 times per second, according to the speed at which the camera is being cranked. Each time it stops the film shifts downward a distance of two centimeters and, when it stops, a shutter opens automatically to enable the photograph to be recorded on the film. The shutter then quickly shuts until the film stops again. This produces a series of photographs two centimeters high by two and a half centimeters wide[3] from one end of the strip of film to the other. Once the film is exposed, it is automatically fed into another canister, which is also hermetically protected from daylight. When we look at the images obtained after they are developed, we can see that a gesture, such as someone raising an arm, is depicted by five or six different images and that the person's arm occupies a higher position in each one; its movement has been broken down and reproduced in its sequential phases. If the film were to run without stop and without a shutter to mask its movement of descent, we would see a streak in the space occupied by the arm instead of a series of distinct images. The stopping and starting of the strip of film is performed, according to the make of camera, by a cam, a Maltese cross, or a claw mechanism moving both horizontally and vertically to grasp the film by the perforations found on each of its sides. There is no point in entering into detail here about the different film advancement mechanisms used. However the film is fed through the machine, and whatever the system used to stop it, the principle remains the same: to take a given number of sequential photographs of a moving object at very close and regular intervals.

I will abstain from giving any technical description of the kinematograph camera itself, because countless books on the subject exist and provide all the necessary information. My goal is to study, not the kinematograph camera, but rather kinematographic views.

The Different Kinds of Kinematographic Views

There are four broad categories of kinematographic views. Or, in any event, all such views can be tied to one or another of these categories. There are so-called *natural views*, *scientific views*, *artificially arranged scenes*, and so-called *transformation views*. I have deliberately named these kinds of kinematographic views in the order in which they have appeared since the first screenings. In the beginning, views were exclusively of natural subjects. Later, the kinematograph was employed as a scientific machine before finally being used in the theater. From the start, it had enormous success, at first because of people's curiosity about animated photographs. But once the kinematograph was put in the service of theatrical art, its success was triumphal. Since then, this marvelous instrument's popularity has grown with every passing day and has now assumed prodigious proportions.

Natural Views

Everyone working in kinematography began by making natural views. Whatever particular area they devote themselves to, they have all continued to make such films from time to time. These views kinematographically reproduce scenes from ordinary life, in streets and squares, by the sea, on riverbanks, from boats and trains, in panoramic views, in views of ceremonies, parades, processions, and so forth. In short, documentary photographs, which used to be taken by portable cameras, have been replaced by animated documentary photographs. After taking very simple subjects at first, which were astonishing solely because of the novelty of movement in prints that had always been frozen and immobile, operators today, by traveling around the world, present extremely interesting shows we can watch without stirring. They show us foreign lands we have probably never seen, along with their dress, animals, streets, peoples, and customs—all rendered with photographic fidelity. The landscapes of the Indies, Canada, Algeria, China, and Russia, waterfalls, snow-covered countries and their sports, misty or sunny lands: everything has been filmed for the pleasure of people who do not like to stir. Many operators specialize in this kind of work because it is the easiest. If you have an excellent instrument, if you are a good operator-photographer, if you know how to choose a vantage point, if you are unafraid of traveling or of moving heaven and earth to obtain the permits that are often required, then you have all the qualifications required in this branch of the industry. This is undoubtedly a great deal, but we will see further on that all this is only the infancy of the art. Any photographer can take views from nature, but not everyone can artificially arrange scenes.

Scientific Views

Soon after the appearance of animated photographs, several people had the idea of using the kinematograph to record anatomical studies of human and animal movement on film. Before the invention of the kinematograph proper, Mr. Marey had already succeeded in photographing a bird in flight and a galloping horse with truly extraordinary results by using a camera with several lenses triggered in sequence to break down their movement.[4] Today, thanks to the kinematograph, the automatic device of the highest order, this has become mere child's play. Others[5] have attached microscopes to the kinematograph and presented us with quite curious enlargements of the workings of extremely tiny creatures. Finally, others have used the kinematograph to record and reproduce a teacher performing surgery for a special audience of students,[6] or to give practical lessons about glass blowing, steam or electric machines in motion, pottery-making, and all sorts of industries. Strictly speaking, this special branch of kinematography could be placed in the category of natural views, since the operator limits himself, as before, to filming what is happening in front of him, except in microscopic studies, which require special instruments and know-how. In any event, I did not want to pass over this special function of the kinematograph.

Artificially Arranged Scenes

We now come to artificially arranged scenes, or genre scenes. Any subject of any sort in which the action is prepared as it is in the theater and performed by actors in front of the camera falls into this category. There are countless kinds of such views, including comic skits, comic opera, burlesque, somber drama, comedy, peasant stories, so-called chase scenes, clown acts, acrobatic acts, graceful, artistic, or whimsical dance turns, ballet, opera, stage plays, religious scenes, risqué subjects, tableaux vivants, war scenes, actualities and reenactments of sensational news items, accidents, catastrophes, crimes and attacks—the list goes on and on. The kinematograph knows no bounds. Any subject dreamt up by the imagination is suitable, and the kinematograph seizes upon them. This category and the following one have, in particular, made the kinematograph immortal, because the subjects conceived by the imagination are infinitely varied and inexhaustible.

So-called Transformation Views

I now come to the fourth category of kinematographic views, which exhibitors call transformation views. I find this description unsuitable, however. Since I was the one who created this special field, perhaps you will allow me to say that the term fantastic views would be far more correct. For, while a certain number of these views do contain scene changes, metamorphoses, and transformations, a large number of them have none at all. Instead, they have lots of trick effects, theatrical machinery, mise en scène, optical illusions, and a whole series of procedures that can only be called trick shots, hardly an academic term but one that has no equivalent in refined discourse. In any event, this category is far more widespread, because it encompasses everything from natural views (both unstaged and without trick effects, even if taken out of doors)[7] to the most imposing theatrical performances. It includes all the illusions that can be produced by sleight-of-hand, optical effects, photographic tricks, set design and theatrical machinery, lighting effects, dissolving effects (dissolving views, the English call them), and the entire arsenal of fantastic and magical compositions capable of driving the most fearless person mad. While I don't mean to disparage the two former categories, I am going to speak only about the latter two, for the very simple reason that there I will be entirely on firm ground and able, consequently, to describe them with full knowledge of the facts. Since the day—and this goes back ten years—when countless publishers of kinematographic views began to throw themselves into making natural views and comic scenes, whether good, bad, or excellent, I abandoned the simplest types and began to specialize in subjects whose interest lies in their difficulty of execution. Since then, I have dedicated myself to them over all others.[8] This, by the way, is what earned me a visit from Roger Aubry,[9] who asked me to describe for the readers of this *Annuaire* how artistic kinematographic views are conceived and made. I do so with a pleasure heightened by the fact that I love with a passion the great art form to which I have devoted my life. This art offers such a variety of ways to experiment, it demands so much work of all kinds and requires such sustained attention that I sincerely do not hesitate to proclaim it the most engaging and worthy of the arts, for it makes use of almost all of them. The stage, drawing, painting, sculpture, architecture, mechanical skills, manual labor of all kinds— all are employed in equal measure in this extraordinary profession. The amazement of those who happen to watch part of our work always affords me the utmost pleasure and amusement. The same phrase invariably comes to their lips: "Really, it's extraordinary! I never imagined that so much space and equipment were needed, that so much work was required to obtain these views! I didn't have any idea at all how they were made." Alas, afterward they know little more, for one must, as they say, roll up one's sleeves, and for a long time, to obtain a thorough knowledge of the innumerable difficulties to be surmounted in a profession in which everything, even the seemingly impossible, is achieved, and the most fanciful dreams, the most incredible creations are given the semblance of reality. Finally, needless to say, you must absolutely achieve the impossible, since you photograph it and render it visible!!!

The Acting Studio

For the special kind of view that concerns us, a studio has to be contrived ad hoc. Briefly, it is a combination, made of iron and glass, of a photographic studio (on a gigantic scale) and a theatrical stage. The camera booth and operator are located at one end, while at the other end is a floor, constructed exactly like a theater stage and fitted with trapdoors, scenery slots, and uprights. Of course, on each side of the stage there are wings with storerooms for sets, and behind it there are dressing rooms for the actors and extras. Under the stage are the workings for the trapdoors and buffers necessary for the appearances and disappearances of the diabolical gods in fairy plays and slips in which flats can be collapsed during scene changes. Overhead, there is a grate with the pulleys and winches needed for maneuvers requiring power (flying characters or vehicles, the oblique flights of angels, fairies, and swimmers, etc.). Special rollers help to move the canvas panoramas while electric lamps are used to cast the image of apparitions. In short, we have a quite faithful, small-scale likeness of a fairy theater. The stage is about ten meters wide with an additional three meters of wings both stage left and stage right. The length of the whole, from the proscenium to the camera, is seventeen meters.[10] Outside, there are metal sheds for the construction of wooden props, sets, etc., and a series of storerooms for construction materials, props, and costumes.

Lighting with Daylight and Artificial Light

The ceiling of the studio is part frosted glass and part regular glass. In summer, when the sun strikes the sets through the windows, the results could be disastrous because the shadows of the roof's iron beams would be conspicuous on the backdrops below. Moving shutters, operated by wires that enable them to be opened and closed in the wink of an eye, protect against this problem. These shutters are made of tracing paper (the kind used by architects for drawing their plans); when closed, they provide a softly filtered light similar to that of frosted glass. Even lighting is extremely difficult to obtain throughout the filming of a scene that can last four hours or more for a subject that, when projected, lasts two to four minutes. When it is cloudy, and damnably dark cumulus clouds delight in constantly crossing in front of the sun, the photographer's friend, exasperation is quickly seen in the person who directs the operators, assistants, stagehands, actors, and extras. You must be patient throughout all kinds of ordeals; sometimes it is better to wait for daylight to return and at other times it is better to close the shutters if there is too much light or to open them if there is not enough. All this must be done without losing sight of a thousand details inhering in the work at hand. If I am not crazy by now, I probably never will be, because fleecy, cloudy, and misty skies have tried my patience severely. Throughout my career they have caused innumerable failures and given rise to enormous costs; each tableau that has to be started over or is impossible to perform because bad weather interferes with the acting doubles, triples, or quadruples in cost, depending on whether you attempt it two, three, or four days in a row. I have watched scenes, the ballet in *Faust and Marguerite*[11] among them, performed for eight straight days at a cost of 3,200 francs, even though they last only two and a half minutes. It is enough to drive you mad.

After much trial and error, and even though it has often been said to be impossible, I have recently succeeded in creating artificial lighting with special electric equipment consisting of stage lights, runners, and stays, like those used in the theater. These create a complete daylight effect and in the future will protect me from the sore trials of the past.[12] Praise the Lord! I will not go mad . . . at least on account of the clouds. Diffuse light is created with a large number of arc lamps and mercury-vapor tubes in different combinations. This artificial light is used at the same time as daylight, and its intensity varies according to need.

Composing and Preparing Scenes

Composing a scene, play, drama, fairy play, comedy, or artistic scene naturally requires, first of all, a scenario drawn from the imagination. Then, you must seek effects that will have an impact on the audience, create sketches and models of the sets and costumes, and come up with the view's star attraction, without which it has no chance of success. As far as illusions or fairy plays are concerned, inventing, combining, and outlining the tricks and the preliminary study of their composition require special care. The mise en scène is also prepared in advance, as are the movements of the extras and the positions of the workers. It is exactly like preparing a play for the theater, with the exception that the author must know how to work out everything on paper by himself. As a result, he must be the author, metteur en scène, set designer, and often an actor if he wants to obtain a unified whole. Whoever devises a scene should direct it, because it is completely impossible for it to succeed if ten different people get involved. Above all, you have to know exactly what you want and spell out exactly what everyone's task will be. You cannot lose sight of the fact that rehearsals don't last three months like in the theater, but only fifteen minutes at most. If you lose time, the daylight dwindles—and goodbye photography. Everything, especially the snags to be avoided during the filming, must be anticipated. And, in the scenes involving machinery, there are many such snags.

Sets

The sets are produced by following a chosen model. They are constructed in wood and cloth in a workshop adjoining the acting studio and painted in distemper like theatrical sets, except that the painting is executed exclusively in grisaille, using all the intermediate gradations of gray from jet black to pure white. This gives them the look of funerary decorations and they have a strange effect on those seeing them for the first time. Colored sets come out very badly. Blue becomes white while red, green, and yellow become black, completely ruining the effect.[13] It is thus necessary to paint sets in the manner of photographers' backdrops. The painting, unlike that of theatrical sets, is very carefully done. The finish, correctness of the perspective, and trompe l'œil are skillfully executed to tie the painting to real objects, just like in panoramas. All this is necessary to give verisimilitude to the entirely artificial objects that the camera will photograph with absolute precision. Anything poorly made will be faithfully reproduced by the camera, so you must open your eyes and carry everything out with meticulous care. This is the only thing I know. In material matters the kinematograph must do better than the theater and not accept the conventional.

Props

Props are made of wood, canvas, cardboard, plaster, molded pasteboard, and molded clay. Everyday objects can also be used. But if you want to get the best photographic results, the best thing to do, even for the chairs, fireplaces, tables, carpets, furniture, candelabra, clocks, and so on, is to use only specially made objects painted in various shades of gray, carefully chosen to fit the object. Major films or strips of film are often colored by hand before they are projected, but if the objects are bronze, mahogany, red, yellow, or green in color, this is not possible, because they become deep black. As a result, they are not transparent when photographed and therefore cannot be made sufficiently translucent for projection. This is something audiences are generally unaware of, and they certainly do not suspect how much time and care it takes to make all these props, which appear to be mere ordinary objects.

Costumes

For the same reason, most costumes must be specially made in tones that photograph well and can later be colored. This is why it is necessary to have an enormous wardrobe of costumes of all sorts, from all periods and countries and of different classes, along with their accessories, not to mention the hats, wigs, weapons, and jewels belonging to the greatest lords or the worst low-life. The costume wardrobe, however large it may be, is always inadequate. Even with ten thousand costumes in our current repertoire, we occasionally have to go to theatrical costumers to complete the platoons, particularly for parades or processions, when many similar costumes are needed. Naturally, you also need costumers and seamstresses to repair and maintain the costumes. The same is true for the linens, tights, shoes, and accessories.

Actors and Extras

Contrary to general belief, it is very difficult to find good performers for the kinematograph. An excellent actor in the theater, even a star, is worth absolutely nothing in a kinematographic scene. Even professional mimes are often bad, because their pantomime is performed according to conventional principles, like mimes in ballet who have a special, immediately recognizable performance style. These performers, although they are greatly superior within their specialty, are put off balance as soon as they come into contact with the kinematograph. This is because kinematographic miming requires extensive training and special qualities. There is no longer an audience for the actor to address, either verbally or with gestures. The camera is the only viewer, and nothing is worse than looking at it and performing to it. This is what invariably happens at first to actors accustomed to the stage but not to the kinematograph. Actors must realize that they have to make themselves understood to the deaf viewers watching them while remaining completely silent. Their performances must not be showy and yet be very expressive. Few gestures are used, but they must be very distinct and clear. They must create perfect physiognomies and strike just the right pose. I have seen many scenes performed by well-known actors who were not good because the principal element of their success, speech, is lacking in the kinematograph. In the theater, they are accustomed to speaking well and using gestures only secondarily to speech, while in the kinematograph, speech is nothing and the gesture is everything. Some of them, however, and Galipaux[14] is one, have made some good scenes. Why? Because he is used to performing solo pantomime in his monologues, and because he is endowed with a very expressive physiognomy. He knows how to make himself understood without speaking, and his gestures, even if deliberately exaggerated—which is necessary in pantomime and especially in photographed pantomime—are always spot on. An actor's gestures, when accompanying his speech, are very telling, but they are no longer comprehensible when he mimes. If you say "I am thirsty" in the theater, you do not close your hand and bring your thumb to your mouth to simulate a bottle. It's completely unnecessary, because everyone heard that you are thirsty. In pantomime, however, you are obviously obliged to make this gesture.

That's all quite simple, isn't it? And yet, nine times out of ten, this does not work for anyone not accustomed to miming. Nothing can be improvised; everything must be learned. It is also advisable to consider how the camera will render a gesture. In a photograph, the characters overlap each other, and the greatest care must always be taken to make the principal characters stand out and to moderate the fervor of the supporting characters, who are always inclined to gesticulate at the wrong time. This produces a jumble of bustling people in the photograph. The audience no longer knows whom to look at and no longer understands the action. The action must take place in sequential phases, not simultaneously. The actors must consequently pay attention and perform only in turn, at the precise moment when their participation is necessary. There is one more thing that I have very often had difficulty in making clear to performers who are always inclined to show off and get themselves noticed to the great detriment of the action and the overall effect: generally speaking, they are too eager. A lot of tact is needed to moderate this excessive eagerness without giving offense! As strange as it may seem, every performer in my rather large troupe has been chosen after twenty or thirty tests in which I did not find who I was looking for, even though all were very fine actors in the Parisian theaters in which they worked.

Not everyone has what it takes, and eagerness, unfortunately, does not replace these qualities. Those who do take to it quickly, while others never will. Female performers who are good at mime are rare. Many are fine, intelligent, beautiful women who wear their costume and makeup well, but when they must mime a somewhat difficult scene, woe is me! A thousand times woe! Those who have never witnessed the sweat worked up by a metteur en scène have never seen anything. I hasten to add that there are, fortunately, exceptions to the rule who perform with grace and intelligence. The conclusion: forming a good kinematographic troupe is a long and difficult business. Only those with no concern for art satisfy themselves with the first people who come along and make the scene confusing and uninteresting.

Expenses

The expenses associated with kinematographic views can vary greatly according to the kind of subject being filmed. Today, film stock costs approximately half a franc per meter, for both the negative and the positive print. The raw material, therefore, costs about 10 francs for 20 meters of positive or negative film, or 20 francs total, if only one print is made. This, of course, is a pittance. The most costly thing, if you're shooting your subject in the Indies, the Americas, or elsewhere, is the travel expenses, which add considerably to the cost of the subject being filmed. If you're shooting artificially arranged scenes, this cost of 20 francs per meter can multiply to no end, which depends on the cost of obtaining the negative. Some people create scenes with four or five characters played by second-rate actors right in the street or a garden, on a country road or farm, and so on. In such cases, the manufacturing cost will not be high. Others, on the contrary, will use a large number of people, including some highly paid actors, along with sets, props, and costumes. In this case, costs become quite high. To give you a better idea, a large historical piece, fairy play, or opera made up of 30 or 40 tableaux requires two and a half to three months of preparation and 20 to 30 filming sessions using 20 to 30 actors, 150 to 200 extras, a couple of dozen stagehands, dancers, wardrobe people and hairdressers, costumers, and the rest. Some tableaux, especially those involving trick effects, have to be started over several times before they are perfect. In short, once the piece is finished it will have cost 12, 15, or even 18 to 20,000 francs in expenses of all kinds. Its total length will be 400 meters, for a projection time of 22 to 23 minutes. The audience, paying a franc or a half-franc admission, has no idea of this important detail. This is also why the cost of prints necessarily varies a great deal, according to the film publisher and the kind of work they do.[15] People are also generally unaware that the fees paid to good actors are so high that most of them earn more in a month with a film manufacturer than they do with the theater to which they belong. This is an excellent new source of income for actors, for whom the kinematograph has been a greatly appreciated way to supplement their incomes.

Trick Effects

It is impossible in this already long chat to explain in detail how kinematographic trick effects are done. That would require a special study. Moreover, practice alone leads to an understanding of the details of the procedures employed, some of which involve unheard-of difficulties. I can say without boasting, since everyone in the profession recognizes it, that I was the one who successively came up with all the so-called "mysterious" kinematographic techniques. The publishers of artificially arranged scenes have all more or less followed the path I laid down, and one of them, the head of the world's largest kinematographic company,[16] known for its mass, low-cost production, told me himself: "Thanks to you, the kinematograph has managed to sustain itself and has become an unprecedented success. By applying animated photographs to the theater, to its infinite variety of subjects, you prevented its decline, which would otherwise have rapidly occurred with natural scenes, whose inevitable similarities would have quickly bored the audience." I can tell you without bashfulness that this glory—if glory it is—pleases me most. Do you want to know how the idea of using trick effects in kinematography first came to me? Very simply, upon my word. One day, when I was photographing as usual in the Place de l'Opéra, the camera I used in the early days (a primitive thing in which the film tore or frequently caught and refused to advance) jammed and produced an unexpected result. It took a minute to disengage the film and to start the camera up again.[17] In the meantime, the passersby, horse trolleys, and other vehicles had, of course, changed positions. When I projected the strip of film, which I had stuck back together[18] at the point of the break, I suddenly saw a Madeleine-Bastille horse trolley change into a hearse and men become women. The substitution or stop-camera trick had been discovered. Two days later, I carried out the first metamorphoses of men into women and the first sudden disappearances that, in the beginning, had such great success.[19] Thanks to this very simple trick, I made the first fairy plays: *Le Manoir du Diable* (*The Haunted Castle*),[20] *Le Diable au Couvent* (*The Devil in a Convent*),[21] *Cendrillon* (*Cinderella*),[22] and the rest. One trick led to another. With the success of this new kind of film, I used my ingenuity to find new techniques and dreamt up, in turn, dissolving scene-changes (created by a special device in the camera); apparitions, disappearances, and metamorphoses created using superimpositions[23] on black backgrounds or separate sections of the set; and superimpositions on already-exposed white backgrounds (something everyone declared to be impossible before they saw it). I cannot discuss the subterfuge I used to create these superimpositions because my imitators have not yet penetrated their full secret. Then came tricks with decapitated heads,[24] with the doubling of characters, and scenes performed by a single character who, through doubling, portrays all by himself up to ten similar characters[25] staging a scene together. Finally, by using my special knowledge of illusions acquired through twenty-five years of practice at the Robert-Houdin theater,[26] I introduced to the kinematograph mechanical, optical, magic, and other tricks. When all these techniques are competently used together, I do not hesitate to say that it is possible today to achieve the most impossible and improbable things in kinematography.

I will conclude by saying that the simplest tricks, much to my chagrin, make the greatest impact, while those achieved through superimposition, which are much more difficult, are hardly appreciated, except by those who understand the problems involved. Views performed by a single actor, in which the film is exposed up to ten times in the camera, are so difficult that they become a veritable Chinese puzzle. The actor, playing different scenes ten times, must remember precisely to the second, while the film is running, what he was doing at the same time in previous passages and his exact location on stage. This alone makes it possible to show ten characters played by one actor with the necessary precision. If, at some point in the procedure, the actor makes an untoward gesture, if his arm moves in front of a character already photographed, this will be superimposed and out of focus, which reveals the secret of the trick. You can see from this just how difficult it is and how angry you can get when, after three or four hours of sustained work and attention, a sprocket hole in the film tears after the seventh or eighth superimposition, forcing you to abandon the film and do everything over again. For it is impossible to repair a film with a torn sprocket hole when the image is still latent and cannot be developed until the tenth and last superimposition is recorded.

Perhaps this is all "Greek" to the uninitiated, but I repeat that more detailed explanations would lead us too far astray.

In any case, intelligently used trick effects make it possible today to reveal the supernatural, the imaginary, and even the impossible, and to create truly artistic tableaux that give true pleasure to those who understand that every branch of art contributes to their creation.

Difficulties and Bothers

Apart from the obstacles related to the execution of such scenes mentioned above, others still can hinder the kinematographer. These include varying light conditions, clouds passing in front of the sun, accidents involving the camera, the film jamming in the camera, film tearing when it is too thin, emulsion that is not adequately light-sensitive, stains or dots on some film after development, making them unusable, and imperceptible holes that become great boulders when enlarged and projected. It is thus a great relief to find, after the film is developed, that the negative is perfect. No one outside the fold has the patience, perseverance, and will necessary for success; I cannot help but smile when I hear people say, "Why are these views so expensive?" I know all too well, but how to make this understood to someone who is unfamiliar with the work and values only one thing in a view: a low cost!

Taking the View: The Operator

Needless to say, the operator for this special kind of work must be highly experienced and very much up to date with a host of little tricks of the trade. A difficult sort of view cannot be taken by a beginner. He would invariably ruin the most easily achieved tricks if he forgot even the smallest thing while turning the crank. Cranking the handle one time too many, forgetting a number while counting out loud during a take or a moment's distraction can make everything go wrong. What is needed is someone who is calm, attentive, thoughtful, and capable of withstanding annoyance and frayed nerves, because annoyance and frayed nerves are practically inevitable when you are dealing with endless problems and almost constant unpleasant surprises. These observations will help you understand why taking fantastic views is so difficult, as they depend on the metteur en scène, the stagehands, the actors, and the operator taking the view. Perfect harmony, getting everyone to pay attention, and precise cooperation are hard to obtain when, at the same time, you are struggling against material problems of all sorts.

This will suffice to explain why, after having thrown themselves into this new genre, the majority of photographers have abandoned it. You have to be more than a mere operator for all this. While kinematographers are a dime a dozen, the ones who have succeeded in doing something different than the others are far less common. There is no more than one per country, if that, since every country in the world depends on French manufacturers for artistic views.

Rehearsals and Filming

A word now on the actual filming of the subject. When a tableau is ready, the sets finished and all their praticables in place, as well as props and trick effects if there are any, the tableau's[27] costumes are laid out in the actors' dressing rooms for the following day. Just like in the theater, they arrive on time. This is indispensable, because the sun doesn't wait. After a succinct explanation of the characters they are going to play, they are given their costumes. They dress and put on their makeup; in short, they get ready the way they do in the theater. They are not exempt from the laws governing the painting of the set, however, for which only black and white are used. Rouge is not used on their cheeks or lips, because if it were they would be turned into Negroes. Makeup is done exclusively in black and white. This too is a special art requiring some training, because there are limits to observe in order to obtain the types required without becoming ridiculous.

The actors, hurried along by the assistants, go down to the stage. There, the metteur en scène, who is usually the author, first explains the overall scene to be performed and then has the actors partially rehearse the various parts of the action: the principal action first and then the secondary episodes. He directs their movements and the positioning of the extras and must act out each character's part in order to indicate their gestures, entrances, exits, and position on the stage. He takes great care to separate these groups so that their pantomime will not be confused and the viewer will be able to follow the continuity of the principal action involving the leading characters without tiring. All this requires considerable practice and absolute precision in the explanations. Intelligent actors and bit performers are essential, so that they understand right away what is being asked of them.

You cannot lose track of the fact that the merciless sun is turning and that if everything is not understood, solved and ready to photograph in time, the hour of full daylight will pass and you will have to postpone everything until the next day, at twice the expense. When everything is ready to go, you move on to the dress rehearsal. If something isn't right, you fix it and start again. Finally, everything is ready. The actors perform the scene, speaking their lines the way they do in the theater, which gives a greater fidelity to their acting. The operator runs the camera and everything that happens is recorded in a regular manner. If a second tableau is to be performed, the set is changed as soon as the first tableau is finished, all the actors run to their dressing rooms to change their costumes, and then everyone comes back to the stage.

The same work of sorting out difficulties, explaining, and rehearsing starts over, and the second tableau is played and photographed. If we're in a rush, I don't stop to think while at the same time not forgetting anything, because, except in summer, there are few favorable hours in the day and you cannot waste a second. A complicated tableau sometimes requires two or three days to complete. It is not unusual to spend eight or nine hours on a tableau which will last two minutes when projected. This is especially true in scenes involving transformations and superimpositions, hence their high cost.

Developing the Negative and Making Prints

I said at the outset that I wasn't going to enter into great detail about the technical ins and outs of the kinematograph.

Kinematography is really just photography, pure and simple. Suffice to say, for the uninitiated, that the exposed strips of film are developed in two ways, depending on the manufacturer: either on frames, around which the film is wrapped, the gelatin facing out; or on drums or cylinders, on which the film is placed in a spiral, also with the gelatin facing out.[28] In the former case, the frames are lowered into grooved vats of developer, where they stay for the amount of time needed for developing. The person doing the job takes them out from time to time and inspects them by holding them up to the light, just like ordinary photographic plates. If you are using drums to develop the film, these are placed in semicylindrical vats, in which they turn on their axis. Rotation is produced either by turning a hand crank, exactly like the cylinders used to roast coffee in grocery stores, or by electric motor, which makes it possible for a single person to monitor the development of several drums at the same time.

Washing and fixing the film are done by taking the frames or drums from one vat to another containing water and hyposulphite. Finally, the film is given a last wash. The frames are plunged into running water just like photographic plates, while the drums are turned quickly in water that is constantly refreshed. Washing by rotation is much quicker and more energetic, which is better for the manufacturing process. Finally, the film is stretched onto very large cylinders of about one and a half meters in diameter, which are turned electrically at high speed. The film is dry in about an hour.

As for making prints, this is done by pressing unexposed film against a developed negative, with the gelatin side of each touching. The two strips of film are inserted together into a device identical to the device used to take the view, except that the lens is replaced by a square window, in front of which is placed an artificial light. The light prints the image exactly the same way that positive glass projection plates are made.

The kinematograph today has become a colossal industry employing more than 80,000 people in different parts of the world. That's hard to believe but a fact nonetheless, and its success is growing every day. Why? Because an interesting show is an irresistible attraction, and because the kinematograph has made it possible to give superb shows in all those countries lacking theaters or other distractions at an affordable price, because the *impresario*,[29] once he has paid for the film, doesn't have to pay the actors every day.

Oh, if it could only be like this for theater directors!!! But that's the way it is. Only photographed actors who have performed imperturbably and flawlessly in kinematographic views are this easy to deal with. They cannot be uneven, good one day and bad the next; if they perform well at first, they will be excellent forever. What an advantage!!!

G. Méliès
Director of the Robert-Houdin Theater

Notes

Acknowledgments

1. This volume has since been published in English translation. See Gaudreault, *From Plato to Lumière*.

2. These seminars took place at the Université de Montréal, the Université Laval, the University of São Paulo, Université Paris 1–Panthéon-Sorbonne, Université Paris 3–Sorbonne Nouvelle, the University of Bologna, the University of Liège, the Nordic Academy for Advanced Study in Vatnahalsen, Norway, the University of Buenos Aires, the École normale supérieure in Paris, and the École européenne supérieure de l'image in Angoulême.

3. In particular Karine Boulanger, Philippe Gauthier, Dominique Noujeim, Louis Pelletier, and Lisa Pietrocatelli.

4. See Paci, *Comédie musicale* and *Machine à voir*.

Introduction

1. This symposium was held as part of the thirty-fourth congress of the International Federation of Film Archives (FIAF), organized by David Francis (at the time an archivist of the National Film Archive in London) in collaboration with Eileen Bowser (at the time an archivist in the Film Department of the Museum of Modern Art in New York).

2. For a compilation of these films, see Gaudreault, ed., *Cinema 1900–1906*, vol. 2.

3. The specialists invited to Brighton were already relatively prepared for the change; in the months leading up to the conference, most of them had written articles proposing new approaches to early cinema. These texts were included in the conference proceedings. See Holman, ed., *Cinema 1900–1906*. Most of the papers presented at Brighton were also published in French in *Cahiers de la cinémathèque* 29 (1979) in a special issue edited by André Gaudreault.

4. Crary, *Techniques of the Observer*, 7.

5. I addressed the expression "cinéma des premiers temps," basically the French equivalent of "early cinema," at the 1996 Cerisy conference on the theme "Georges Méliès and Cinema's Second Century." The substance of this critique can be found in

Chapter 2 of the present volume. I also critiqued the expression "early cinema" in my article "From 'Primitive Cinema' to 'Kine-Attractography,'" in *Cinema of Attractions Reloaded*, ed. Strauven.

6. See Gaudreault, *Cinema delle origini*. The present volume follows the French edition of the book which is different from the Italian edition. Extensive new material had been added and it had been completely revised. While most of the hypotheses found in the Italian edition have been buttressed, others have been refined or simply abandoned.

7. There are many reasons to praise the work of the Lumière brothers, but inventing cinema as such is not one of them.

8. Méliès, "Vues cinématographiques."

9. Ibid., 362. See p. 136 in the present volume, where Méliès declares, "Consequently, my intention is primarily to examine unknown aspects of *how kinematographic views are made*, in particular the difficulties audiences are unaware of but which are encountered at every step of executing works that appear quite simple and natural." My emphasis.

Chapter 1. Looking at Early Cinema in a New Light

1. Sadoul, *Histoire générale du cinéma*.

2. Jacobs, *Rise of the American Film*.

3. Mitry, *Histoire du cinéma*.

4. On this topic, see Gaudreault and Gunning, "Early Cinema as a Challenge."

5. I am thinking, for example, of the Italian scholar Gian Piero Brunetta, about whom it would be difficult to say whether he is primarily a film historian or a film theorist. The same is true of people such as Tom Gunning and Ben Brewster in the United States and of Noël Burch and François Jost in France, who also work on both fronts.

6. Comolli, in a series of four articles entitled "Technique et idéologie." The first of these four articles appeared in an English translation by Diana Matias under the title "Technique and Ideology" in *Film Reader* 2 (January 1977): 128–40, and the latter two, under the same title and by the same translator, in Philip Rosen, ed., *Narrative, Apparatus, Ideology*.

7. Comolli, "Technique and Ideology," 424.

8. Mottram, "Fact and Affirmation," 338–39.

9. Mitry, *Histoire du cinéma* and *Esthétique et psychologie du cinéma*. An abridged English translation of the latter exists, entitled *The Aesthetics and Psychology of the Cinema*.

10. We should note in passing that history and aesthetics in Mitry, rather than being in symbiosis, are dealt with in separate volumes.

11. Comolli, "Technique et idéologie," 55–56. (Note that this section of Comolli's multipart essay was not included in the English translation quoted in note 7 above.)

12. Deslandes (in collaboration with Jacques Richard on volume 2), *Histoire comparée du cinéma*.

13. Deslandes was one of the few historians working before 1970 to give detailed

references for (almost) all the sources he used. In addition to giving his volumes a more scholarly character, this has made it possible for others to continue his work. It is impossible, for example, to make use today of a filmmaker's filmography if its author (Mitry, for example) does not explain why (for which reasons and using which sources that a later historian might consult) he attributes a particular film to the filmmaker in question.

14. Burch, *Life to those Shadows*, *passim*. Burch began using this expression at least as early as 1977.

15. Polan, "Poétique de l'histoire," 35.

16. The era of "serious" filmographies probably began with the Malthête family's work on Georges Méliès. See Malthête, Malthête-Méliès, and Quévrain, *Essai de reconstitution*. The most recent updating of this filmography can be found in Malthête and Mannoni, *Méliès, magie et cinéma*. Solid Lumière and Edison filmographies have also been published. See Aubert and Seguin, *Production cinématographique des frères Lumière* (book accompanied by a CD-ROM); and Musser, *Edison Motion Pictures*.

17. Italy has a particular penchant for silent film festivals, for which they alone seem to have the secret: in addition to the festival in Pordenone-Sacile (Le Giornate del cinema muto), there is also the festival in Bologna (Cinema ritrovatto). These are very popular events attended by hundreds of scholars year after year from around the world. We should also note French efforts in the field, with the Rencontres cinématographiques d'Avignon in the late 1980s and the CinéMémoire festival in the 1990s.

18. This is the case, to give but one example, of DOMITOR, the International Association Dedicated to the Study of Early Cinema, which presents a program of period films at its biennial conferences. Another sign that the collaboration between archivists and scholars remains strong today is the fact that these conferences are organized in close collaboration with the local film archive, or archives as the case may be.

19. See in particular the groundbreaking volume by Lagny, *De l'histoire du cinéma*; and Allen and Gomery, *Film History*.

20. The present author and the research team he led in collaboration with Tom Gunning in the early 1990s tried to put these principles into practice in a research project whose results included the publication *Pathé 1900*, ed. André Gaudreault in collaboration with Tom Gunning and Alain Lacasse. See also the more recent *Filmographie des "vues" tournées au Québec*, edited by André Gaudreault, Germain Lacasse, and Pierre Véronneau, available at the following address: http://cri.histart.umontreal.ca/grafics/ (accessed 11 September 2010).

21. Polan, "Poétique de l'histoire," 31.

22. Jacobs, *Rise of the American Film*.

23. Sadoul, *Histoire générale du cinéma*.

24. Mitry, *Histoire du cinéma*.

25. Cutting up film history like this into ten-year periods is practically an archetype of "primitive" (if I may say so!) historical thinking, one found regularly in film histories. An additional example can be found in *The History of the British Film* by Low (with

Roger Manvell in the case of the first volume), a four-volume work published beginning in 1948, which goes back and forth between temporal criteria (taking decades as its unit of measurement) and criteria related to social history. Volume 1 deals with the period 1896–1906; volume 2 with 1906–1914; volume 3 with 1914–1918; and volume 4 with 1918–1929.

26. Mitry, *Histoire du cinéma*, vol. 1, 469–70.

27. Ibid., vol. 2, 12.

28. In particular, in my case, at the time of my participation in the first Cerisy conference on Méliès in 1981 (with, as it turns out, Jean Mitry in attendance), not long after the Brighton congress in 1978.

29. Noël Burch, "Porter, or Ambivalence," 91. Emphasis in the original.

30. Sadoul, in *Cinquantenaire du Cinéma*, 24–25. Quoted by Malthête, "Bulletin 26," 19.

31. Morin, *Cinema*. This distinction is also found in the very title of the volume on which Deslandes and Richard collaborated: *Histoire comparée du cinéma*, vol. 2: *Du cinématographe au cinéma, 1896–1906*. Note that the English translator of Morin's book has chosen to use the terms Cinematograph, cinematography, and cinematographic, thereby risking confusion, in the latter two cases, with quite different contemporary meanings. By choosing to use kinematograph, kinematography, et cetera, my translator and I believe we have sidestepped these problems and been able to use a widespread period term in English no longer in general use to suggest a more generic phenomenon than that associated with the Lumière Cinématographe, highlighting in the process the "alien quality" of early cinema I discuss in Chapter 2 below.

32. It is interesting to note that, for Morin, the passage from kinematograph to cinema occurs at the very dawn of Georges Méliès's film career around 1896. For Morin, Méliès's arrival made this transformation possible. In my approach, which is more historical and theoretical (while Morin's approach is more anthropological), the transformation in question takes place, rather, in the early 1910s, or virtually at the end of Méliès's film career.

33. For an example of the use of the term "kinematographer" (*cinématographiste* in the original), see the text by Méliès reproduced as Appendix B in the present volume. On page 149, he writes: "Apart from the obstacles related to the execution of such scenes mentioned above, others still can hinder the *kinematographer*. These include varying light conditions." My emphasis. Méliès uses this term on three occasions in his text.

34. Gunning, "Whole Town's Gawking," 189.

35. Mitry, *Histoire du cinéma*, vol. 1, 120.

36. Ibid., 256.

37. See the afterword, "Cinema: Between Literariness and Intermediality," in my volume *From Plato to Lumière*. For a commentary on Mitry's hypotheses on theatricality and narrativity, see also Gunning, *D.W. Griffith and the Origins of American Narrative Film*.

38. Mitry, *Histoire du cinéma*, vol. 1, 221.

39. Ibid., 240.

40. Ibid., 254.

41. Ibid., 229.

42. Mitry, "De quelques problèmes," 121.

43. Ibid., 116.

44. See Benveniste, *Problems in General Linguistics*, 208–11.

45. Gadamer, *Truth and Method*.

46. Duby and Lardeau, *Dialogues*, 40.

47. In French, I employ the term *exhibiteur*, which was used in film circles at the time but today is not standard French (the "proper" term today would be *exploitant*). In order to convey in English that exhibition practices of the day were significantly different from what they became under institutional cinema, I adopt here the English term *exhibitioner*, a now rarely used synonym of exhibitor. It should be noted that, unlike the French, "exhibitioner" was never, to my knowledge, used in English-speaking film circles.

48. As Jacques Malthête has rightly remarked (in a personal communication), it was only with Jacques Deslandes (in the second volume of his *Histoire comparée du cinéma*, written in the late 1960s in collaboration with Jacques Richard) that the lecturer's presence began to be felt in film history. It would have been surprising had this not been the case, considering the emphasis placed by this volume on film exhibition in fairground settings, where lecturers proliferated.

49. My thanks to Jean-Pierre Sirois-Trahan and Jacques Malthête for pointing out some of these examples. It would probably be possible to find a few others in Sadoul's work, but they would in any event still be few in number.

50. Sadoul, *Histoire générale du cinéma*, vol. 2, 97.

51. Ibid., 128. My emphasis.

52. Ibid., 268.

53. Ibid., 431. Sadoul is quoting a news story by a French journalist in New York about film exhibition in the United States (*Ciné-Journal*, 30 November 1909).

54. Ibid., 524.

55. Ibid., vol. 4, 215.

56. This is the expression used by Coissac in his volume *Manuel pratique* (p. 23) to describe what he saw as cinema's only destiny. The same author eventually came to believe in cinema's future and, in an about-face, wrote one of the first film histories: *Histoire du Cinématographe*. I will return to this volume later in my discussion.

57. Albert Laffay, *Logique du cinéma*, 81–82. This book was an anthology of articles initially published in the late 1940s in the journal *Les Temps modernes*.

58. Sopocy, "Narrated Cinema." About this same time, the Japanese lecturer, the *benshi*, was rediscovered in the work of Noël Burch, who also participated in the Brighton congress. See Noël Burch, *To the Distant Observer*.

59. For a more thorough discussion of the film lecturer, see Lacasse's essential volume *Le Bonimenteur de vues animées*.

60. Most of the researchers who participated in the Brighton congress and in the film screenings that preceded it have been highly prolific since, publishing dozens of articles we might describe as having been influenced by their experience at Brighton.

They have also published a number of book-length studies, among them Eileen Bowser's *Transformation of Cinema*; Noël Burch's *Life to Those Shadows*; Gunning's *D.W. Griffith and the Origins of American Narrative Film*; Musser's *Emergence of Cinema*; Salt's *Film Style and Technology*; and Sopocy's *James Williamson*. I take the liberty of adding to this list my own *From Plato to Lumière*, first published in French in 1988.

Chapter 2. The Emergence of the Kinematograph

1. This is the expression proposed by de Kuyper in "Cinéma de la seconde époque," 28–35.

2. Benjamin, "On the Concept of History," 392.

3. I first used this term (*extranéité* in French) at a conference in Paris in 1993 (Gaudreault and Simard, "Extranéité du cinéma.")

4. Here I am adapting for historical purposes a concept of film narratology formulated by Jost in his book *L'Œil-caméra*.

5. I will return to this specific point of vocabulary in greater depth in Chapter 4.

6. Gadamer, *Truth and Method*, 264.

7. In a previous English translation of my discussion of this concept, I spoke of it as the process of "putting it all together," when all other aspects of the film production process—putting in sequence, putting in frame, putting in place, et cetera—are joined. See Giraud, *Lexique français du cinéma*, 123, s.v. "Film"; and Gaudreault, *From Plato to Lumière*, 94.

8. I refer the reader once again to the text by Méliès, "Kinematographic Views," reproduced as Appendix B in the present volume. See p. 150: "While kinematographers are a dime a dozen, the ones who have succeeded in doing something different from the others are far less common. There is no more than one per country, if that, since every country in the world depends on French manufacturers for artistic views."

9. In a paper given at the conference *Le Cinéma, cent ans après* in Montreal in November 1995 (this paper was later published, but without the comment quoted here). See Mariniello, "Histoire du cinéma."

10. Georges Méliès, "Kinematographic Views," reproduced as Appendix B in the present volume. My emphasis. See p. 147 for the comment quoted.

11. Deslandes, *Boulevard du cinéma*, 71.

12. Méliès's complete comment reads as follows (ibid., 30–31): "My film career has been so tied up with my career at the Robert-Houdin theater that one can barely tell them apart. Because in the end it was my penchant for tricks, my passion for the fantastic, which determined my vocation as the 'magician of the screen,' as I am known. Obviously, I made a lot of nontrick views, but because of my obligations at the time, to carry out some of my film work for the theater, to stick with magic and amuse my young audience at matinee shows, fantastic films clearly dominate my work in the cinema." See also Deslandes and Richard, *Histoire comparée du cinéma*, vol. 2, 448 and 503.

13. See Appendix B.

14. For an up-to-date and annotated list of Méliès's stage tricks, see Malthête and Mannoni, *Méliès, images et illusions*, 33–46.

15. Pougin, *Dictionnaire historique et pittoresque du théâtre,* s.v. "féerie," 360, 364. My thanks to Églantine Monsaingeon for bringing this volume to my attention.

16. For more about this colorful character in the history of the exhibition of animated pictures in Canada, see Duigou and Lacasse, *Marie de Kerstrat.*

17. Aumont, "Quand y a-t-il cinéma primitif?" 17–32.

18. Or, at least, it prevents us from "thinking about film history differently," to take up the title of an article by Rick Altman, "Penser l'histoire du cinéma autrement." (This article does not exist in English, but its argument was taken up in the chapter "Crisis Historiography" in Altman's book *Silent Film Sound.*) Altman is a "new generation" historian whose work and ideas over the past fifteen or twenty years have been completely in keeping with my argument here. *Silent Film Sound,* with its applications of his "crisis historiography," is a veritable summa on the history of sound in so-called "silent" cinema.

19. For a genesis of these expressions in French, see the book of which the present volume is a translation: Gaudreault, *Cinéma et attraction,* 83. I will leave it to English-language scholars to trace the history of these terms in English. A brief and far from conclusive survey by me and the translator of these lines, however, has turned up the following: It would appear that the term "primitive cinema" came to English from the French, and at a much later date, possibly as late as Noël Burch's work (largely published in translation from French) in the early 1980s. "Early cinema" too seems to have appeared in English much later than the French "cinéma des premiers temps." Its first use as a historical category may date from a 1979 article by Charles Musser, immediately following the 1978 Brighton congress ("The Early Cinema of Edwin Porter"). A few years later, in the first published anthologies of the work of many of the "Brighton generation" historians, the term had still not taken root: In the Brighton proceedings edited by Roger Holman in 1982, some authors employed "early film" (or "early films," with less claim to describing a historical category), while others used "early cinema" (*Cinema 1900–1906,* vol. 1). The following year, an article by Tom Gunning, whose name would later become synonymous with "early cinema" studies in the United States, still employed the expression "early film" ("An Unseen Energy Swallows Space," 355–66 in Fell, ed., *Film before Griffith*). In that same volume, "early cinema" is the term used in an article by André Gaudreault, in a translation by John Fell that was perhaps influenced by the presence of the word "cinema" in the French expression "cinéma des premiers temps" ("Temporality and Narrativity in Early Cinema, 1895–1908"). Finally, one might even argue that "early film" was the more natural choice in English and enjoyed the advantage of a certain distance from the institution "cinema"; it may be that "early cinema" prevailed because of the pervasive French influence in the field—in which case the present author assumes his share of the blame, in light of his "early" translated article noted above! We have been able to trace the systematic use of "early film" as far back as Low's multivolume history of early British cinema (we refer to the three volumes covering 1896–1918) published immediately after World War II, *The History of the British Film*—A.G. and T.B.

20. Méliès, "En marge de l'histoire du cinématographe," 29.

21. Jost, "Invention du cinéaste."

22. At the Cerisy conference "Nouvelles approches de l'histoire du cinéma" in the summer of 1985. See Gaudreault and Gunning, "Early Cinema as a Challenge."

23. Giraud, *Lexique français du cinéma*, 91.

24. Coissac, *La théorie et la pratique des projections*. An abridged version of this volume, entitled *Manuel pratique du conférencier-projectionniste*, was published by the same publisher in 1908.

25. Coissac, *Histoire du cinématographe*, 359.

26. A hapax, or hapax legomenon, is defined by the *Oxford English Dictionary* as "a word or form of which only one instance is recorded in a literature or an author."

27. Coissac, *Histoire du cinématographe*, 359.

28. Giraud, *Le Lexique français du cinéma des origines à 1930*, 110.

29. In discussion with Wanda Strauven, the editor of a volume on early cinema to which I was contributing, and my translator and the author of the following comments, Timothy Barnard, the term "kine-attractography" was agreed upon to translate "cinématographie-attraction." Barnard writes: In the first place, "cinématographie" in French is most emphatically not the same as "cinematography" in English, ruling out any sort of direct translation such as "cinematography-attraction." "Attractography" fancifully extends the tradition of the multitude of "graphs" introduced to the market, or the language, at the beginning of the past century (the kinetograph, cinematograph, vitagraph, biograph, motiograph, etc.) and even well beyond (at least until 1957, with the introduction of the Mutoscope Voice-o-Graph, the street-corner recording booth in which Jean-Pierre Léaud, for example, records a 45-rpm love song in Jean-Luc Godard's *Masculin Féminin* [1966]). *Attractography*, however, is not merely yet another "graph," but the genus to which all these species belong: It is the cultural series created by mechanical devices that use celluloid film to produce attractions. At the same time, *attractography* was created by adopting the popular penchant for word play and word creation using a common suffix and the connector "o," whose lasting appeal is attested to by the "voice-o-graph." Even before the early twentieth century's plethora of "graphs" came the early nineteenth century's "ramas": the 1820s saw, after the panorama, the diorama, cosmorama, georama, uranorama, neorama, et cetera. And the popular practice of creating even more fanciful words based on such attractions goes back at least as far as Balzac's *Père Goriot* (1834–35), in which it is related that "The recent invention of the diorama, carrying optical illusion farther than in panoramas, had brought into some of the ateliers the jest of throwing superfluous 'ramas' into one's talk": "souporamas," "healthoramas," "cornoramas" and the like. (We hope, however, to have avoided Balzac's historical anachronism: his novel is set in 1819, three years before the introduction of the diorama.) Finally, "kine" identifies the cultural series for the reader (on its own, *attractography* could mean anything) at the same time as it refuses to identify it with the institution "cinema." Beginning with Edison in 1888 and extending right into the 1920s, "kine" was an accepted and common form in English; indeed, it is the standard English phonetic transcription of the Greek—even the Lumière Cinématographe was initially known in English as the kinematograph. Once

again, even in the case of the word *cinema,* English seems to have followed the French rather than its own rules and inclinations.

Chapter 3. Attraction and the Kinematograph

1. On this topic, see my article "Les vues cinématographiques selon Eisenstein."
2. On this topic, see in particular Gunning, "Whole Town's Gawking."
3. See Gaudreault and Gunning, "Early Cinema as a Challenge."
4. Eisenstein, "Montage of Attractions."
5. "L'attraction dans les films." This text came to my attention long after the 1985 Cerisy conference.
6. *La Nature,* January 11, 1896 (quoted in Giraud, *Lexique français du cinéma,* 48, s.v. "Attraction"). In 1985, Tom Gunning and I were unaware of Giraud's volume.
7. *Le Progrès* (Lyon), July 17, 1906 (quoted in Giraud, *Lexique français du cinéma,* 48, s.v. "Attraction").
8. Delluc, *"Roi de la mer,"* 30.
9. Fouquet, "Attraction," 1. This text also came to my attention long after the 1985 Cerisy conference.
10. In their respective thoughts on the matter, which each of them has communicated to me personally.
11. At the time, Tom Gunning and I had no idea how important the concept of attraction was in the twenty or thirty years prior to Eisenstein's formulation in 1923 of his theory of the montage of attractions.
12. On the topic of the role of attractions in early cinema, see Strauven, ed., *Cinema of Attractions Reloaded,* and Paci, *Machine à voir.* Paci employs Eisenstein's ideas about the "montage of attractions" (which she correlates with theories of distanciation from Shklovsky to Brecht) and the concept of the attraction, which she elevates to the level of category, to examine the specific relationship film may have with the viewer. She proposes that we view film history as riddled with moments in which attraction reigns in works that, in their relationship with the viewer, are on the outer reaches of the narrative model.
13. Giraud, *Lexique français du cinéma,* 48, s.v. "Attraction."
14. Gunning, "Attractions, truquages et photogénie," 179. The term used in this French-language article by Gunning is "manifestation visuelle."
15. Ibid., 182.
16. Gunning, "Whole Town's Gawking," 193.
17. Georges Méliès, "Importance du scénario," 32. This passage is quoted in Sadoul, *Georges Méliès,* 115, although with variations. These variations are due to the fact that Sadoul translated back into French the Spanish version of an original text by Méliès. My thanks to Jacques Malthête for this clarification.
18. See Gaudreault and Gunning, "Early Cinema as a Challenge."
19. This expression is David Bordwell's ("Textual Analysis, etc.," 129).
20. Recall the meaning of profilmic, defined by Étienne Souriau as "everything that exists in the world . . . but especially what is intended to be filmed; in particular,

anything that has been placed before a camera and captured on film" (*Univers filmique*, 8).

21. I employ the term here in the manner I defined it in chapter nine of my book *From Plato to Lumière*, which alters Souriau's definition of it: For me what pertains to the filmographic is any effect, any effect whatsoever, that derives from the cinematic apparatus and which, without affecting in any concrete way the profilmic during the film's shooting, transforms the viewer's perception of this profilmic material when the film is screened. These activities include, on the one hand, all the practices related to the overall procedure of *shooting* a film: camera movements, framing, filming, et cetera; and on the other all the practices that form part of the overall procedure of *editing*: matching shots, creating syntagma, synchronization, trick effects, et cetera.

22. For a more detailed discussion of each of these paradigms, see Gaudreault and Kessler, "L'acteur comme opérateur de continuité," and Gaudreault and Marion, "Le cinéma naissant."

23. This term was used in English in the day to describe this kind of film.

24. The following is a description of this view: "This gives a correct view of the famous Boyton Water Chute, and is full of life and motion" (F. Z. Maguire & Co, *Catalogue* [March 1898], 32).

25. The following is a description of this view by the editors of the recently published Lumière filmography: "Pedestrians walking by and various vehicles on the square." Aubert and Seguin, *La production cinématographique des frères Lumière*, 228.

26. True, such views are not that numerous. Several Lumière views, for example, give the impression of having been shot on the fly when in fact they were the product of real collaboration between those filming and those being filmed.

27. It should be noted that, given the peculiar nature of the Edison system, the very first filmstrips made for kinetoscopes, beginning in 1891, were shot in a studio, the "Black Maria," and could not for this very reason belong to the first paradigm, that of pure recording. Because they required an element of mise en scène, these strips belong, even if they arrived first, to what I describe here as the "second" paradigm, that of monstration.

28. On this question, see Gaudreault (with the assistance of Jean-Marc Lamotte), "Fragmentation and Segmentation in the Lumière 'Animated Views.'"

29. The operator interrupted the shooting of the film (by ceasing to crank the camera handle) when he realized that the figures in the parade, over whom he had no control, were about to leave a gaping hole in their ranks as they passed in front of the camera.

30. This view, alone in the Lumière system, is made up of three partial views, whose titles reflect the fact that this assemblage is an amalgam of segments: *L'arrivée en voiture*; *La remise des décorations*; *La sortie de la chambre de commerce*. Each of these three segments functions as a punctiliar view, with no close communication between them.

31. A staged film that was produced by creating several superimpositions by stopping the camera, thereby framing the image in the same way from beginning to end.

32. A film made up of a dozen punctiliar tableaux without any direct communication between one and the next.

Chapter 4. Intermediality and the Kinematograph

1. We might even go so far as to say that intermediality has become a fashionable topic in cinema studies (in particular, but not only, since early cinema came to the fore), if we are to judge from the number of conferences held around the world these past few years that refer to it. We might also note the work of the Centre for Research into Intermediality (CRI) at the Université de Montréal, which I helped to found, which is far from limited to cinema studies alone (http://cri.histart.umontreal.ca/; accessed 11 September 2010).

2. Francœur, *Les signes s'envolent*, 69–70n.

3. Deslandes, *Le boulevard du cinéma*, 29–30.

4. Odin's ideas are themselves derived from the work of Christian Metz, particularly those found in his book *The Imaginary Signifier*, with its very interesting hypotheses about the institution cinema from a psychoanalytical perspective. Metz, moreover, enumerates the qualities of the institution in a way entirely keeping with the approach taken in the present volume: "The ego's position in the cinema . . . on the contrary . . . is foreseen and marked in advance by the institution (the equipment, the disposition of the auditorium, the mental system that internalizes the two)" (*Imaginary Signifier*, 53).

5. Odin, "Pour une sémio-pragmatique du cinéma," 71.

6. Ibid., 70.

7. Berrendonner, *Éléments de pragmatique linguistique*, 95.

8. Odin, "Pour une sémio-pragmatique du cinéma," 70.

9. Robert, *L'Institution du littéraire au Québec*, 149–50.

10. Moisan, *L'Histoire littéraire*, 55.

11. For a more in-depth discussion of this topic, see Gaudreault and Marion, "A Medium Is Always Born Twice."

12. Lourau, *Analyse institutionnelle*, 48, quoted by Odin, "Sémio-pragmatique du cinéma et de l'audio-visuel," 41. The French term used is "bric-à-brac."

13. de Kuyper, "Le théâtre comme mauvais objet," 69.

14. Altman, "De l'intermédialité au multimédia," 38.

15. Robert, *L'Institution du littéraire au Québec*, 159.

16. Anciens Établissements Pathé Frères, *Catalogue* 4 (March 1902). I discuss this document in greater depth in Chapter 5.

17. Odin, "Approche sémio-pragmatique," 28.

18. Schaeffer, *Qu'est-ce qu'un genre littéraire?* 171.

19. I owe this expression to Denis Simard, who came up with it during one of the many discussions we have had on the subject.

20. Metz, *Language and Cinema*, 122. Emphasis in the original. See also p. 37 of *Imaginary Signifier*, where Metz remarks that some "very historically circumscribed

genres" (such as documentary, newsreels, advertising films) may very well be hazy institutions but are full-fledged institutions just the same.

21. Todorov, *Notion de littérature*, 34.

22. Vincent Pinel and Pierre Jenn adopt this view in, respectively, *Louis Lumière, inventeur et cinéaste* and *Georges Méliès cinéaste*. This choice of words is not that of Pinel and Jenn alone (whom I use here as examples simply because the word *cinéaste* appears in the very title of their books): I myself have used this incriminated term in recent years, as have most French-speaking film scholars, to describe the first crank turners.

23. There are a dozen or so uses of the word *operator* in Méliès's article "Kinematographic Views" (Vues cinématographiques). To give just one example, he states (on page 149 of the present volume): "Needless to say, the *operator* for this special kind of work must be highly experienced and very much up to date with a host of little tricks of the trade. A difficult sort of view cannot be taken by a beginner." My emphasis.

24. There are at least half a dozen occurrences of the expression "natural views" (*vues de plein air*) in Méliès's article and four examples of the expression "artificially arranged scenes" (*sujets composés*). Here is one example, under the heading "The Different Kinds of Kinematographic Views" on page 138 of the present volume: "There are four broad categories of kinematographic views. Or, in any event, all such views can be tied to one or another of these categories. There are so-called *natural views, scientific views, artificially arranged scenes*, and so-called *transformation views*." Emphasis in the original.

25. Giraud, *Lexique français du cinéma*, 143, s.v. "Mise."

26. According to Jacques Malthête, in a letter to the present author, there were exactly 58 cuts. Despite appearances—the fragments of the view in question are all "homo-frame," or shot from the same camera position—this film is one of the most fragmented of Méliès's output. For a discussion of the meaning of the expression "homo-frame," see my article "Fragmentation and Segmentation."

27. A direct translation of *cinématographiste* would be "cinematographist," which, with rare exceptions, was not used in English. In English, I have found the term *cinematographist* only once, dating from 1900: "In this particular attention has been given to the needs of *The Amateur Cinematographist*, who, until quite lately, has been much neglected." Hector Maclean, preface to *Animated Photography*. Maclean was in charge of the new edition of this book, which was originally published in 1897. Unless I'm mistaken, the word *cinematographist* appears nowhere else in the book. The *Oxford English Dictionary* (vol. 3, p. 221) gives two further examples: an advertisement from 1898 and a newspaper article from 1903. The earliest confirmed use of the word thus dates to 1898. Because of the rarity of the word *cinematographist,* when not using the French word *cinématographiste* in direct reference to the French context, I will use here the term *kinematographer,* which was quite common at the time in English usage, particularly in Britain. It appears, with decreasing frequency, right into the sound period and lives on today, for example, in the name of an asso-

ciation of British film professionals, the British Kinematograph Sound and Television Society (BKSTS), founded in 1931 as the British Kinematograph Society (BKS). This term has the added merit of distancing us from the Lumière Cinématographe (one of many film recording devices of the day) and of corresponding to the term I use to describe the cultural series in question here, kine-attractography. Similarly, I will use "kinematograph," the generic English-language term of the period (its first use can be dated at least to 1896), instead of *cinematograph,* which refers to a single device among many and which often gives rise to confusion in English when the term *cinematographic,* for example, is wrongly used to mean "cinematic" or simply "film" used as an adjective.

28. All of them taken from Giraud's indispensable *Lexique français du cinéma.*

29. I have trimmed from this list numerous competing terms because I have been unable to determine how widespread they were or because their first documented use came later, in the 1920s. Some examples are *cinéiste, cinégraphe, cinématographieur, écraniste,* and *tourneur.*

30. Giraud, *Le Lexique français du cinéma,* 65–66, s.v. "Cinéaste."

31. See Appendix B in the present volume, 150.

32. Ibid., 143.

33. Ibid., 143. "Composing a scene, play, drama, fairy play, comedy, or artistic scene naturally requires, first of all, a scenario drawn from the imagination."

34. In 1900 Méliès had in fact made a film entitled *L'Homme-Orchestre* (*The One-Man Band*).

35. See Appendix B in the present volume, 142.

36. Canudo, "Naissance d'un sixième art." The essay was reprinted in Canudo, *Usine aux images,* 40. Published in English translation as "The Birth of a Sixth Art," trans. Ben Gibson et al., *Framework* 13 (Autumn 1980) and reprinted with modifications in Richard Abel, *French Film Theory and Criticism,* vol. 1. Note that the passage quoted here is not included in these translations and appears to be translated here for the first time. My emphasis.

37. Émile Maugras and Maurice Guégan, *Cinématographe devant le droit,* 109. The book's authors were also closely tied to the magnates of the film business, a newly created "race." As the authors indicate in their book, one of them (Maugras) was a "member of the board of directors of Omnia-Pathé" and "Chairman of the Board of Cinéma-théâtre Pathé," while the other (Guégan) was a "member of the board of directors of Cinéma National Pathé."

38. Ibid., 25–26. Emphasis in the original.

39. Ibid., 109.

40. *Illustration,* 30 May 1896, 442. Quoted in Giraud, *Lexique français du cinéma,* 93, s.v. "Cinématographiste."

41. *Nature,* 30 October 1897, 350. Quoted in Giraud, *Lexique français du cinéma,* 93, s.v. "Cinématographiste."

42. See Appendix B in the present volume, 149.

43. Ibid., 150.

44. Pierre Courtet-Cohl kindly provided me with this reproduction. This is what he said about it (in an e-mail to the author, 14 March 2006): "Please find attached the first page of a small notebook of my grandfather's, entirely written in his own hand. . . . Unfortunately, it bears no date, but I don't think it would be mistaken to date it to 1910 or 11. On this page he summarizes his films made from 1908 until during the Great War. You might ask why the first page wasn't written in 1908: because the first four years appear to have been written down all at once, using the same ink and the same handwriting, a regularity that is broken after 1911. The actual size of the page is 8cm x 13cm." Note also that the word *cinématographiste* is found in the very title of a commemorative exhibition dedicated to Cohl in 1988 at the Cinémathèque québécoise in Montreal, in collaboration with Pierre Courtet-Cohl. The expression also makes its way into Raymond Maillet's title of the catalogue for this event: *Émile Cohl cinématographiste 1857–1938*.

45. The interesting thing is that the two brief synopses of the film that I have been able to find on the Internet (both on 29 April 2007) get around the problem of unfamiliarity with the term *cinématographiste* by using the most common terms in use today to describe the filmmaker in French: *réalisateur* in the case of one and *metteur en scène* in the case of the other. The first synopsis reads: "Léonce, wrapped up in his work as a *réalisateur*, leaves the conjugal home. His wife suspects him of infidelity." The second reads: "Poupette discovers a woman's hair on the coat of her husband Léonce, a very popular metteur en scène. Racked with suspicion, she decides to set a trap for him in order to get to the bottom of it." The first synopsis can be found at http://www.seances.org/html/cycle.asp?id=315#l (accessed 11 September 2010) and the second at http://dvdtoile.com/Filmographie.php?id=16941 (accessed 11 September 2010).

46. As I mentioned in chapter 2, Méliès himself used the term *cinématographiste* as late as 1926 to describe the first metteurs en scène.

47. Gaudreault, *From Plato to Lumière*, chapter 9.

48. John J. Frawley, Affidavit, 24 June 1902.

49. James H. White, Affidavit, 9 June 1902.

50. Henry de Grandsaignes d'Hauterives, an important exhibitioner of animated views in Canada, quoted in the anonymous "Épopée napoléonienne," 5.

51. Anonymous, "Nos lieux d'amusements," 2.

52. Jost, "Invention du cinéaste," 57.

Chapter 5. A Problematic Institutional Space

1. Simard, "De la nouveauté," 44.

2. In 1904, this journal was renamed *The Optical Lantern and Cinematograph Journal*.

3. For more on the topic of the production models employed by the Pathé company, see Laurent Le Forestier's unpublished and highly instructive doctoral dissertation, *L'Industrialisation du mode de production des films Pathé*, and his recent book *Aux sources de l'industrie du cinéma*.

4. Bousquet, *Catalogue Pathé*, 1904, 3. My emphasis.

5. Latham Eidoloscope program, quoted in Musser, *Emergence of Cinema*, 98. My emphasis.

6. Bousquet, *Catalogue Pathé*, 1900, 31. My emphasis.

7. *Catalogue Gaumont*, 1903, 35. My emphasis.

8. The reader will note that the initials of the names Georges Ménard and Georges Méliès are the same. Jacques Malthête's analysis of the text led him to date it to 1906 (personal communication).

9. Georges Ménard, quoted without precise indication of its source in Bernard Chardère, *Lumières sur Lumière*, 128. This text is reproduced more completely—without emphasis—in Deslandes, *Boulevard du cinéma*, 99–101. (Deslandes, however, dates the catalogue of the Robert-Houdin theater in which Ménard's text appears to circa 1912.) Emphasis in the original.

10. I should make clear that when I speak of Edison and Lumière, I am sometimes referring to these individuals themselves and sometimes to the people they worked with closely. We know Edison did not work with the same intensity on all the research that went into the invention and perfection of the Kinetograph and other procedures associated with it and that a good share of the work was carried out by his assistant, William K. L. Dickson. As for the two Lumière brothers, they did not have entirely the same role to play. In addition, they themselves shot only a limited number of films.

11. Creton, "Figures de l'entrepreneur," 152.

12. According to Henri Bousquet, most of them already had "stage experience" before beginning to work for Pathé. See Bousquet, "Âge d'or," 59.

13. A lot would be gained in particular by examining the output of Vitagraph, which appears to have had a leading role in the United States similar in many respects to that of Pathé in France and elsewhere in the world. Unfortunately, little is yet known about this company.

14. Even by the late 1920s, Méliès remained a worthy representative of kine-attractography: for him, a lateral tracking shot was "a set moving horizontally," a vertical tracking shot was a set moving "up and down, letting us see the different parts of a room," dolly forwards were "characters who suddenly get bigger," and close-ups "feet or hands that become enormous to let us see a detail." See the article (written by Méliès in 1929, according to Deslandes, in *Histoire comparée du cinéma*, vol. 2, *Du cinématographe au cinéma*—but Jacques Malthête reports, in correspondence with the present author, that Deslandes was mistaken and that the text in question was written by Maurice Noverre, inspired of course by Méliès himself) initially published in *Le Nouvel art cinématographique* in January 1930 and quoted by Deslandes and Richard in *Histoire comparée du cinéma*, vol. 2, 469–70.

15. Recently I and Philippe Gauthier (a Ph.D. candidate at the Université de Montréal/the Université de Lausanne and a research assistant at GRAFICS) published an article on this film and other early occurrences of the same device in other Pathé films (including *Terrible angoisse* [*Terrible Anguish*, 1906], *Ruse de mari* [*Artful Husband*], *Les Chiens policiers* [*Police Dogs*] and *Le Cheval emballé* [*Runaway Horse*], all 1907]). See Gaudreault and Gauthier, "Crosscutting, a Programmed Language."

16. On the question of the "origin" of crosscutting, see Gunning, *D.W. Griffith and the Origins of American Narrative Film*, passim. (Note, however, that Gunning uses the term "parallel editing" instead of crosscutting throughout this book.) I am currently in the process of collaborating on a book with Philippe Gauthier on the history and importance of this editing configuration in early cinema, forthcoming from Columbia University Press.

17. The viewer thus sees the door burst open four times on screen (although from a diegetic perspective it bursts open only twice) because, each time the character passes through the door, the same action is shown from two different camera positions, one on each side of the door (inside and out).

18. For the moment because I hope to follow up on this volume with the publication of work I have been carrying out over the past few years with my colleague Philippe Marion of the Université de Louvain.

19. Bousquet, *Catalogue Pathé*, 1901, 3.

20. Coissac, *Manuel pratique*, 23.

21. This work was begun by Églantine Monsaingeon, a research assistant at GRAFICS at the time, in her master's thesis *Des genres et des modes*.

22. This is well known. For a discussion of the context of this "adaptation," see Schwartz's volume, *Spectacular Realities*.

23. See the work of Frank Kessler and Sabine Lenk.

24. Whether by chance or necessity, *L'Histoire d'un crime* includes an entire scene in flashback, one of the great devices of the film language yet to come. This flashback, moreover, is more theatrical than cinematic in nature (it takes place inside a rectangular opening in the stage set showing the prisoner in his cell, stretched out on a straw mattress), but we might ask ourselves whether the appearance at such an early date of a kind of flashback in this "breakthrough film" isn't the sign of something, if only on the level of the script. Note that this flashback is not present in the wax-figure tableaux.

25. Henri Bousquet informs us that "Years later, Zecca remarked that he did not place his hopes in drama and acrobatic films but rather in fairy plays." See the interview with Zecca in *L'Image*, published in 1932 and reported by Bousquet in "Âge d'or," 52.

26. Pathé, *Scènes à grand spectacle* catalogue, March 1902.

27. See the Afterword to my volume *From Plato to Lumière* entitled "Cinema, Between Literariness and Intermediality," 151–64.

Conclusion

1. Gadamer, *Truth and Method*, 292.

2. I allude here to the title of a book by Noël Burch, *To the Distant Observer*.

3. Sorlin, "Promenade dans Rome," 7.

4. I use the word "impression" here in its figurative sense. The *OED* describes this as "An effect, especially a strong effect, produced on the intellect, conscience, or feelings."

5. Or, not to forget all those who contributed to the invention of the "basic device," what we should perhaps call the *Edison tradition* and the *Lumière tradition*, Edison and Lumière being the two names visible at the tip of the iceberg.

6. "Specimens" in the sense "There were some curious specimens among my visitors" (Thoreau); "phenomena" in the sense "Something very notable or extraordinary; a thing, person or animal remarkable for some unusual quality" (*OED*).

7. Even though Edison's place in the series "chronophotography" seems obvious in many respects, it is clear that his work was a qualitative leap and did not have the same goals as chronophotography. As François Albera has pointed out to me in personal correspondence, the term "specimen" is indicative of this difference. Marey's specimens were highly ordinary (the ordinary man, the ordinary line, the ordinary horse): they were not "curious specimens"; they were not "phenomena" in the sense of curiosities.

8. Jost, "Pourquoi le cinéma des débuts?" 15–16.

9. The problem raised by Jost is important enough in his eyes for him to title the section of his article that addresses it as follows: "Epistemological Obstacles," foremost among which is the "demon of analogy" (ibid., 15).

10. Albera, "Leçon(s) d'histoire du cinéma." This was the most recent issue published when the French edition of the present volume went to press.

11. Ibid., 22.

12. Ibid., 19. My emphasis.

13. Ibid., 19–20. My emphasis.

14. These two texts, which were published a few months apart, were written at about the same time, although their authors in no way acted in concert. I know each author well and took pains to verify this. For Odin's text, see "Présentation" in the thematic issue of the journal *Cinémas* "La théorie du cinéma, enfin en crise."

15. Ibid., 9–10. Emphasis in the original.

16. Gaudreault and Simard, "Extranéité du cinéma," 19. Delivered at an international conference on the first twenty years of French cinema at the Université de la Sorbonne in 1993, organized by Jean A. Gili, Michèle Lagny, Michel Marie, and Vincent Pinel.

17. Ibid., 19.

18. Ibid., 21.

Appendix A

1. My thanks to Nicolas Dulac, a doctoral candidate in a joint program at the Université de Montréal and Université Paris 3, and a research assistant at GRAFICS, for revising my responses and suggesting certain adjustments to them.

2. Here is another concept that must be handled with care when writing history, as I explain below.

3. Throughout this discussion the participants refer indirectly to Thomas Kuhn's work on paradigm shifts, found in his book *The Structure of Scientific Revolutions*—Trans.

4. Thus in the Introduction I remark: "Between these two dates (1890 and the 1910s), there was a time when what I call kine-attractography reigned. The principles and products of kine-attractography have little in common with those of cinema, apart from the fact that each paradigm is based on the use of moving pictures" (p. 7).

5. Recently, Philippe Marion and I have used the expression "paradigm of representational systems" (*paradigme des régimes de représentation*) to describe these paradigms

as a whole. Gaudreault and Marion, "Pour une nouvelle approche." I should point out that it is by sheer chance that this article on film history was published in an issue of the journal dedicated to film theory guest-edited by Roger Odin.

6. Gaudreault and Marion, "Pour une nouvelle approche."

7. Christophe Huss, for example, in a series of articles in the Montreal daily newspaper *Le Devoir*—articles whose very titles are signs of a program unto itself. See in particular his article entitled "Votre cinéma n'est pas un cinéma. . . . Retransmissions en direct des représentations: le directeur général a fait entrer le Met dans une nouvelle ère" of 17 December 2007, about the live transmission in several Montreal movie theaters of Gounod's *Romeo and Juliet* at New York's Metropolitan Opera: "I'm anxious to see the return of the *metteur en images* Brian Large, because his colleague Gary Halvorson is a prisoner of his nervousness. His constant changes of shot in Act I were extremely annoying. He calmed down a little afterwards. These *broadcasts* have no need of a virtuoso, agitated *cineaste*; all they require is a mere *witness* to the action on stage. On the plus side, most of Gary Halvorson's shots and compositions are aesthetically beautiful." See also his article "Musique classique: *Salomé* ouvre la saison du Met dans les cinémas" of 11–12 October 2008: "Because the wall was very close to the orchestra pit, the action 'leapt up at us,' especially because the indescribable Gary Halvorson (the *metteur en image*) makes excessive use of low-angle shots." And, finally, his article entitled "Opéra au cinéma: Une pimpante *Fille du régiment*," published 28 April 2008: "The production was *filmed* by Gary Halvorson, who I have run down here in the past but who on Saturday delivered his most decent effort, the one least disturbed by his ego." (In these quotations, the emphasis is mine.) Apart from the fact that Huss has Halvorson in his sights, these articles teach us many things. In particular, that this critic favors the description "metteur en image(s)" to describe the agent responsible for the new layer of meaning to which the recording and transmission give rise. Huss also tells us that this kind of performance is in the end a mere *broadcast*, and that one should do no more than to "film" the opera. We also learn that, for Huss, the *metteur en images* of live-broadcast operas should not do "too much," should remain a mere "witness" and, above all, not take himself for a cineaste projecting his ego into, onto, or between the images!

8. Thierry Lefebvre, "*Voyage dans la lune*, film composite." Forthcoming in an English translation under the title "*A Trip to the Moon*: A Composite Film," trans. Timothy Barnard, in Matthew Solomon, ed., *Fantastic Voyages of the Cinematic Imagination: Georges Méliès's Trip to the Moon* (Albany, State University of New York Press, 2011).

9. Rather than quoting parts of these texts in my responses, I direct the reader to them directly (each of the following articles is cowritten with Philippe Marion): "The Cinema as a Model"; "A Medium Is Always Born Twice"; and "Un Art de l'emprunt."

10. Carou, *Cinéma français et les écrivains*.

11. Gaudreault and Odin, "Cinématographe, un 'enfant prodige.'"

12. See, for example, http://www.newscientist.com/article/mg19426101.700 -interview-shades-of-meaning.html (accessed 11 September 2010).

13. This text appeared on the invitation to the first public screenings offered by the Lumière brothers and can be found in Bessy and Lo Duca, *Louis Lumière inventeur*, 107.

14. Recall the four quotations of commentators of the day found on page 85 of my book.

15. Bousquet, *Catalogue Pathé*.

16. This was the year of a conference at which I delivered a paper later published as Gaudreault and Simard, "Extranéité du cinéma."

17. Including the Centre for Research on Intermediality (CRI) at the Université de Montréal at http://cri.histart.umontreal.ca (accessed 11 September 2010).

18. Strauven, ed., *Cinema of Attractions Reloaded*.

19. A *catalogue raisonné* in French is a term used in art history and criticism for a complete catalogue of an artist's work with commentary. *Raisonné* alone means reasoned or thought out, and this is the sense the author wishes to impart through this play on words—Trans.

Appendix B

1. 16th year (Paris: Librairie Plon, 1907), 362–92. This article was initially published in English in a heavily abridged translation by Stuart Liebman in *October* 29 (Summer 1984). A longer version was later translated by Liebman for publication in Abel (ed.), *French Film Theory and Criticism*. It appears here in its complete form; Stuart Liebman's translation has been revised by and additional passages have been translated by Timothy Barnard following the original version established by Jacques Malthête, whose introduction to the text prefaces the present translation and whose notes follow. André Gaudreault would like to thank Stuart Liebman for his kind permission to reprint and revise his translation.

2. When the kinematograph appeared, films—a new and necessarily hazy concept—were described in different ways according to whether one was referring to the physical object, its content, its scene breakdown, or its length. In the well-documented case of Georges Méliès, it has been possible to establish the following brief glossary in French for the years 1896–1912: *vue* ["view"], a general term used for the most part to describe a film's content, but not limited to actualities or documentaries; *bande* ["filmstrip"], a term used to describe the physical object; *scène* ["scene"], a fictional view (sometimes described as a *fantaisie* ["fantasy"], *paysannerie* ["a story depicting country life"], or a *bouffonnerie* ["buffoonery"]); *pièce* ["play"], a great *scène* or *tableau* film (often a *féerie* ["fairy play"]; for a definition of *tableau*, see note 27 below); and *film*, a general term used to describe both the object and its content (this word appears without exception in every Méliès catalogue). See Malthête, "Historiographie méliésienne."

3. More precisely, 18 by 24 mm.

4. It appears that Méliès has confused the battery of cameras used by Eadweard Muybridge (1830–1904) in his experiments (12 cameras in 1878, 24 in 1879) with the film-based chronophotograph of Étienne-Jules Marey (1830–1904), which used a single lens.

5. Such as Francis Martin Duncan (1873–1961), whose "micro-Bioscope" films were produced by Charles Urban from 1903 on. See Lefebvre, "Film scientifique et grand public."

6. Méliès is referring to the surgical films of Dr. Eugène-Louis Doyen (1859–1916). For more information on the work of this pioneer, see Lefebvre, *La Chair et le celluloïd*.

7. This part of the sentence is somewhat obscure (the *Annuaire* gives "non préparées ou truquées," but Méliès in all probability wrote "préparées ou truquées," thus a typographical error?) because it is hard to imagine how at the time an "unstaged" or "without trick effects" outdoor view could become a "fantastic view." The remark beginning "In any event" and ending "the most fearless person mad" was, however, reproduced without modification in 1929 in *La Revue du cinéma*, p. 22 (see Appendix B, at A).

8. Méliès's films were manufactured under the trade name Star Film. The first trademark was registered in Paris on 20 November 1896, in the form of a single black star with five points. On 27 December 1902, the famous black star between the words "Méliès" and "Star Film" was registered. Contrary to a widely held belief, Star Film never referred to anything more than the brand name of a "Manufacture de films pour cinématographes" owned by Méliès. Nevertheless, on 7 January 1898, he incorporated a company called "L'Étoile, Société générale de cinématographe," which apparently had a very short life. This last piece of information was provided to me by Marc Durand.

9. Roger Aubry is known for having devised an airborne photographic camera using a kite. He was a member of the Société de photographie in 1902 and registered a patent for an "automatic airborne photographic device" in 1909 and another for a "film-based aviation photographic device" in 1920. Information about these patents was provided to me by Marie-Sophie Corcy.

10. For more information on Méliès's first studio, see Malthête, "Les Deux studios de Georges Méliès." Built in 1897, this studio was destroyed in December 1945 (see *L'Écran français* 28 [9 January 1946]: 4; this article was communicated to me by Laurent Mannoni).

11. Méliès is referring to the tableau "Les Reines de beauté (grand ballet)" ("Ballet of the Celebrated Women of Antiquity") in the film *Damnation du docteur Faust* (*Faust and Marguerite*, 1904, 260 meters, nos. 562–74; the film is extant).

12. In the end this setup was little used by Méliès (see Noverre, "Œuvre de Georges Méliès," 80; and Bessy and Lo Duca, *Georges Méliès, mage*, 194. Recall that in 1897 Méliès had already worked with artificial light in his laboratory in the Passage de l'Opéra when filming the singer Paulus.

13. The orthochromatic emulsion of the day was sensitive only to the short-wavelength colors blue and ultraviolet.

14. Félix Galipaux (1860–1931) acted in at least one Méliès film, *Le Raid Paris–Monte-Carlo en automobile* (*An Adventurous Automobile Trip*, 1905, 200 meters, nos. 740–749; the film is extant). The "special leaflet" devoted to this particular film, in its description of the first tableau, remarks, "Two automobilists (the well-known actors Maurel and Fragson) enter into a wager to reach the Côte d'Azur from Paris in less than two hours. . . . The two drivers are seen off from the Place de l'Opéra by a large, cheering crowd, attracted by the announcement of their extravagant bet. Many well-known performers, including Galipaux of the Palais-Royal and Noté of the Opéra, the remarkable mime Séverin and the divine operetta singer Jane Yvon, are seen wishing the drivers

bon voyage." In 1904 Galipaux had acted in the Pathé film *Premier cigare d'un collégien* (*Boy's First Smoke*, no. 844) and two phono-cine scenes, *La Lettre* (no. 1037) and *Au téléphone* (no. 1038) (Bousquet, *Catalogue Pathé des années 1896 à 1914*, vol. 4, 1896–1906, 887 and 889).

15. In 1905–06, Méliès sold his black-and-white films measuring less than 140 meters for two francs per meter and his films measuring more than 140 meters for two and a half francs (a franc at the time was worth approximately US$3 today). Coloring, which Méliès always ensured was executed with great care, cost between a franc and a half and a franc and three quarters per meter. This means that fairy plays in color could reach four and a quarter francs per meter. Pathé films of the same period, especially color films, were decidedly more affordable at two francs per meter for black and white, no more than three francs per meter for coloring with stencils or tinting, and no more than two francs, ten centimes, for toning (see Malthête, "Historiographie méliésienne").

16. This "head" appears to be Charles Pathé (1863–1957), who would write some thirty years later: "Mr. Méliès has the distinction of having brought about considerable progress in the field of kinematographic entertainment. He was the first to leave the beaten paths on which we were all walking. We were using as subjects the everyday events of public life. . . . Mr. Méliès was the first to produce transformation scenes, one of the most important of which was *Voyage dans la lune* (*A Trip to the Moon*). As the director of the Robert-Houdin theater on the Boulevard des Italiens, he was familiar with the entertainment business and with audiences. His virtues were many." (Charles Pathé, *De Pathé Frères à Pathé Cinéma: Pour les amis de Charles Pathé* [Nice: private printing, 1940], partially reprinted by Bernard Chardère in *Premier Plan* 55 [June 1970]: 41–42.)

17. Méliès no longer made explicit reference to this unverifiable and yet widely cited episode in his final two major texts: the series of seven articles published in 1926 in *Ciné-Journal* under the title "En marge de l'histoire du cinématographe" (reproduced in Malthête, *Méliès, images et illusions*, 135–44) and Méliès's "Mémoires," published in 1936 in Bessy and Lo Duca, *Georges Méliès, mage*, 169–217.

Three years after the publication of the series of seven articles in *Ciné-Journal*, Maurice Noverre, despite having been strongly inspired by Méliès, said no more on the topic, and in fact rather less (Maurice Noverre, *Le Nouvel Art cinématographique* 4 [October 1929]: 66]; and ibid. 5 [January 1930]: 83]. Méliès took up Noverre's October 1929 article almost word for word in his memoirs (Bessy and Lo Duca, *Georges Méliès, mage*, 180).

Nevertheless, Méliès appears to have spoken late in life about the Place de l'Opéra episode, as reported by Henry, "Évolution du cinéma, I—Les Débuts," 31–35: "One day I was shooting in the Place de l'Opéra and as a hearse passed into the field of vision my 'mill' suddenly jammed. A screw had come loose. I fixed the problem in two minutes and continued shooting. . . . But imagine my surprise when projecting the film, seeing the hearse transformed into a Madeleine-Bastille horse trolley. The substitution was so quick that Merlin the Magician could not have repudiated it. For me, my *Corbillard évanoui* ("Vanished Hearse") was a revelation." Note the reversal with respect to the substitution described in the 1907 text.

Another reference to the famous episode, related by Méliès himself, appears in Jeanne and Ford, *Histoire encyclopédique du cinéma*, vol. 1, 46. The authors quote Méliès as reported by Francis Ambrière in the journal *L'Image* 19 (n.d.): "I was filming in the Place de l'Opéra. Suddenly my camera stopped working. While I was examining the mechanism, ask yourself if the people in the street had changed! At the time it didn't occur to me and I completed my strip of film. But when I developed it, what a surprise! I had begun to shoot a horse trolley coming from the Boulevard des Capucines; when the vehicle reached the entrance to the Boulevard des Italiens, it changed into a hearse! The principle of transformation scenes had been discovered!"

18. The importance of the expression "stuck back together" (*ressoudée* in the French) may not have been recognized by the earliest film historians. We now know that the art of stop-camera kinematography was tied to fantastic editing of the negative, painstakingly reworked to match up appearances, disappearances, and substitutions (see Malthête, "Le Collage magique" and the references cited there).

Even though he was always loath to expound on the ways in which he executed his trick effects, Méliès appears to have alluded to these himself in 1926 in "En marge de l'histoire du cinématographe," p. 9: "In this way a number of trick effects, laboriously executed in sequence and skillfully matched up, make up a film in which the operator appears to be endowed with an extraordinary dexterity and a wonderful talent for impeccable execution." In 1929, Noverre was more explicit: "Méliès also matched up his own negatives. These difficult matches required a great deal of patience and concentration when working on views which almost always contained major trick effects. He also supervised the production of positive prints in the laboratory to ensure their quality" (*Le Nouvel Art cinématographique* 4 [1929], op. cit., 75).

19. *Escamotage d'une dame chez Robert-Houdin* (*The Vanishing Lady*, 20 meters, no. 70, made in the fall of 1896; the film is extant) is the first known example of the stop-camera technique in Méliès's work and was used here for each of its three functions: appearance, disappearance, and substitution.

20. A film 75 meters in length, nos. 78–80, made in late 1896. The film is extant.

21. A film 60 meters in length, nos. 185–187, made in 1899. The film is extant.

22. A film 120 meters in length, nos. 219–224, made in 1899. The film is extant.

23. The French term used here is *superposition*; later, *surimpression* became the standard term. Méliès, curiously enough, makes a distinction between *superpositions* and *surimpressions*, but in 1936, in his memoirs ("En marge de l'histoire du cinématographe"), he employs only *surimpressions*. Similarly, in both texts he employs the term *film* rather than *bande*, *scène* or *pièce*, *cinéma* rather than the *cinématographe* or *cinématographie*, and *studio* or *atelier*. He also employs *cinéaste* rather than *cinématographiste* and *caméra* instead of *appareil*.

24. See Malthête, "Quand Méliès n'en faisait qu'à sa tête."

25. In fact, it seems clear that Méliès never went beyond exposing a strip of film seven times, when he brought seven musicians to life on the screen in *L'Homme-Orchestre* (*The One Man Band*, 1900, 40 meters, nos. 262–263; the film is extant). He also created a music lover with six heads in *Le Mélomane* (*The Melomaniac*, 1903, 50 meters,

nos. 479–480; the film is extant). This did not prevent Noverre from commenting: "nos. 262–263, *L'Homme-Orchestre*, the first view with twelve superimpositions of the same character, Méliès himself playing all sorts of instruments" ("Gala Méliès," 87). Nor did it prevent Méliès from declaring to Coissac: "I remember a little film, *L'Homme-Orchestre*, where I alone played eighteen parts! . . . which required eighteen superimpositions on the same negative, which sometimes tore, requiring us to start over in part" (Coissac, *Histoire du cinématographe*, 378).

26. In 1907 Méliès had, in fact, been director of the Robert-Houdin theater for only nineteen years. He had rented this magic theater from Count Rohan-Chabot in 1888 and had purchased the business from the widow of Émile Robert-Houdin, the son of the theater's founder. It is possible, however, that Méliès began attending the theater regularly as early as 1882.

27. The word *tableau* merits careful explanation. Méliès uses the term in the present text in its theatrical sense, as the subdivision of an act corresponding to a change of set (he also described as *tableaux* the scale models he made for the sets of his films). Elsewhere, I have described this as a *plan-décor* ("set-shot") in order to make its idea clear: the action, recorded in front of a single set by a camera whose position does not change, may be fragmented at the stage of editing the negative into *plans-trucages* ("trick-shots"), which the single *plan-décor* helps to mask. On the other hand, according to the Méliès catalogue, action unfolding in the same *plan-décor* can be subdivided into several sections that are also called *tableaux*. The purpose of these divisions is unclear. It appears that the accumulation of these *tableaux* of a special nature was intended mostly for publicity purposes. Thus the famous *Voyage dans la lune* (*A Trip to the Moon*, 1902, 260 meters, nos. 399–411; the film is extant), for which the catalogue vaunts 30 tableaux ("A major spectacle in 30 tableaux") contained only eighteen *plan-décors*—in other words, seventeen set changes. This no doubt is the meaning of the "tableaux" mentioned in the present text above (under the rubric "Expenses"): "To give you a better idea, a large historical piece, fairy play, or opera [is] made up of 30 or 40 tableaux." We might mention the extreme case represented by the film *Le Sacre d'Édouard VII* (*Coronation of Edward VII*, 1902, 107 meters; the film is extant), a film made in a single *plan-décor* which the explanatory text cuts up into no fewer than ten *tableaux*. (See Malthête, "Méliès et le conférencier.")

28. Méliès chose the latter option. See Noverre, "L'Œuvre de Georges Méliès," and Méliès, "Mes Mémoires," in Bessy and Lo Duca, *Georges Méliès, mage*, 183–84.

29. In 1907, this word meant the director of a stage-entertainment business.

Works Cited in the Present Volume

This section provides information about books and specific articles cited in the present volume. The reader may find a complementary (and extended) bibliography specifically on early cinema on page 185 of this book.

The two bibliographies are independent of one another; therefore, a book listed in the Works Cited in the Present Volume might also appear in the General Bibliography on Early Cinema.

Abel, Richard. *French Film Theory and Criticism*. 2 vols. Princeton, N.J.: Princeton University Press, 1988.

Albera, François. "Leçon(s) d'histoire du cinéma (en France)." *1895*, no. 50 (2006): 9–27.

Allen, Robert Clyde, and Douglas Gomery. *Film History: Theory and Practice*. New York: Knopf, 1985.

Altman, Rick. "De l'intermédialité au multimédia: Cinéma, médias, avènement du son." *Cinémas* 10, no. 1 (1999): 37–53.

———. "Penser l'histoire du cinéma autrement: Un modèle de crise." *Vingtième siècle*, no. 46 (1995): 65–74.

———. *Silent Film Sound*. New York: Columbia University Press, 2004.

"L'attraction dans les films." *Ciné pour tous* 118 (November 1923): 10–11.

Aubert, Michelle, and Jean-Claude Seguin. *La Production cinématographique des frères Lumière*. Paris: Mémoires du cinéma et Bibliothèque du film, 1996.

Aumont, Jacques. "Quand y a-t-il cinéma primitif? ou Plaidoyer pour le primitif." In *Le Cinéma au tournant du siècle/Cinema at the Turn of the Century*, edited by Claire Dupré La Tour, André Gaudreault, and Roberta E. Pearson, 17–32. Quebec City: Nota Bene, 1999.

Benjamin, Walter. "On the Concept of History." In *Walter Benjamin: Selected Writings*, vol. 4, edited by Howard Eiland and Michael W. Jennings, 389–400. Cambridge, Mass.: Harvard University Press, 2003.

Benveniste, Émile. *Problems in General Linguistics*. Coral Gables, Fla.: University of Miami Press, 1971.

Berrendonner, Alain. *Éléments de pragmatique linguistique*. Paris: Minuit, 1982.

Bessy, Maurice, and Giuseppe-Maria Lo Duca. *Georges Méliès, mage*. Paris: J.-J. Pauvert, 1961.

Bordwell, David. "Textual Analysis, etc." *Enclitic* (Fall 1981/Spring 1982): 125–36.

Bousquet, Henri. "L'Âge d'or." In *Pathé: Premier empire du cinéma*, edited by Jacques Kermabon, 47–73. Paris: Centre Georges Pompidou, 1994.

———. *Catalogue Pathé des années 1896 à 1914*. Vol. 4, *1896–1906*. Bures-sur-Yvette: Édition Henri Bousquet, 1996.

Bowser, Eileen. *The Transformation of Cinema 1907–1915*. New York: Charles Scribner's Sons, 1990.

Burch, Noël. *Life to Those Shadows*. Berkeley: University of California Press, 1990.

———. "Porter, or Ambivalence." *Screen* 19, no. 4 (1978–79): 91–106.

———. *To the Distant Observer: Form and Meaning in the Japanese Cinema*. Berkeley: University of California Press, 1979.

Canudo, Riciotto. "La Naissance d'un sixième art: Essai sur la cinématographe." *Entretiens idéalistes*, 25 Oct. 1911.

Carou, Alain. *Le Cinéma français et les écrivains*. Paris: AFRHC, 2002.

Catalogue Gaumont. 1903. Grafics Collection. p. 35.

Chardère, Bernard. *Lumières sur Lumière*. Lyon: Presses universitaires de Lyon, 1987.

Coissac, G.-Michel. *Histoire du cinématographe: De ses origines à nos jours*. Paris: Cinéopse/Gauthier-Villars, 1925.

———. *Le Manuel pratique du conférencier-projectionniste*. Paris: Maison de la Bonne Presse, 1908.

———. *La Théorie et la pratique des projections*. Paris: Maison de la Bonne Presse, 1906.

Comolli, Jean-Louis. "Technique and Ideology: Camera, Perspective, Depth of Field," trans. Diana Matias. In *Narrative, Apparatus, Ideology: A Film Theory Reader*, edited by Philip Rosen, 421–43. New York: Columbia University Press, 1986.

———. "Technique et idéologie." *Cahiers du cinéma*, nos. 229–231, 233–235 (1971–1972).

Crary, Jonathan. *Techniques of the Observer: On Vision and Modernity in the Nineteenth Century*. Cambridge, Mass.: MIT Press, 1990.

Creton, Laurent. "Figures de l'entrepreneur, filières d'innovation et genèse de l'industrie cinématographique: Lumière, Pathé et Méliès." In *Georges Méliès, l'illusionniste fin de siècle?* edited by Jacques Malthête and Michel Marie, 133–64. Paris: Presses de la Sorbonne Nouvelle, 1997.

De Kuyper, Éric. "Le cinéma de la seconde époque." *Cinémathèque*, no. 2 (1992): 58–68.

———. "Le théâtre comme mauvais objet." *Cinémathèque*, no. 11 (1997): 63–75.

Delluc, Louis. "Le Roi de la mer." In *Cinéma et Cie*. (Paris: Bernard Grasset, 1919). Originally published in *Le Film*, July 9, 1917.

Deslandes, Jacques. *Le Boulevard du cinéma à l'époque de Georges Méliès*. Paris: Éditions du Cerf, 1963.

Deslandes, Jacques, and Jacques Richard. *Histoire comparée du cinéma*. Vol. 2, *Du cinématographe au cinéma 1896–1906*. Tournai: Casterman, 1968.

Duby, Georges, and Guy Lardeau. *Dialogues*. Paris: Flammarion, 1980.

Duigou, Serge, and Germain Lacasse. *Marie de Kerstrat*. Rennes: Ouest-France, 2002.

Eisenstein, Sergei. "The Montage of Attractions (1923)." In *Selected Works*. Vol. 1, *Writings, 1922–1934*, edited by Richard Taylor, 33–38. London: British Film Institute, 1988.

Fell, John L., ed. *Film before Griffith*. Berkeley: University of California Press, 1983.

Fouquet, E.-L. "L'Attraction." *L'Echo du cinéma* 11 (28 June 1912): 1.

Francœur, Louis. *Les Signes s'envolent: Pour une sémiotique des actes de langage culturels*. Quebec City: Presses de l'Université Laval, 1985.

F. Z. Maguire & Co. *Catalogue* (March 1898) GRAFICS Collection.

Gadamer, Hans-Georg. *Truth and Method*. New York: Crossroad, 1988.

Gaudreault, André, ed. *Les Cahiers de la Cinémathèque* 29 (1979).

———, ed. *Cinema 1900–1906: An Analytical Study*. Vol. 2, *Analytical Filmography*. Brussels: FIAF, 1982.

———. *Cinema delle origini: O della "cinematografia-attrazione."* Milan: Il Castoro, 2004.

———. *Cinéma et attraction: Pour une nouvelle histoire du cinématographe*. Paris: CNRS, 2008.

———. "Fragmentation and Segmentation in the Lumière 'Animated Views.'" *Moving Image* 3, no. 1 (2003): 110–31.

———. *From Plato to Lumière: Narration and Monstration in Literature and Cinema*. Toronto: University of Toronto Press, 2008.

———. "From 'Primitive Cinema' to 'Kine-Attractography.'" In *The Cinema of Attraction Reloaded*, edited by Wanda Strauven, 85–104. Amsterdam: Amsterdam University Press, 2006.

———, ed. In collaboration with Tom Gunning and Alain Lacasse. *Pathé 1900: Fragments d'une filmographie analytique du cinéma des premiers temps*. Paris: Presses de la Sorbonne Nouvelle, 1993.

———. "Temporality and Narrativity in Early Cinema, 1895–1908." In *Film before Griffith*, edited by John L. Fell, 311–29. Berkeley: University of California Press, 1983.

———. "Les Vues cinématographiques selon Eisenstein, ou: Que reste-t-il de l'*ancien* (le cinéma des premiers temps) dans le *nouveau* (les productions filmiques et scripturales d'Eisenstein)?" In *Eisenstein: L'Ancien et le nouveau*, edited by Dominique Chateau, François Jost, and Martin Lefebvre, 23–43. Paris: Sorbonne/Colloque de Cerisy, 2001.

Gaudreault, André, and Philippe Gauthier. "Crosscutting, a Programmed Language." In *The Griffith Project*, Vol. 12, edited by Paolo Cherchi Usai, 30–47. London: British Film Institute, 2008.

Gaudreault, André, and Tom Gunning. "Early Cinema as a Challenge to Film History." In

The Cinema of Attraction Reloaded, edited by Wanda Strauven, 365–80. Amsterdam: Amsterdam University Press, 2006.

Gaudreault, André, and Frank Kessler. "L'Acteur comme opérateur de continuité ou, les aventures du corps mis en cadre, mis en scène et mis en chaîne." In *L'uomo visibile: L'attore dal cinema delle origini alle soglie del cinema moderno/The Visible Man: Film Acting from Early Cinema to the Eve of Modern Cinema*, edited by Laura Vichi, 23–32. Udine, Italy: Forum, 2002.

Gaudreault, André, Germain Lacasse, and Pierre Véronneau, eds. *Filmographie des "vues" tournées au Québec*. Available at http://cri.histart.umontreal.ca/grafics/fr/filmo/default.asp (accessed 2 November 2010).

Gaudreault, André, and Jean-Marc Lamotte. "Fragmentation and Segmentation in the Lumière 'Animated Views.'" *The Moving Image* 3, no. 1 (Spring 2003).

Gaudreault, André, and Philippe Marion. "A Medium Is Always Born Twice." *Early Popular Visual Culture* 3 (May 2005): 3–15.

———. "Le Cinéma naissant et ses dispositions narratives." *Cinéma & Cie*, no. 1 (2001): 34–41.

———. "Pour une nouvelle approche de la périodisation en histoire du cinéma." *Cinémas* 17, nos. 2–3 (Spring 2007): 215–32.

Gaudreault, André, and Roger Odin, "Le Cinématographe, un 'enfant prodige.'" In *La Decima musa: Il Cinema e le altre arti/The Tenth Muse: Cinema and Other Arts*, edited by Leonardo Quaresima and Laura Vichi, 67–81. Udine, Italy: Forum, 2001.

Gaudreault, André, and Denis Simard. "L'Extranéité du cinéma des premiers temps." In *Les Vingt premières années du cinéma français*, edited by Jean Gili, Michèle Lagny, Michel Marie, and Vincent Pinel, 15–28. Paris: Presses de la Sorbonne Nouvelle, 1995.

Giraud, Jean. *Le Lexique français du cinéma des origines à 1930*. Paris: CNRS, 1958.

Gunning, Tom. "Attractions, truquages et photogénie: L'Explosion du présent dans les films à truc français produits entre 1896 et 1907." In *Les Vingt premières années*, 177–93.

———. *D. W. Griffith and the Origins of American Narrative Film: The Early Years at Biograph*. Urbana: University of Illinois Press, 1991.

———. "An Unseen Energy Swallows Space." In *Film before Griffith*, edited by John L. Fell, 355–66. Berkeley, University of California Press, 1983.

———. "The Whole Town's Gawking: Early Cinema and the Visual Experience of Modernity." *Yale Journal of Criticism* 7, no. 2 (1994): 189–209.

Henry, Pierre. "Évolution du cinéma, I—Les Débuts." *Cinéa et Ciné Pour Tous réunis* 24 (April 1932): 31–35.

Hepworth, Cecil M. *Animated Photography*, 2d ed. London: Hazell, Watson & Viney, 1897.

Holman, Roger, ed. *Cinema 1900–1906: An Analytical Study*. Vol. 1. Brussels: International Federation of Film Archives, 1982.

Jacobs, Lewis. *The Rise of the American Film: A Critical History*. New York: Teachers College Press, 1971.

Jeanne, René, and Charles Ford, *Histoire encyclopédique du cinéma*. Vol. 1, *Le Cinéma français 1895–1929*. Paris: Robert Laffont, 1947.

Jenn, Pierre. *Georges Méliès cinéaste*. Paris: Albatros, 1984.

Jost, François. "L'Invention du cinéaste." In *Prima dell' autore*, edited by Anja Franceschetti and Leonardo Quaresima, 53–62. Udine, Italy: Università degli Studi di Udine, 1997.

———. *L'Œil-caméra: Entre film et roman*. Lyon: Presses universitaires de Lyon, 1987.

———. "Pourquoi le cinéma des débuts?" *Cinéma & Cie*, no. 1 (2001): 13–23.

Lacasse, Germain. *Le Bonimenteur de vues animées: Le Cinéma "muet" entre tradition et modernité*. Paris: Méridiens Klincksieck, 2000.

Laffay, Albert. *Logique du cinéma*. Paris: Masson, 1964.

Lagny, Michèle. *De l'histoire du cinéma: Méthode historique et histoire du cinéma*. Paris: Armand Colin, 1992.

Lefebvre, Thierry. *La Chair et le celluloïd: Le Cinéma chirurgical du docteur Doyen*. Brionne: Jean Doyen, 2004.

———. "Film scientifique et grand public: Une rencontre différée." In *É.-J. Marey: Actes du colloque du centenaire*, edited by Dominique de Font-Réaulx, Thierry Lefebvre, and Laurent Mannoni, 159–67. Paris: Arcadia, 2006.

Le Forestier, Laurent. *Aux sources de l'industrie du cinéma: Le modèle Pathé, 1905–1908*. Paris: L'Harmattan, 2006.

———. *L'Industrialisation du mode de production des films Pathé entre 1905 et 1908*. Unpublished Ph.D. diss., Université Paris 3/Sorbonne Nouvelle, 2000.

Lourau, René. *L'Analyse institutionnelle*. Paris: Minuit, 1970.

Low, Rachael, and Roger Manvell. *The History of the British Film*. Vol. 1, *1896–1906*. London: George Allen and Unwin, 1948.

Maclean, Hector. Preface to *Animated Photography*, by Cecil Hepworth. 2d ed. London: Hazwell, Watson & Viney, 1897.

Maillet, Raymond. *Émile Cohl cinématographiste, 1857–1938*. Montreal: Cinémathèque québécoise, 1988.

Malthête, Jacques. "Bulletin 26." *Cinémathèque Méliès* (1995): 19.

———. "Le Collage magique chez Edison et Méliès avant 1901." *CinémAction* 102 (2002): 96–109.

———. "Les Deux studios de Georges Méliès." In *Méliès, magie et cinéma*, edited by Malthête and Laurent Mannoni, 134–69. Paris: Éditions Paris Musées, 2002.

———. "Historiographie méliésienne: Quelques nouveaux repères." In *Georges Méliès, l'illusionniste fin de siècle?*, edited by Malthête and Michel Marie, 25–41. Paris: Presses de la Sorbonne Nouvelle/Colloque de Cerisy, 1997.

———. *Méliès, images et illusions*. Paris: Exporégie, 1996.

———. "Méliès et le conférencier." *Iris*, no. 22 (Fall 1996): 117–29.

———. "Quand Méliès n'en faisait qu'à sa tête." *1895* 27 (September 1999): 21–32.

Malthête, Jacques, Madeleine Malthête-Méliès, and Anne-Marie Quévrain. *Essai de reconstitution du catalogue français de la Star-Film, suivi d'une analyse catalographique des films de Georges Méliès recensés en France*. Bois d'Arcy, France: Publications du Service des Archives du Film du CNC, 1981.

Malthête, Jacques, and Laurent Mannoni, eds. *Méliès, magie et cinéma*. Paris: Paris Musées, 2002.

Mariniello, Silvestra. "L'Histoire du cinéma contre le cinéma dans l'histoire." In *Le Cinéma en histoire: Institution cinématographique, réception filmique et reconstitution historique*, edited by André Gaudreault, Germain Lacasse, and Isabelle Raynauld, 13–27. Paris: Méridiens Klincksieck, 1999.

Maugras, Émile, and Maurice Guégan. *Le Cinématographe devant le droit*. Paris: V. Giard & E. Brière, 1908.

Méliès, Georges. "En marge de l'histoire du cinématographe." *Cinéma*, no. 884 (6 Aug. 1926).

———. "Importance du scénario." In *Georges Méliès*, edited by Georges Sadoul. Paris: Seghers, 1961.

———. "Les Vues cinématographiques: Causerie par Geo. Méliès." *Annuaire général et international de la photographie*. Paris: Librairie Plon, 1907.

Metz, Christian. *The Imaginary Signifier: Psychoanalysis and the Cinema*. Bloomington: Indiana University Press, 1982.

———. *Language and Cinema*. Paris: Larousse, 1971.

Mitry, Jean. *The Aesthetics and Psychology of the Cinema*. Bloomington: Indiana University Press, 1997.

———. "De quelques problèmes d'histoire et d'esthétique du cinéma." *Les Cahiers de la Cinémathèque* 10–11 (Summer–Fall 1973): 112–41.

———. *Esthétique et psychologie du cinéma*. 2 vols. Paris: Éditions Universitaires, 1963–65.

———. *Histoire du cinéma*. 5 vols. Paris: Éditions Universitaires, 1967–80.

Moisan, Clément. *L'Histoire littéraire*. Paris: Presses Universitaires de France, 1990.

Monsaingeon, Églantine. "Des genres et des modes." Unpublished master's thesis, Université de Montréal, 1999.

Morin, Edgar. *The Cinema, or the Imaginary Man*. Minneapolis: University of Minnesota Press, 2005.

Mottram, Ron. "Fact and Affirmation: Some Thoughts on the Methodology of Film History and the Relation of Theory and Historiography." *Quarterly Review of Film* 5, no. 3 (1980): 335–47.

Musser, Charles. "The Early Cinema of Edwin Porter." *Cinema Journal* 19, no. 1 (1979): 1–38.

———. *Edison Motion Pictures, 1890–1900: An Annotated Filmography*. Washington, D.C.: Smithsonian Institution Press, 1997.

———. *The Emergence of Cinema: The American Screen to 1907*. New York: Charles Scribner's Sons, 1990.

Noverre, Maurice. "La Gala Méliès." *Le Nouvel art cinématographique* 5 (January 1930).

———. "L'Œuvre de Georges Méliès: Étude rétrospective sur le premier 'Studio cinématographique' machiné pour la prise de vues théâtrales." *Le Nouvel art cinématographique* 3 (July 1929).

———. "L'Œuvre de Georges Méliès: Étude rétrospective sur la première entreprise industrielle de cinématographie théâtrale (1896–1914)." *Le Nouvel Art cinématographique* 4 (October 1929).

Odin, Roger. "Approche sémio-pragmatique, approche historique: De l'intérêt du dialogue." *Ars Semeiotica* 17, nos. 1–4 (1994).

———. "Pour une sémio-pragmatique du cinéma." *Iris*, no. 1 (1983): 67–82.

———. "Présentation." *Cinémas* 17, nos. 2–3 (2007): 9–32.

———. "Sémio-pragmatique du cinéma et de l'audio-visuel," In *Towards a Pragmatics of the Audiovisual*; vol. 1, edited by Jürgen E. Müller, 33–46. Münster, Germany: Nodus.

Paci, Viva. *La Comédie musicale et la double vie du cinéma*. Paris / Udine, Aléas / Forum (forthcoming) 2011.

———. *La Machine à voir*. À propos de cinéma, attraction, exhibition. Lillie Presses Universitaires du Setentrion, (forthcoming) 2011.

Pathé. *Scènes à grand spectacle*. Catalogue. GRAFICS Collection. March 1902.

Pinel, Vincent. *Louis Lumière, inventeur et cinéaste*. Paris: Nathan, 1994.

Polan, Dana. "La Poétique de l'histoire: *Metahistory* de Hayden White." *Iris*, no. 2 (1984).

Pougin, Arthur. *Dictionnaire historique et pittoresque du théâtre et des arts qui s'y rattachent*. Paris: Librairie de Firmin-Didot, 1885.

Robert, Lucie. *L'Institution du littéraire au Québec*. Ste. Foy: Presses de l'Université Laval, 1989.

Sadoul, Georges. In *Cinquantenaire du cinéma (28 décembre 1895–28 décembre 1945)*, 24–25. Paris: Prisma, 1946.

———. *Georges Méliès*. Paris: Seghers, 1961.

———. *Histoire générale du cinéma*. 6 vols. Paris: Denoël, 1946–1975.

Salt, Barry. *Film Style and Technology: History and Analysis*. London: Starword, 1992.

Schaeffer, Jean-Marie. *Qu'est-ce qu'un genre littéraire?* Paris: Seuil, 1989.

Schwartz, Vanessa R. *Spectacular Realities: Early Mass Culture in Fin-de-Siècle Paris*. Berkeley: University of California Press, 1998.

Simard, Denis. "De la nouveauté du cinéma des premiers temps." In *Le Cinéma en histoire: Institution cinématographique, réception filmique et reconstitution historique*, edited by André Gaudreault, Germain Lacasse, and Isabelle Raynauld, 30–56. Paris: Méridiens Klincksieck, 1999.

Sopocy, Martin. "A Narrated Cinema: The Pioneer Story Films of James A. Williamson." *Cinema Journal* 18, no. 1 (1978): 1–28.

———. *James Williamson: Studies and Documents of a Pioneer of the Film Narrative*. Madison, N.J.: Fairleigh Dickinson University Press, 1998.

Sorlin, Pierre. "Promenade dans Rome." *Iris*, no. 2 (1984): 5–24.

Souriau, Étienne. *L'Univers filmique*. Paris: Flammarion, 1953.

Strauven, Wanda, ed. *The Cinema of Attractions Reloaded*. Amsterdam: Amsterdam University Press, 2006.

Todorov, Tzvetan. *La Notion de littérature et autres essais*. Paris: Seuil, 1987.

General Bibliography
on Early Cinema

Compiled by Nicolas Dulac and Santiago Hidalgo
under the supervision of André Gaudreault
and with the assistance of Lisa Pietrocatelli
and Carolina Lucchesi Lavoie.

A bibliography is an essential part of a book such as this one dealing in large part with historiography. The bibliography provided here includes some of the essential publications dealing with early cinema—if not in their entirety, at least in part. Various volumes dealing with historiographical questions have also been included here. While not exhaustive, this bibliography nevertheless provides the reader with an overview of some of the research carried out over the past thirty years in the field and should serve as a practical guide for researchers and students of early cinema.

The bibliography is divided into three categories: books; journals; and filmographies, catalogues, and bibliographies. Note that in order to limit this bibliography to a manageable length, individual journal articles and book chapters have not been included in it. Thematic journals and special issues of journals on the topic of early cinema, however, have been included. Readers seeking specific articles, apart from those cited in this volume (which you can find in the section Works Cited in the present volume), are invited to consult the excellent database maintained by the International Federation of Film Archives (FIAF), which appears under "Early Cinema Filmographies, Catalogues, and Bibliographies" in this bibliography. Some older work in the field has been included here, either because of its historical importance or because of its prominence in classical writings on film history. It should be noted, finally, that apart from a few essential works in Italian, the books and journals given here are in English or French.

Please note that bibliographical references for material found in Jacques Malthête's notes to the text by Georges Méliès that appear in Appendix B in this volume are included in the notes themselves and are not a part of the bibliography, except in cases of overlap.

Books on Early Cinema

Abel, Richard. *Americanizing the Movies and "Movie-Mad" Audiences, 1910–1914.* Berkeley: University of California Press, 2006.

———. *The Ciné Goes to Town: French Cinema, 1896–1914.* Berkeley: University of California Press, 1994.

———, ed. *Encyclopedia of Early Cinema.* London: Routledge, 2005.

———. *The Red Rooster Scare: Making Cinema American (1900–1910).* Berkeley: University of California Press, 1999.

———, ed. *Silent Film.* New Brunswick, N.J.: Rutgers University Press, 1996.

Abel, Richard, and Rick Altman, eds. *The Sounds of Early Cinema.* Bloomington: Indiana University Press, 2001.

Abel, Richard, Giorgio Bertellini, and Rob King, eds. *Early Cinema and the "National."* New Barnet, Hertfordshire, U.K.: John Libbey, 2008.

Albera, François, Marta Braun, and André Gaudreault, eds. *Arrêt sur image, fragmentation du temps: Aux sources de la culture visuelle moderne / Stop Motion, Fragmentation of Time: At the Roots of the Modern Visual Culture.* Lausanne, Switzerland: Payot-Lausanne, 2003.

Albera, François, and Roland Cosandey, eds. *Cinéma sans frontières 1896–1918: Aspects de l'internationalité dans le cinéma mondial: Représentations, marchés, influences et réception / Images Across Borders: Internationality in World Cinema: Representations, Markets, Influences and Reception.* Lausanne, Switzerland: Payot-Lausanne, 1995.

Allen, Robert C. *Vaudeville and Film, 1895–1915.* New York: Arno, 1980.

Allen, Robert C., and Douglas Gomery. *Film History: Theory and Practice.* New York: Knopf, 1985.

Altman, Rick. *Silent Film Sound.* New York: Columbia University Press, 2004.

Andriopoulos, Stefan. *Possessed: Hypnotic Crimes, Corporate Fiction, and the Invention of Cinema.* Chicago: University of Chicago Press, 2008.

Anthony, Barry. *The Kinora: Motion Pictures for the Home 1896–1914.* London: Projection Box, 1996.

Anthony, Barry, and Richard Brown. *A Victorian Film Enterprise: The History of the British Mutoscope and Biograph Company.* Trowbridge, U.K.: Flicks, 1999.

Armatage, Kay. *The Girl from God's Country: Nell Shipman and the Silent Cinema.* Toronto: University of Toronto Press, 2003.

Aronson, Michael. *Nickelodeon City: Pittsburgh at the Movies, 1905–1929.* Pittsburgh: University of Pittsburgh Press, 2008.

Auerbach, Jonathan. *Body Shots: Early Cinema's Incarnations.* Berkeley: University of California Press, 2007.

Aumont, Jacques, André Gaudreault, and Michel Marie, eds. *Histoire du cinéma: nouvelles approches.* Paris: Publications de la Sorbonne, 1989.

Bakker, Gerben. *Entertainment Industrialised: The Emergence of the International Film Industry, 1890–1940.* Cambridge, U.K.: Cambridge University Press, 2008.

Balshofer, Fred J., and Arthur C. Miller. *One Reel a Week.* Berkeley: University of California Press, 1967.

Banda, Daniel, and José Moure. *Le Cinéma: Naissance d'un art, premiers écrits (1895–1920)*. Paris: Flammarion, 2008.

Barnes, John. *The Beginnings of the Cinema in England 1894–1901*. 5 vols. Exeter, U.K.: University of Exeter Press, 1996–1998.

Barnouw, Erik. *Documentary: A History of the Non-Fiction Film*. New York: Oxford University Press, 1974.

———. *The Magician and the Cinema*. Oxford: Oxford University Press, 1981.

Barsam, Richard M. *Nonfiction Film: A Critical History*. New York: Dutton, 1973.

Baumann, Shyon. *Hollywood Highbrow: From Entertainment to Art*. Princeton, N.J.: Princeton University Press, 2007.

Bean, Jennifer M., and Diane Negra, eds. *A Feminist Reader in Early Cinema*. Durham, N.C.: Duke University Press, 2002.

Bean, Shawn C. *The First Hollywood: Florida and the Golden Age of Silent Filmmaking*. Gainesville: University Press of Florida, 2008.

Belloï, Livio. *Le Regard retourné: Aspects du cinéma des premiers temps*. Québec/Paris: Nota Bene/Méridiens Klincksieck, 2000.

Bergsten, Bebe, ed. *Biograph Bulletins, 1896–1908*. Los Angeles: Locare Research Group, 1971.

Bernardi, Daniel, ed. *The Birth of Whiteness: Race and the Emergence of United States Cinema*. New Brunswick, N.J.: Rutgers University Press, 1995.

Bertellini, Giorgio. *Italy in Early American Cinema: Race, Landscape, and the Picturesque*. Bloomington: Indiana University Press, 2010.

Bessière, Irène, and Jean A. Gili, eds. *Histoire du cinéma: Problématique des sources*. Paris: Association française de recherche sur l'histoire du cinéma, 2004.

Bessy, Maurice, and Giuseppe-Maria Lo Duca. *Georges Méliès, mage*. Paris: Pauvert, 1961.

Blom, Ivo. *Jean Desmet and the Early Dutch Film Trade*. Amsterdam, Netherlands: Amsterdam University Press, 2003.

Bordwell, David, Kristin Thompson, and Janet Staiger. *The Classical Hollywood Cinema: Film Style and Mode of Production to 1960*. New York: Columbia University Press, 1985.

Bottomore, Stephen. *I Want to See This Annie Mattygraph: A Cartoon History of the Coming of the Movies*. Pordenone, Italy: Le Giornate del Cinema Muto, 1995.

Bowser, Eileen. *The Transformation of Cinema 1907–1915*. New York: Charles Scribner's Sons, 1990.

Braun, Marta. *Picturing Time: The Work of Etienne-Jules Marey*. Chicago: University of Chicago Press, 1992.

Brewster, Ben, and Lea Jacobs. *Theatre to Cinema: Stage Pictorialism and the Early Feature Film*. Oxford: Oxford University Press, 1997.

Brown, Richard, and Barry Anthony. *A Victorian Film Enterprise: The History of the British Mutoscope and Biograph Company, 1897–1915*. Trowbridge, U.K.: Flicks, 1999.

Brownlow, Kevin. *Behind the Mask of Innocence: Sex, Violence, Prejudice, Crime: Films of Social Conscience in the Silent Era*. Berkeley: University of California Press, 1990.

———. *The Parade's Gone By*. Berkeley: University of California Press, 1976.

Brunetta, Gian Piero. *The History of Italian Cinema: A Guide to Italian Film from Its Origins to the Twenty-First Century*. Princeton, N.J.: Princeton University Press, 2009.

Burch, Noël. *Life to Those Shadows*. Berkeley: University of California Press, 1990.

Burrows, Jon. *Legitimate Cinema: Theatre Stars in Silent British Films, 1908–1918*. Exeter, U.K.: University of Exeter Press, 2003.

Butters, Gerald R. *Black Manhood on the Silent Screen*. Lawrence: University Press of Kansas, 2002.

Canudo, Ricciotto. *L'Usine aux images*. Paris: Séguier et Arte, 1995.

Callahan, Vicki, ed. *Reclaiming the Archive: Feminism and Film History*. Detroit, Mich.: Wayne State University Press, 2010.

Carou, Alain. *Le Cinéma français et les écrivains: Histoire d'une rencontre, 1906–1914*. Paris: Association française de recherche sur l'histoire du cinéma, 2002.

Casetti, Francesco. *Eye of the Century: Film, Experience, Modernity*. New York: Columbia University Press, 2008.

Ceram, C.W. *Archaeology of the Cinema*. London: Thames and Hudson, 1965.

Chabria, Suresh, ed. *Light of Asia: Indian Silent Cinema, 1912–1934*. Le Giornate del Cinema Muto, 1994.

Chanan, Michael. *The Dream That Kicks: The Prehistory and Early Years of Cinema in Britain*. London: Routledge & Kegan Paul, 1980.

Chapman, James, H. Mark Glancy, and Sue Harper, eds. *The New Film History: Sources, Methods, Approaches*. New York: Palgrave Macmillan, 2007.

Chardère, Bernard. *Lumières sur Lumière*. Lyon: Presses universitaires de Lyon, 1987.

Charney, Leo. *Empty Moments: Cinema, Modernity, and Drift*. Durham, N.C.: Duke University Press, 1998.

Charney, Leo, and Vanessa R. Schwartz, eds. *Cinema and the Invention of Modern Life*. Berkeley: University of California Press, 1995.

Chen, Tina Mai, and David S. Churchill, eds. *Film, History, and Cultural Citizenship: Sites of Production*. New York: Routledge, 2007.

Cherchi Usai, Paolo. *Georges Méliès*. Rome: La Nuova Italia, 1983.

———, ed. *The Griffith Project*. 12 vols. London: British Film Institute, 1999–2008.

———. *Silent Cinema: An Introduction*. London: British Film Institute, 2000.

———, ed. *A Trip to the Movies: Georges Méliès, Filmmaker and Magician (1861–1938)*. Rochester, N.Y.: George Eastman House, 1991.

Cherchi Usai, Paolo, and Lorenzo Codelli, eds. *Before Caligari: German Cinema, 1897–1920*. Pordenone, Italy: Biblioteca dell'Immagine, 1990.

Cherchi Usai, Paolo, and Yuri Tsivian, eds. *Silent Witnesses: Russian Films, 1908–1919*. Pordenone, Italy: Biblioteca dell'Immagine, 1989.

Chevaldonné, Yves. *Nouvelles techniques et culture régionale: Les Premiers temps du cinéma dans le Vaucluse (1896–1914)*. Quebec City: Les Presses de l'Université Laval, 2004.

Christie, Ian. *The Last Machine: Early Cinema and the Birth of the Modern World*. London: BBC Educational Developments, 1994.

Coe, Brian. *The History of Movie Photography*. London: Ash and Grant, 1981.

Coissac, G.-Michel. *Histoire du cinématographe: De ses origines à nos jours*. Paris: Cinéopse-Gauthier-Villars, 1925.

Cooper, Mark Garrett. *Love Rules: Silent Hollywood and the Rise of the Managerial Class*. Minneapolis: University of Minnesota Press, 2003.

Corcy, Marie-Sophie, Jacques Malthête, Laurent Mannoni, and Jean-Jacques Meusy, eds. *Les premières années de la société L. Gaumont et Cie: Correspondance commerciale de Léon Gaumont 1895–1899*. Paris: AFRHC, 1999.

Cosandey, Roland, André Gaudreault, and Tom Gunning, eds. *Une invention du diable? Cinéma des premiers temps et religion / An Invention of the Devil? Religion and Early Cinema*. Sainte-Foy, Québec: Presses de l'Université Laval, 1992.

Crafton, Donald. *Before Mickey: Animation Film, 1898–1928*. Chicago: University of Chicago Press, 1993.

———. *Émile Cohl, Caricature, and Film*. Princeton, N.J.: Princeton University Press, 1990.

Crary, Jonathan. *Suspensions of Perception: Attention, Spectacle, and Modern Culture*. Cambridge, Mass.: MIT Press, 1999.

———. *Techniques of the Observer: On Vision and Modernity in the Nineteenth Century*. Cambridge, Mass.: MIT Press, 1990.

Dalle Vacche, Angela. *Diva: Defiance and Passion in Early Italian Cinema*. Austin: University of Texas Press, 2008.

de Cordova, Richard. *Picture Personalities: The Emergence of the Star System in America, 1907–1922*. Urbana: University of Illinois Press, 1990.

de Font-Réault, Dominique, Thierry Lefebvre, and Laurent Mannoni, eds. *EJ Marey: Actes du colloque du centenaire*. Paris: Arcadia, 2006.

de Klerk, Nico, and Daan Hertogs, eds. *Uncharted Territory: Essays on Early Nonfiction Films*. Amsterdam: Nederlands Filmmuseum, 1997.

Delmeulle, Frédéric. *Contribution à l'histoire du cinéma documentaire en France, le cas de l'encyclopédie Gaumont, 1909–1929*. Villeneuve d'Ascq, France: Presses universitaires du Septentrion, 2003.

Deslandes, Jacques. *Le Boulevard du cinéma à l'époque de Georges Méliès*. Paris: Éditions du Cerf, 1963.

———. *Histoire comparée du cinéma. Vol. 1, de la cinématique au cinématographe (1826–1896)*. Tournai, Belgium: Casterman, 1966.

Deslandes, Jacques, and Jacques Richard. *Histoire comparée du cinéma. Vol. 2, du cinématographe au cinéma 1896–1906*. Tournai, Belgium: Casterman, 1968.

Dibbets, Karel, and Bert Hogenkamp, eds. *Film and the First World War*. Amsterdam: Amsterdam University Press, 1995.

Doane, Mary Ann. *The Emergence of Cinematic Time: Modernity, Contingency, the Archive*. Cambridge, Mass.: Harvard University Press, 2002.

Duigou, Serge, and Germain Lacasse. *Marie de Kerstrat*. Rennes, France: Ouest-France, 2002.

Dujardin, Philippe, André Gardies, Jacques Gerstenkorn, and Jean-Claude Seguin, eds.

L'Aventure du cinématographe: Actes du Congrès mondial Lumière. Lyon, France: Aléas, 1999.

Dupré La Tour, Claire, André Gaudreault, and Roberta E. Pearson, eds. *Le Cinéma au tournant du siècle / Cinema at the Turn of the Century*. Québec/Lausanne: Nota Bene/ Payot-Lausanne, 1999.

Eckhardt, Joseph P., and Linda Kowall. *Peddler of Dreams: Siegmund Lubin and the Creation of the Motion Picture Industry*. Philadelphia: National Museum of American Jewish History, 1984.

Elsaesser, Thomas, ed. *A Second Life: German Cinema's First Decades*. Amsterdam: Amsterdam University Press, 1996.

Elsaesser, Thomas, and Adam Barker, eds. *Early Cinema: Space, Frame, Narrative*. London: British Film Institute, 1990.

Everett, Anna. *Returning the Gaze: A Genealogy of Black Film Criticism, 1909–1949*. Durham, N.C.: Duke University Press, 2001.

Ezra, Elizabeth. *Georges Méliès: The Birth of the Auteur*. Manchester, U.K.: Manchester University Press, 2000.

Fell, John, ed. *Film before Griffith*. Los Angeles: University of California Press, 1983.

Fitzsimmons, Linda, and Sarah Street. *Moving Performance: British Stage and Screen, 1890s–1920s*. Trowbridge, U.K.: Flicks, 2000.

Franceschetti, Anja, and Leonardo Quaresima, eds. *Prima dell'autore / Before the Author*. Udine, Italy: Università degli Studi di Udine, 1997.

Frauenfelder, Consuelo. *Le Temps du mouvement: Le cinéma des attractions à Genève (1896–1917)*. Geneva, Switzerland: Presses d'histoire suisse, 2005.

Fuller, Kathryn H. *At the Picture Show: Small-Town Audiences and the Creation of Movie Fan Culture*. Charlottesville: University Press of Virginia, 2001.

Fullerton, John, ed. *Celebrating 1895: The Centenary of Cinema*. Sydney, Australia: John Libbey, 1998.

Fullerton, John, and Astrid Söderbergh Widding, eds. *Moving Images: From Edison to the Webcam*. Sydney, Australia: John Libbey, 2000.

Fullerton, John, and Jan Olsson, eds. *Nordic Exploration: Film before 1930*. Sydney, Australia: John Libbey, 1999.

Gaudreault, André, ed. *American Cinema, 1890–1909: Themes and Variations*. New Brunswick, N.J.: Rutgers University Press, 2009.

———, ed. *Au pays des ennemis du cinéma . . . : Pour une nouvelle histoire des débuts du cinéma au Québec*. Québec: Nuit Blanche, 1996.

———. *From Plato to Lumière: Narration and Monstration in Literature and Cinema*. Toronto: University of Toronto Press, 2009.

Gaudreault, André, Germain Lacasse, and Isabelle Raynauld, eds. *Le Cinéma en histoire: Institution cinématographique, réception filmique et reconstitution historique*. Quebec: Nota Bene, 1999.

Gaudreault, André, Catherine Russell, and Pierre Véronneau, eds. *Le Cinématographe, nouvelle technologie du XXe siècle / The Cinema, A New Technology for the 20th Century*. Lausanne: Payot-Lausanne, 2004.

Gauthier, Philippe. *Le Montage alterné avant Griffith: Le cas Pathé*. Paris: L'Harmattan, 2008.

Gerstner, David A. *Manly Arts: Masculinity and Nation in Early American Cinema*. Durham, N.C.: Duke University Press, 2006.

Gifford, Denis. *Books and Plays in Films, 1896–1915: Literary, Theatrical, and Artistic Sources of the First Twenty Years of Motion Pictures*. London: Mansell, 1987.

Gili, Jean A. *André Deed: Boireau, Cretinetti, Gribouille, Toribo, Foolshead, Lehman . . .* Bologna, Italy: Cineteca Bologna, 2005.

Gili, Jean A., Michèle Lagny, Michel Marie, and Vincent Pinel, eds. *Les Vingt premières années du cinéma français*. Paris: Presses de la Sorbonne Nouvelle, 1995.

Giraud, Jean. *Le Lexique français du cinéma des origines à 1930*. Paris: CNRS, 1958.

Gomery, Douglas. *Shared Pleasures: A History of Movie Presentation in the United States*. Madison: University of Wisconsin Press, 1992.

Gordon, Eric. *The Urban Spectator: American Concept Cities from Kodak to Google*. Hanover, N.H.: Dartmouth College Press, 2009.

Gordon, Rae Beth. *Why the French Love Jerry Lewis: From Cabaret to Early Cinema*. Stanford, Calif.: Stanford University Press, 2001.

Grau, Robert. *The Theatre of Science: A Volume of Progress and Achievement in the Motion Picture Industry*. New York: Benjamin Blom, 1969.

Gray, Frank, ed. *Hove Pioneers and the Arrival of Cinema*. London: University of Brighton, 1996.

Grieveson, Lee. *Policing Cinema: Movies and Censorship in Early-Twentieth-Century America*. Berkeley: University of California Press, 2004.

Grieveson, Lee, and Peter Krämer, eds. *The Silent Cinema Reader*. London: Routledge, 2004.

Griffiths, Alison. *Wondrous Difference: Cinema, Anthropology, and Turn-of-the-Century Visual Culture*. New York: Columbia University Press, 2002.

Guibbert, Pierre, ed. *Les Premiers ans du cinéma français: Actes du Ve colloque international de l'Institut Jean Vigo*. Perpignan, France: Institut Jean Vigo, 1985.

Gunning, Tom. *D.W. Griffith and the Origins of American Narrative Film: The Early Years at Biograph*. Urbana: University of Illinois Press, 1991.

Guy, Alice. *Autobiographie d'une pionnière du cinéma*. Paris: Denoël, Gonthier, 1976.

Guynn, William Howard. *The Routledge Companion to Film History*. New York: Routledge, 2010.

Hammond, Michael. *The Big Show: British Cinema Culture in the Great War, 1914–1918*. Exeter, U.K.: University of Exeter Press, 2006.

Hammond, Paul. *Marvelous Méliès*. London: Fraser, 1974.

Hampton, Benjamin Bowles. *History of the American Film Industry from Its Beginnings to 1931*. New York: Dover, 1970.

Hansen, Miriam. *Babel and Babylon: Spectatorship in American Silent Film*. Cambridge, Mass.: Harvard University Press, 1991.

Hanson, Stuart. *From Silent Screen to Multi-Screen: A History of Cinema Exhibition in Britain since 1896*. Manchester, U.K.: Manchester University Press, 2007.

Harding, Colin, and Simon Popple. *In the Kingdom of Shadows: A Companion to Early Cinema*. London: Cygnus Arts, 1996.

Hastie, Amelie. *Cupboards of Curiosity: Women, Recollections, and Film History*. Durham, N.C.: Duke University Press, 2007.

Haver, Gianni, and Pierre-Emmanuel Jaques. *Le Spectacle cinématographique en Suisse (1895–1945)*. Lausanne, Switzerland: Antipodes, 2003.

Hendricks, Gordon. *The Edison Motion Picture Myth*. Berkeley: University of California Press, 1961.

———. *The Kinetoscope: America's First Commercially Successful Motion Picture Exhibitor*. New York: Arno, 1972.

———. *Origins of the American Film*. New York: Arno, 1972.

Hepworth, Cecil M. *Came the Dawn: Memories of a Film Pioneer*. London: Phoenix House, 1951.

Herbert, Stephen, ed. *A History of Early Film*. 3 vols. London: Routledge, 2000–2002.

———, ed. *A History of Pre-Cinema*. 3 vols. London: Routledge, 2000.

Herbert, Stephen, and Luke McKernan, eds. *A Who's Who of Victorian Cinema: A Worldwide Survey*. London: British Film Institute, 1996.

Higson, Andrew. *Young and Innocent? The Cinema in Britain, 1896–1930*. Exeter, U.K.: University of Exeter Press, 2002.

Holman, Roger, ed. *Cinema 1900–1906: An Analytical Study*. 2 vols. Brussels: International Federation of Film Archives, 1982.

Jacobs, Lewis. *The Rise of the American Film: A Critical History*. New York: Teachers College Press, 1971.

Jeanne, René. *Cinéma 1900*. Paris: Flammarion, 1965.

Jeanne, René, and Charles Ford. *Histoire encyclopédique I: Le cinéma français, 1895–1929*. Paris: Robert Laffont, 1947.

Jenn, Pierre. *Georges Méliès cinéaste*. Paris: Albatros, 1984.

Jesionowski, Joyce. *Thinking in Pictures: Dramatic Structure in D.W. Griffith's Biograph Films*. Berkeley: University of California Press, 1987.

Jost, François. *Le Temps d'un regard: Du spectateur aux images*.Québec/Paris: Nota Bene/ Méridiens Klincksieck, 1998.

Keil, Charlie. *Early American Cinema in Transition. Story, Style, and Filmmaking, 1907–1913*. Madison: University of Wisconsin Press, 2001.

Keil, Charlie, and Ben Singer, eds. *American Cinema of the 1910s: Themes and Variations*. New Brunswick, N.J.: Rutgers University Press, 2009.

Keil, Charlie, and Shelley Stamp. *American Cinema's Transitional Era: Audiences, Institutions, Practices*. Berkeley: University of California Press, 2004.

Keim, Norman O. *Our Movie Houses: A History of Film and Cinematic Innovation in Central New York*. Syracuse, N.Y.: Syracuse University Press, 2008.

Kember, Joe. *Marketing Modernity: Victorian Popular Shows and Early Cinema*. Exeter, U.K.: University of Exeter Press, 2009.

Kember, Joe, and Simon Popple. *Early Cinema: From Factory Gate to Dream Factory*. London: Wallflower Press, 2004.

Kermabon, Jacques, ed. *Pathé, premier empire du cinema*. Paris: Centre Pompidou, 1994.

Kessler, Frank, and Nanna Verhoeff, eds. *Networks of Entertainment: Early Film Distribution 1895–1915*. London: John Libbey, 2007.

King, Rob. *The Fun Factory: The Keystone Film Company and the Emergence of Mass Culture*. Berkeley: University of California Press, 2009.

Kirby, Lynn. *Parallel Tracks: The Railroad and Silent Cinema*. Durham, N.C.: Duke University Press, 1997.

Kobel, Peter. *Silent Movies: The Birth of Film to the Triumph of Movie Culture*. New York: Little, Brown, 2007.

Koszarski, Richard M. *An Evening's Entertainment: The Age of the Silent Feature Picture 1915–1928*. Berkeley: University of California Press, 1994.

Kreimeier, Klaus, and Annemone Ligensa. *Film 1900: Technology, Perception, Culture*. New Barnet, Hertfordshire, U.K.: John Libbey, 2009.

Lacasse, Germain. *Le Bonimenteur de vues animées: Le cinéma "muet" entre tradition et modernité*. Québec/Paris: Note Bene/Méridiens Klincksieck, 2000.

———. *Histoires de scopes: Le Cinéma muet au Québec*. Montreal: Cinémathèque québécoise, 1988.

Lagny, Michèle. *De l'histoire du cinéma: Méthode historique et histoire du cinéma*. Paris: Armand Colin, 1992.

Lant, Antonia, and Ingrid Periz, eds. *Red Velvet Seat: Women's Writings on the First Fifty Years of Cinema*. London: Verso, 2006.

Lastra, James. *Perception, Representation, Modernity: Sound Technology and the American Cinema*. New York: Columbia University Press, 2000.

Lecointe, Thierry. *Le Cinématographe Lumière dans les arènes, 1896–1899*. Montpellier: Union des Bibliophiles Taurins de France, 2007.

Lefebvre, Thierry. *La Chair et le celluloïd: Le Cinéma chirurgical du docteur Doyen*. Brionne, France: Jean Doyen, 2004.

Lefebvre, Thierry, Jacques Malthête, and Laurent Mannoni, eds. *Lettres d'Étienne-Jules Marey à Georges Demenÿ, 1880–1894*. Paris: Association française de recherche sur l'histoire du cinéma, 1999.

Le Forestier, Laurent. *Aux sources de l'industrie du cinéma: Le modèle Pathé, 1905–1908*. Paris: L'Harmattan, 2006.

Leyda, Jay. *Kino: A History of the Russian and Soviet Film*. Princeton, N.J.: Princeton University Press, 1986.

Leyda, Jay, and Charles Musser, eds. *Before Hollywood: Turn-of-the-Century American Film*. New York: Hudson Hills, 1987.

Liesegang, Franz Paul. *Dates and Sources: A Contribution to the History of the Art of Projection and to Cinematography*. London: Magic Lantern Society of Great Britain, 1986.

Low, Rachael. *The History of the British Film*. 4 vols. London: George Allen and Unwin, 1949–1971.

Low, Rachael, and Roger Manvell. *The History of the British Film. Vol. 1, 1896–1906*. London: George Allen and Unwin, 1948.

Lowe, Denise. *An Encyclopedic Dictionary of Women in Early American Films: 1895–1930.* Binghamton, N.Y.: Haworth Press, 2005.

Lyons, James, and John Plunkett. *Multimedia Histories: From the Magic Lantern to the Internet.* Exeter, U.K.: University of Exeter Press, 2007.

Mahar, Karen Ward. *Women Filmmakers in Early Hollywood.* Baltimore: Johns Hopkins University Press, 2006.

Maltby, Richard, and Melvyn Stokes, eds. *American Movie Audiences: From the Turn of the Century to the Early Sound Era.* London: BFI, 1999.

Malthête, Jacques. *Méliès, images et illusions.* Paris: Exporégie, 1996.

Malthête, Jacques, and Laurent Mannoni, eds. *Méliès, magie et cinéma.* Paris: Paris Musées, 2002.

Malthête, Jacques, and Michel Marie, eds. *Georges Méliès, l'illusionniste fin de siècle?* Paris: Presses de la Sorbonne Nouvelle, 1997.

Malthête-Méliès, Madeleine, ed. *Méliès et la naissance du spectacle cinématographique.* Paris: Klincksieck, 1984.

Mannoni, Laurent. *Etienne-Jules Marey, la mémoire de l'œil.* Milan, Italy: Mazzotta, 1999.

———. *Le Grand art de la lumière et de l'ombre: Archéologie du cinéma.* Paris: Nathan, 1994.

———. *Trois siècles de cinéma: De la lanterne magique au cinématographe.* Paris: Cinémathèque française, 1995.

Mannoni, Laurent, Marc de Ferrière le Vayer, and Paul Demeny. *Georges Demenÿ, pionnier du cinéma.* Douai, France: Pagine, 1997.

Mannoni, Laurent, and Donata Pesenti Campagnoni. *Lanterne magique et film peint: 400 ans de cinéma.* Paris: Cinémathèque française, 2009.

Mannoni, Laurent, Donata Pesenti Compagnoni, and David Robinson, eds. *Light and Movement: Incunabula of the Motion Picture, 1420–1896.* Pordenone, Italy: Giornate del Cinema Muto, 1995.

Marcus, Laura. *The Tenth Muse: Writing about Cinema in the Modernist Period.* Oxford: Oxford University Press, 2007.

Marie, Michel, and Laurent Le Forestier, eds. *La Firme Pathé-Frères, 1896–1914.* Paris: Association française de recherche sur l'histoire du cinéma, 2004.

Marks, Martin M. *Music and the Silent Film.* New York: Oxford University Press, 1997.

Mathews, Nancy Mowll, and Charles Musser, eds. *Moving Pictures: American Art and Early Film, 1890–1910.* New York: Hudson Hills, 2005.

May, Lary. *Screening Out the Past: The Birth of Mass Culture and the Motion Picture Industry.* New York: Oxford University Press, 1980.

McMahan, Alison. *Alice Guy Blaché: Lost Visionary of the Cinema.* New York: Continuum, 2002.

Meusy, Jean-Jacques. *Paris-Palaces ou le temps des cinémas (1894–1918).* Paris: CNRS, 1995.

Minguet Batllori, Joan M. *Segundo de Chomón: Beyond the Cinema of Attractions (1904–1912).* Barcelona, Spain: Filmoteca de la Generalitat de Catalunya, 1999.

Mitry, Jean. *Histoire du cinema*. 5 vols. Paris: Éditions Universitaires, 1967–1980.

Moore, Paul S. *Now Playing: Early Moviegoing and the Regulation of Fun*. Albany: State University of New York Press, 2008.

Morin, Edgar. *Le Cinéma ou l'homme imaginaire: Essai d'anthropologie sociologique*. Paris: Éditions de minuit, 1956.

Morris, Peter. *Embattled Shadows: A History of Canadian Cinema 1895–1939*. Montreal: McGill-Queen's University Press, 1978.

Mottet, Jean, ed. *David Wark Griffith*. Paris: Publications de la Sorbonne/L'Harmattan, 1984.

Musser, Charles. *Before the Nickelodeon: Edwin S. Porter and the Edison Manufacturing Company*. Berkeley: University of California Press, 1991.

———. *The Emergence of Cinema: The American Screen to 1907*. New York: Charles Scribner's Sons, 1990.

Musser, Charles, and Carol Nelson. *High-Class Moving Pictures: Lyman H. Howe and the Forgotten Era of Travelling Exhibition, 1880–1920*. Princeton, N.J.: Princeton University Press, 1991.

Nead, Lynda. *The Haunted Gallery: Painting, Photography, Film c. 1900*. New Haven, Conn.: Yale University Press, 2007.

Nissen, Dan, Lisbeth Richter Larsen, Thomas C. Christensen, and Jesper Stub. *Preserve the Show*. Copenhagen: Danish Film Museum, 2002.

Oksiloff, Assenka. *Picturing the Primitive: Visual Culture, Ethnography, and Early German Cinema*. New York: Palgrave, 2001.

Olsson, Jan. *Los Angeles before Hollywood: Journalism and American Film Culture, 1905 to 1915*. Stockholm: National Library of Sweden, 2008.

Pang, Laikwan. *The Distorting Mirror: Visual Modernity in China*. Honolulu: University of Hawaii Press, 2007.

Pathé, Charles. *De Pathé Frères à Pathé-Cinéma: Pour les amis de Charles Pathé*. Lyon: SERDOC 1970 reprint.

Pearson, Roberta E. *Eloquent Gestures: The Transformation of Performance Styles in the Griffith Biograph Films*. Berkeley: University of California Press, 1992.

Pearson, Roberta E., and William Uricchio. *Reframing Culture: The Case of the Vitagraph Quality Films*. Princeton, N.J.: Princeton University Press, 1993.

Peiss, Kathy. *Cheap Amusements: Working Women and Leisure in Turn-of-the-Century New York*. Philadelphia: Temple University Press, 1986.

Petro, Patrice. *Aftershocks of the New: Feminism and Film History*. New Brunswick, N.J.: Rutgers University Press, 2002.

Phillips, Ray. *Edison's Kinetoscope and its Films: A History to 1896*. Trowbridge, U.K.: Flicks, 1997.

Pisano, Giusy. *Une archéologie du cinéma sonore*. Paris: CNRS, 2004.

Pisano, Giusy, and Valérie Pozner, eds. *Le Muet a la parole*. Paris: Association française de recherche sur l'histoire du cinéma, 2005.

Popple, Simon, and Vanessa Toulmin, eds. *Visual Delights: Essays on the Popular and Projected Image in the 19th Century*. Trowbridge, U.K.: Flicks, 2000.

————, eds. *Visual Delights Two: Exhibition and Reception*. London: John Libbey, 2005.

Porter, Laraine, and Bryony Dixon. *Picture Perfect: Landscape, Place and Travel in British Cinema before 1930*. Exeter, U.K.: University of Exeter Press, 2007.

Pratt, George. *Spellbound in Darkness: A History of the Silent Film*. Greenwich, N.Y.: New York Graphic Society, 1974.

Quaresima, Leonardo, and Laura Vichi, eds. *La decima musa: Il cinema e le altre arti / The Tenth Muse: Cinema and Other Arts*. Udine, Italy: Forum, 2001.

Quaresima, Leonardo, Alessandra Raengo, and Laura Vichi, eds. *I limiti della rappresentazione: Censura, visibile, modi di rappresentazione nel cinema / The Bounds of Representation: Censorship, the Visible, Modes of Representation in Film*. Udine: Forum, 2000.

————, eds. *La nascita dei generi cinematografici / The Birth of Film Genres*. Udine: Forum, 1999.

Rabinovitz, Lauren. *For the Love of Pleasure: Women, Movies, and Culture in Turn-of-the-Century Chicago*. New Brunswick, N.J.: Rutgers University Press, 1998.

Ramsaye, Terry. *A Million and One Nights: A History of the Motion Picture through 1925*. New York: Simon and Schuster, 1986.

Redi, Riccardo, ed. *Méliès*. Rome: Di Giacomo, 1987.

Rittaud-Hutinet, Jacques. *Auguste et Louis Lumière: Les 1000 premiers films*. Paris: Philippe Sers, 1990.

————. *Le cinéma des origines: Les frères Lumière et leurs opérateurs*. Seyssel, France: Champ Vallon, 1985.

Robinson, David. *George Méliès: Father of Film Fantasy*. London: BFI, 1993.

————. *From Peep Show to Palace: The Birth of American Film*. New York: Columbia University Press, 1996.

Rose, Bernice B., ed. *Picasso, Braque and Early Film in Cubism*. New York: Pace Wildenstein, 2007.

Rosen, Philip. *Change Mummified: Cinema, Historicity, Theory*. Minneapolis: University of Minnesota Press, 2001.

Rosenzweig, Roy. *Eight Hours for What We Will: Workers and Leisure in an Industrial City, 1870–1920*. Cambridge, U.K.: Cambridge University Press, 1983.

Rossell, Deac. *Lanterna Magica—Magic Lantern*. Stuttgart, Germany: Füsslin, 2008.

————. *Living Pictures: The Origins of the Movies*. Albany: State University of New York Press, 1998.

Russell, Catherine. *Experimental Ethnography: The Work of Film in the Age of Video*. Durham, N.C.: Duke University Press, 1999.

Sadoul, Georges. *Histoire générale du cinema*. 6 vols. Paris: Denoël, 1946–1975.

————. *Lumière et Méliès*. Paris: L'Herminier, 1985.

Salt, Barry. *Film Style and Technology: History and Analysis*. London: Starword, 2nd edition, 1992.

Schlüpmann, Heide. *The Uncanny Gaze: The Drama of Early German Cinema*. Urbana: University of Illinois Press, 2010.

Schwartz, Vanessa R. *Spectacular Realities: Early Mass Culture in Fin-de-Siècle Paris*. Berkeley: University of California Press, 1998.

Seguin, Jean-Claude. *Alexandre Promio ou les énigmes de la lumière*. Paris: L'Harmattan, 2000.

Simmon, Scott. *The Invention of the Western Film: A Cultural History of the Genre's First Half-Century*. Cambridge, U.K.: Cambridge University Press, 2003.

Simon, Joan, ed. *Alice Guy Blaché: Cinema Pioneer*. New Haven, Conn.: Yale University Press, 2009.

Singer, Ben. *Melodrama and Modernity: Early Sensational Cinema and Its Contexts*. New York: Columbia University Press, 2001.

Skaff, Sheila. *The Law of the Looking Glass: Cinema in Poland, 1896–1939*. Athens: Ohio University Press, 2008.

Slide, Anthony. *Aspects of American Film History Prior to 1920*. Metuchen, N.J.: Scarecrow Press, 1978.

———. *The Big V: A History of the Vitagraph Company*. Metuchen, N.J.: Scarecrow Press, 1987.

———. *Early American Cinema*. Metuchen: Scarecrow Press, 1994.

———. *Nitrate Won't Wait: A History of Film Preservation in the United States*. Jefferson, N.C.: McFarland, 2000.

Sloan, Kay. *The Loud Silents: Origins of the Social Problem Film*. Urbana: University of Illinois Press, 1988.

Smith, Terry. *Impossible Presence: Surface and Screen in the Photogenic Era*. Chicago: University of Chicago Press, 2001.

Solomon, Matthew. *Disappearing Tricks: Silent Film, Houdini, and the New Magic of the Twentieth Century*. Urbana: University of Illinois Press, 2010.

Sopocy, Martin. *James Williamson: Studies and Documents of a Pioneer of the Film Narrative*. Madison, N.J.: Fairleigh Dickinson University Press, 1998.

Spehr, Paul C. *The Movies Begin: Making Movies in New Jersey 1887–1920*. Newark, N.J.: Newark Museum, 1977.

———. *The Man Who Made Movies: W. K. L. Dickson*. New Barnet, Herts, U.K.: John Libbey Publishing, 2008.

Staiger, Janet. *Bad Women: Regulating Sexuality in Early American Cinema*. Minneapolis: University of Minnesota Press, 1995.

———. *Interpreting Films: Studies in the Historical Reception of American Cinema*. Princeton, N.J.: Princeton University Press, 1992.

Stamp, Shelley. *Movie-Struck Girls: Women and Motion Picture Culture after the Nickelodeon*. Princeton, N.J.: Princeton University Press, 2000.

Stewart, Jacqueline Najuma. *Migrating to the Movies: Cinema and Black Urban Modernity*. Berkeley: University of California Press, 2005.

Streible, Dan. *Fight Pictures: A History of Boxing and Early Cinema*. Berkeley: University of California Press, 2008.

Strauven, Wanda, ed. *The Cinema of Attractions Reloaded*. Amsterdam: Amsterdam University Press, 2006.

Thompson, Kristin. *Exporting Entertainment: America in the World Film Market, 1907–1934*. London: BFI, 1985.

Tosi, Virgilio. *Cinema before Cinema: The Origins of Scientific Cinematography*. London: British Universities Film and Video Council, 2005.

Toulet, Emmanuellle. *Cinématographe, invention du siècle*. Paris: Gallimard, 1988.

Toulmin, Vanessa. *Electric Edwardians: The Story of the Mitchell and Kenyon Collection*. London: British Film Institute, 2006.

Toulmin, Vanessa, Simon Popple, and Patrick Russell, eds. *The Lost World of Mitchell and Kenyon: Edwardian Britain on Film*. London: British Film Institute, 2004.

Tsivian, Yuri. *Early Cinema in Russia and Its Cultural Reception*. London: Routledge, 1994.

Urban, Charles. *A Yank in Britain: The Lost Memoirs of Charles Urban, Film Pioneer*. Hastings, U.K.: Projection Box, 1999.

Vardac, A. Nicholas. *Stage to Screen: Theatrical Method from Garrick to Griffith*. Cambridge, Mass.: Harvard University Press, 1949.

Verhoeff, Nanna. *The West in Early Cinema: After the Beginning*. Amsterdam: Amsterdam University Press, 2006.

Vichi, Laura, ed. *L'uomo visibile: L'attore dal cinema delle origini alle soglie del cinema moderno / The Visible Man: Film Actor from Early Cinema to the Eve of Modern Cinema*. Udine, Italy: Forum, 2002.

Vivié, Jean. *Prélude au cinema: De la préhistoire à l'invention*. Paris: L'Harmattan, 2006.

Waller, Gregory, ed. *Moviegoing in America: A Sourcebook in the History of Film Exhibition*. Malden, Mass.: Blackwell, 2001.

Whissel, Kristen. *Picturing American Modernity: Traffic, Technology, and the Silent Cinema*. Durham, N.C.: Duke University Press, 2008.

Williams, Christopher, ed. *Cinema: The Beginnings and the Future*. London: University of Westminster Press, 1996.

Youngblood, Denise. *The Magic Mirror: Moviemaking in Russia, 1908–1918*. Madison: University of Wisconsin Press, 1999.

Zhang, Zhen. *An Amorous History of the Silver Screen: Shanghai Cinema, 1896–1937*. Chicago: University of Chicago Press, 2005.

Zone, Ray. *Stereoscopic Cinema and the Origins of 3-D Film, 1838–1952*. Lexington: University Press of Kentucky, 2007.

Early Cinema Journals

The following four journals are among the few periodicals that deal almost exclusively with early cinema or, at the very least, with silent cinema, and are key references in the field:

1895. Revue de l'Association française de recherche sur l'histoire du cinéma. In print since September 1986.

Early Popular Visual Culture (previously *Living Pictures: The Journal of the Popular and Projected Image before 1914*). This periodical is not only about early cinema, but also on visual culture in general. In print since Summer 2001.

Griffithiana. Billingual journal (English and Italian). In print since November 1978.

KINtop. Jahrbuch zur Erforschung des frühen Films. Annual German journal in print from 1992 to 2006.

Special Issues on Early Cinema

Abel, Richard, and Rick Altman, eds. "Global Experiments in Early Synchronous Sound." Special issue, *Film History* 11, no. 4 (1999).

Allen, Robert C., ed. "Film History." *Journal of Film and Video* 37, no. 1 (winter 1985).

Bean, Jennifer M., and Diane Negra, eds. "Early Women Stars." Special issue, *Camera Obscura* 16, no. 48 (2001).

Bertellini, Giorgio, ed. "Early Italian Cinema." Special issue, *Film History* 12, no. 3 (2000).

Bottomore, Stephen, ed. "Cinema Pioneers." Special issue, *Film History* 10, no. 1 (1998).

———, ed. "Early British Cinema." Special issue, *Film History* 16, no. 1 (2004).

———, ed. "Early Cinema." Special issue, *Film History* 11, no. 3 (1999).

Cherchi Usai, Paolo, ed. "Philosophy of Film History." Special issue, *Film History* 6, no. 1 (1994).

De la Bretèque, François, ed. "La Maison Gaumont a cent ans." *Cahiers de la cinémathèque*, nos. 63–64 (1995).

Dulac, Nicolas, and Bernard Perron, eds. "Configurations de l'alternance / Configuring Alternation." *Cinéma & Cie*, no. 9 (2007).

Gaudreault, André, ed. "Archives, Document, Fiction: Film before 1907 / Le cinéma avant 1907." *Iris* 2, no. 1 (1984).

———, ed. "Le Cinéma des premiers temps." *Cahiers de la Cinémathèque*, no. 29 (1979).

Gaudreault, André, and Germain Lacasse, eds. "Le Bonimenteur de vues animées / The Moving Picture Lecturer." *Iris*, no. 22 (1996).

Gaudreault, André, Jacques Malthête and Madeleine Malthête-Méliès, eds. "Propos sur les vues animées." *Dossiers de la Cinémathèque*, no. 10 (1982).

Gosser, Mark H., ed. "Archaeology of Cinema." *Quarterly Review of Film Studies* 9, no. 1 (1984).

Guibbert, Pierre, ed. "D. W. Griffith encore et toujours." *Cahiers de la Cinémathèque*, no. 17 (1975).

Gunning, Tom, ed. "Early Cinema." *Persistence of Vision*, no. 9 (1991).

Hastie, Amelie, and Shelley Stamp, eds. "Women and the Silent Screen." Special Issue, *Film History* 18, no. 2 (2006).

Higashi, Sumiko, ed. "In Focus: Film History, or a Baedeker Guide to the Historical Turn." *Cinema Journal* 44, no. 1 (2004): 94–143.

Jost, François, ed. "Par où continuer / What's Next?" *Cinéma & Cie, International Film Studies Journal*, no. 1 (2001).

Kessler, Frank, Sabine Lenk, and Martin Loiperdinger, eds. "Early Non-fiction Cinema." *Historical Journal of Film, Radio, and Television* 15, no. 4 (1995).

Lefebvre, Thierry, Laurent Mannoni, and Michel Marie, eds. "Cinéma des premiers temps: Nouvelles contributions françaises." *Théorème*, no. 4 (1996).

Maule, Rosanna, ed. "Femmes et cinéma muet: Nouvelles problématiques, nouvelles méthodologies." *Cinémas* 16, no. 1 (2005).

——, ed. "Representational Technologies and the Discourse on Early Cinema's Apparatus / Les Technologies de représentation et le discours sur le dispositif cinématographique des premiers temps." *Cinéma & Cie, International Film Studies Journal*, no. 3 (2003).

Mitry, Jean, ed. "Le cinéma muet italien." *Cahiers de la Cinémathèque*, nos. 26–27 (1979).

Nash, Melanie, and Jean-Pierre Sirois-Trahan, eds. "Dispositif(s) du cinéma (des premiers temps)." *Cinémas* 15, no. 1 (2003).

Oms, Marcel, ed. "D. W. Griffith hier et aujourd'hui." *Cahiers de la Cinémathèque*, no. 6 (1972).

Rossel, Deac, ed. "A Chronology of Cinema, 1889–1896." Special issue, *Film History* 7, no. 2 (1995).

Russel, Catherine, and Pierre Véronneau, eds. "Le Cinéma muet au Québec et au Canada: nouveaux regards sur une pratique culturelle." *Cinémas* 6, no. 1 (1995).

Sobchack, Vivian, ed. "The Silent Cinema." *Journal of Popular Film and Television* 15, no. 3 (1987).

"United States of America vs. Motion Picture Patents Company and Others." *Film History* 1, no. 3 (1987).

Early Cinema Filmographies, Catalogues, and Bibliographies

American Film Institute. *Catalog of Motion Pictures Produced in the United States: Feature Films, 1911–1920*. Berkeley: University of California Press, 1988.

Aubert, Michelle, and Jean-Claude Seguin. *La Production cinématographique des frères Lumière*. Paris: Mémoires du cinéma et Bibliothèque du film, 1996.

Bousquet, Henri. *Catalogue Pathé des années 1896 à 1914*. 4 Vols. , *1896–1906*. Paris: Henri Bousquet, 1993.

Bowser, Eileen, ed. *Biograph Bulletins: 1908–1912*. New York: Farrar, Strauss and Giroux, 1973.

Catalog of Copyright Entries: Motion Pictures, 1894–1912. Washington, D.C.: Library of Congress, Copyright Office, 1951.

Catalog of Copyright Entries: Motion Pictures, 1912–1939. Washington, D.C.: Library of Congress, Copyright Office, 1953.

Chirat, Raymond, ed. *Catalogue des films français de fiction de 1908 à 1918*. Paris: Cinémathèque française, 1995.

Cosandey, Roland. *Cinéma 1900: Trente films dans une boîte à chaussures*. Lausanne: Payot-Lausanne, 1996.

Dagrada, Elena, ed. *Bibliographie internationale du cinéma des premiers temps / International Bibliography on Early Cinema*. Madison, Wisc.: DOMITOR, 1995.

Early Rare British Filmmakers' catalogues. London: British Film Institute, 1983.

FIAF International Film Archive Database. CD-ROM. Brussels: FIAF, 2006.

FIAF International Index to Film Periodicals. http://fiaf.chadwyck.com/home.do (accessed 11 September 2010).

Gaumont Pathé Archives. http://www.gaumontpathearchives.com (accessed 11 September 2010).

Gifford, Denis. *The British Film Catalogue, 1895–1994.* 2 vols. London: Fitzroy Dearborn, 2001.

Hagener, Malte, and Michael Töteberg. *Film: An International Bibliography.* Stuttgart, Germany: J.B. Metzler, 2002.

Hecht, Hermann, and Ann Hecht, eds. *Pre-Cinema History: An Encyclopaedia and Annotated Bibliography of the Moving Image before 1896.* London: Bowker-Saur/BFI, 1993.

Malthête, Jacques, Madeleine Malthête-Méliès, and Anne-Marie Quévrain. *Essai de reconstitution du catalogue français de la Star-Film, suivi d'une analyse catalographique des films de Georges Méliès recensés en France.* Bois d'Arcy, France: Publications du Service des Archives du Film du CNC, 1981.

Mannoni, Laurent. *Le Mouvement continué: Catalogue illustré de la collection des appareils de la cinémathèque française.* Milan, Italy: Mazzotta, 1996.

Moving Image Collections. http://mic.loc.gov/index.php (accessed 11 September 2010).

Musser, Charles. *Edison Motion Pictures, 1890–1900: An Annotated Filmography.* Washington, D.C.: Smithsonian Institution Press, 1997.

———, ed. *Motion Picture Catalogs by American Producers and Distributors, 1894–1908.* Frederick, Md.: University Publications of America, 1984.

National Film Archive Catalogue. Part I: Silent News Films (1895–1933). London: British Film Institute, 1965.

———. *Part II: Silent Non-Fiction Films (1895–1934).* London: British Film Institute, 1960.

———. *Part III: Silent Fiction Films (1895–1930).* London, British Film Institute, 1966.

Niver, Kemp R., ed. *Biograph Bulletins, 1896–1908.* Los Angeles: Locare Research Group, 1971.

———. *Early Motion Pictures: The Paper Print Collection in the Library of Congress.* Washington, D.C.: Library of Congress, 1985.

Savada, Elias, ed. *The American Film Institute Catalog of Motion Pictures Produced in the United States: Film Beginnings, 1893–1910.* 2 vols. Metuchen, N.J.: Scarecrow Press, 1995.

Spehr, Paul C. *American Film Personnel and Company Credits, 1908–1920: Filmographies Recorded by Authoritative Organizational and Personal Names from Lauritzen and Lundquist's American Film-Index.* Jefferson, N.C.: McFarland, 1996.

Toulet, Emmanuelle. *Bibliographie internationale du cinéma des premiers temps: Travaux des membres de Domitor.* Quebec City: Domitor, 1987.

Workers of the Writers' Program of the Work Projects Administration in the City of New York. *The Film Index: A Bibliography.* 3 vols. New York: Museum of Modern Art; White Plains, NY: Kraus, 1941–1985.

Index

André Gaudreault is a professor at the Département d'histoire de l'art et d'etudes cinématographiques at the Université de Montréal, the author of *From Plato to Lumière: Narration and Monstration in Literature and Cinema,* and the editor of *American Cinema 1890–1909: Themes and Variations.*

Timothy Barnard is a film historian, publisher, and translator.

The University of Illinois Press
is a founding member of the
Association of American University Presses.
. . . .

Composed in 9.5/14 Officina Serif STD
with Officina Serif and Sans display
by Celia Shapland
at the University of Illinois Press
Manufactured by Cushing-Malloy, Inc.

University of Illinois Press
1325 South Oak Street
Champaign, IL 61820-6903
www.press.uillinois.edu